Marx's Theory of Price and its Modern Rivals

Marx's Theory of Price and its Modern Rivals

Howard Nicholas
Senior Lecturer, Economics of Development

palgrave
macmillan

First published 2011 by
PALGRAVE MACMILLAN

Palgrave Macmillan in the UK is an imprint of Macmillan Publishers Limited, registered in England, company number 785998, of Houndmills, Basingstoke, Hampshire RG21 6XS.

Palgrave Macmillan in the US is a division of St Martin's Press LLC, 175 Fifth Avenue, New York, NY 10010.

Palgrave Macmillan is the global academic imprint of the above companies and has companies and representatives throughout the world.

Palgrave® and Macmillan® are registered trademarks in the United States, the United Kingdom, Europe and other countries

ISBN 978-0-230-30257-0

This book is printed on paper suitable for recycling and made from fully managed and sustained forest sources. Logging, pulping and manufacturing processes are expected to conform to the environmental regulations of the country of origin.

A catalogue record for this book is available from the British Library.

Library of Congress Cataloging-in-Publication Data

Nicholas, Howard, 1954–
    Marx's theory of price and its modern rivals / Howard Nicholas.
        p. cm.
    Includes index.
    ISBN 978–0–230–30257–0 (hardback)
        1. Prices. 2. Microeconomics. 3. Marxian economics. I. Title.
    HB221.N52 2011
    335.4'12–dc23   2011021114

10   9   8   7   6   5   4   3   2   1
20 19 18 17 16 15 14 13 12 11

Printed and bound in Great Britain by
CPI Antony Rowe, Chippenham and Eastbourne

Contents

Preface

The present work has had a very long gestation. It was born out of my PhD studies in the late 1970s and early 1980s in which I attempted to understand Marx's theory of money and the role it plays in his explanation of business cycles. As with so many who have undertaken PhDs, once completing this study it dawned on me how little I really understood of the subject. With hindsight this should not have been surprising given the sheer scope of the endeavour, my own ignorance of the subject matter at the time, and the relative paucity of writings in this area, including those by Marx. Perhaps the real benefit of the study for me was the questions it raised in my mind rather than the answers it provided me with. In attempting to answer some of these questions in my post-doctoral research work, I kept being drawn to the theory of price, Marx's theory of price, as the necessary point of departure for a fuller understanding of not only his theory of money and role it played for him in the cyclical movement of the capitalist system but, more fundamentally, its importance for his general explanation of the latter. Hence, the present work.

Once I settled on this point of departure I soon came to realise that a comprehensive understanding of Marx's theory of price would require me to: address certain of the major criticisms of this theory from those within and without the Marxist school of thought, certainly if I was to convince anyone, including myself, of its scientific rigour; assess other interpretations of it, mostly to ascertain whether I was saying anything different; and, compare Marx's explanation of prices with other explanations, both Classical and modern, to demonstrate the specificity and pre-eminence of Marx's explanation. To be perfectly frank, in the early phases of my post-doctoral studies I was not entirely certain of either the scientific rigour or superiority of Marx's theory of price, or that I had much to add to what had already been said about this theory. I was even inclined towards the view that many of the criticisms levelled against Marx's theory of price, particularly those emanating from the Sraffian school, were more than justified. However, as I delved deeper into Marx's own writings, and reflected on these, not only did my doubts dissipate, but I became increasingly convinced that many traditional and modern interpretations of Marx's theory of price, by friends and foes alike, seriously misrepresented it.

In writing this book I have sought to present what I understand to be Marx's theory of price in as intelligible and accessible a manner as possible. However, I have to admit, and apologise in advance for the fact, that the end product still presumes a certain familiarity with Marxist and non-Marxist theories of price on the part of the reader. I consider this to be unavoidable since the purpose of the book is to interpret and expand on Marx's own writings on price in a way which allows it to be compared with other, particularly modern, theories, and not simply to regurgitate these writings. Accordingly, I see this book as being particularly useful for Master's and PhD level students, teachers of economics, researchers, and those with a keen interest in the foundations of economic thinking.

A book with such a long gestation period such as the present one could not have been written without considerable support and encouragement. In this regard I would like to thank my parents, Heloise and Brian, my wife, Nicolien, and my children, Jeske, Bram and Kasper. In one way or another, and to different degrees, they have all made sacrifices over considerable periods of time to allow me to bring this work to fruition. I would also like to thank all my past students, colleagues, and friends, who have in one way or another contributed to the development of my knowledge and understanding, and the countless authors whose work I have explicitly and implicitly drawn from. And last, but not least, I would like to thank Eri for her painstaking archival and referencing work.

1
Introduction

This book focuses on Marx's theory of price. Its aim is to provide an interpretation of this theory which is consistent with the logic, if not the written word, of Marx's analysis in *Capital*, his most developed work in political economy, or 'economics', as the subject matter of much of this work is now referred to. The motivation for doing so is twofold. Firstly, to contribute to the recent revival in interest in Marx's economic analysis of capitalism, noting in passing that any theory purporting to explain the dynamics of the capitalist system, as Marx's does, requires most fundamentally a theory of price. The theory of price, it needs emphasising, both reflects and conditions general theories of the economic system. Secondly, to shift the focus of economic debate back to its foundations, there being nothing more foundational than the theory of price. Presently, the focus of economic debate is the alleged causes of, and required policy responses to, the recent severe crisis of the global capitalist system. What is apparent is that much of this debate is poorly informed, if at all, by any coherent theoretical analysis, causing a growing number of economists to argue for a reconsideration of the foundations.[1] It is in this context that the present work can be argued to have a particular significance.

The hostility to Marx's work has, needless to say, a long history, with many of the most concerted attacks directed at his theory of price – seen as a sort of 'Achilles heel' of his analysis of capitalism. It has been argued, *inter alia*, that Marx's theory of price is little more than a **repetition** of that of the Classical economist David Ricardo, that it is **unintelligible**, and, perhaps most damaging of all, that it is **inconsistent**. The view that Marx's theory of price is little more than a repetition of Ricardo's is a long-standing one, and taken as a veritable matter of fact in non-Marxist circles. One of the high priests of economic orthodoxy in the last century, Paul Samuelson, famously referred to Marx as 'a minor Post-Ricardian' (1957, p. 911). The intelligibility criticism was made most trenchantly by Joan Robinson in her withering indictment of Marx's labour theory of value, which she dismissed as a 'rigmarole of words' (1964, p. 39). The inconsistency criticism refers to the so-called 'transformation problem' in *Capital*. Beginning with Böhm-Bawerk (1975)[1896], the problem is deemed to be that Marx did not show, and, indeed, could not show, that values determine prices in a capitalist system when the values of all commodities, including inputs, are transformed into prices. More recently, in the wake of the work of Piero Sraffa (1960), a charge of **redundancy** has been added to the preceding list of criticisms. It is contended that the journey from value to price is **unnecessary** since price can be calculated far more simply and consistently by reference to the technical conditions of production and distribution of net product between wages and profits.[2]

It is not just those hostile to Marx's work who have cast doubt on the validity of his explanation of prices. Even those who might be considered to be sympathetic to the bulk of his economic analysis in *Capital* express certain reservations when it comes to his theory of price. One cause for doubt is the above-mentioned transformation problem. It is perhaps fair to say that many, if not the majority, of those sympathetic to Marx's economic analysis accept that it contains a transformation problem as argued by his critics, and a considerable proportion of these accept that the problem is an intractable one. Another cause for doubt is the phenomenon of monopoly. Beginning with Hilferding (1981)[1910], and continuing with Baran (1957), Baran and Sweezy (1966), Sweezy (1968), Meek (1973), Howard and King (1975), etc., the argument advanced is that the tendency towards an increasing concentration and centralisation of capital has caused competitive capitalism to give way to a very different form of capitalism, namely monopoly capitalism. Most importantly, it is argued that in this phase of capitalism there are various artificial and natural barriers to the free movement of capital thereby negating the operation of the law of value and invalidating much of Marx's analysis of capitalism, particularly his explanation of prices.[3]

Needless to say, the literature is replete with defences of Marx against these criticisms. A great many expositions of his theory of price have sought to distinguish it from that of Ricardo in an attempt to avoid it being tarred with the same brush so to speak (e.g., Meek, 1973; Fine, 1982; Pilling, 1986). However, it is probably fair to say that no consensus has emerged regarding precisely how the two theories differ. The reason, as will be argued below, appears to be a failure to agree on

Marx's explanation of price and in particular his understanding of **value**.

On the question of intelligibility, it is agreed by all except the most devout defenders of Marx that his presentation in *Capital* is certainly impenetrable to any but the most persevering reader. Francis Wheen suggests that it was sheer incomprehension rather than political enmity that explains the muted reaction to Volume 1 of *Capital* following its publication in 1867 (2006, p. 84). Subsequent to the publication of *Capital*, there have been numerous attempts to *précis* and interpret this work in a way that makes it more **intelligible**.[4] However, at least partly because of considerable divergences in such interpretations, but, ironically, also partly because of the impenetrable nature of many of the interpretations themselves, it would appear that the intelligibility criticism is still far from being satisfactorily addressed.

Most attention has unquestionably been paid by defenders of Marx's price theory to the **consistency** criticism. To some extent, this is because it has been the main focus of critics of Marx's theory of price, but also because a large number of other criticisms of this theory are seen as in one way or another bound up with this one. Up to the 1980s it was common for most Marxists to accept that Marx's transformation procedure was indeed inconsistent in the state in which he left it, but that it could be made consistent following one or another of a number of transformation procedures involving solutions of sets of simultaneous equations. It was also accepted that these solutions required the sacrifice of one of two fundamental equalities postulated by Marx; the equalities of, on the one hand, aggregate values and prices, and, on the other hand, aggregate surplus value and profits. The reason for the sacrifice was the assumed need for an invariance condition to make the solution to the simultaneous equations determinate.[5] A majority of Marxists favoured sacrificing the aggregate values and prices equality, arguing that the real purpose of Marx's value theory was an explanation of profit not prices *per se*.[6] This view of Marx's price theory naturally opened the door for an acceptance of the above-mentioned redundancy criticism, and with it an alternate explanation of price offered by either Post Keynesians in general or Sraffa in particular (see Chapters 7 and 8 for a discussion of these explanations). From the early 1980s onwards, by way of a reaction to what was seen as a capitulation to the critics of Marx, there has been a growing tendency in the Marxist camp to posit solutions to the transformation problem which do not require sacrifice of either of the equality postulates. The best-known among these are the so-called New Interpretation (NI) and the Temporal Single

System Interpretation (TSSI). However, and as will be argued in greater detail in Chapter 5, these interpretations have in the process of defending Marx tended either to deny the relevance of his value theory for an explanation of price, or to interpret Marx as having what amounts to a trivial explanation of the latter.

Somewhat less attention has been paid by defenders of Marx's theory of price to the monopoly criticism; that Marx's theory is premised on the existence of competition whereas the economic reality of today is the prevalence of all manner of artificial and natural monopolies. The main reason for this inattention is no doubt the somewhat muted nature of the criticisms in this regard. Orthodox (Neoclassical) economists are naturally reluctant to pursue this line of criticism since most of their explanations of price similarly presume the existence of a competitive environment. Within the Marxist school the criticisms have become more muted as a result of, on the one hand, the migration of many of the critics to the Post Keynesian school, and, on the other hand, a growing awareness that the process of concentration and centralisation of capital has not resulted in the elimination of the competitive process, certainly not as caricatured by Marx. As Meek noted in his critical remarks on the relevance of Marx's labour theory of value to the explanation of price in present-day capitalism:

> One must be careful, however, not to exaggerate the extent to which the coming of monopoly capitalism has invalidated the traditional analyses based on the assumption of free competition. Monopoly does not mean the end of competition, and may even at times (e.g., during periods of price war) mean an intensification of competition. (1973, p. 286)

Which means, as Meek also notes, that the theory of monopoly price should be regarded as a supplement and not an alternative to the theory of competitive price (*Ibid.*, p. 287).

My intention in this book is to argue that: a) Marx has an intelligible, logical and consistent theory of price; b) his concept of value is at the very heart of this explanation; c) his theory of price is neither a mere repetition of Ricardo's theory, nor has it been made redundant by Sraffa's or Post Keynesian contributions; d) it has not been invalidated by tendencies towards concentration and centralisation in capitalism, and e) it warrants more serious consideration than it has hitherto been accorded by those interested in understanding the economy – whether or not they are sympathetic to Marx's purpose in the study of capitalism, *viz.* its overthrow, and especially given the growing dissatisfaction with the foundations of mainstream economic thinking.

To this end, I begin by presenting in Chapters 2 and 3 what I consider to be Marx's theory of price. In Chapter 2, I look at Marx's explanation of price in the context of the simple circulation of commodities, explaining at the outset of the chapter why he chose to begin with the explanation of price in such an economic setting. I build on this in Chapter 3 when considering his explanation of price in competitive capitalism, including his explanation of price formation in monopoly sectors. I contend that Marx chose to begin his explanation of price in capitalism with a consideration of price in the simple circulation of commodities because the latter captures the essence of the former and not because of its supposed historical antecedence. In both Chapters 2 and 3, I pay particular attention to Marx's understanding of price – its emergence, purpose, formation and nature – and the meaning he ascribes to the different concepts he uses. I argue that it is an appreciation of this understanding of price by Marx, and clarity with regard to the precise meaning of the concepts he uses, that permits one to make sense of his explanation of price magnitudes in terms of values. I then move to a consideration of Marx's views on the theories of price in the works of Adam Smith and David Ricardo in Chapter 4. My primary aim in this chapter is to show the distinctiveness of Marx's contribution in comparison with the so-called Classical theories, and notwithstanding the fact that he most certainly drew inspiration from these theories, particularly that of Ricardo. In Chapter 5, I appraise various 'traditional' and 'new' interpretations of Marx's theory of price. I argue that these interpretations attribute to Marx explanations of price which are more in keeping with those of Ricardo. In Chapters 6 to 8, I critically assess more modern theories of price – the Neoclassical, Post Keynesian and Sraffian – mostly, but not exclusively, with a view to developing further an understanding of Marx's theory. In outlining and critically appraising both the Neoclassical and Post Keynesian theories of price, I pay attention to differences within each theory where I consider these to be relevant. In the presentation and analysis of the Neoclassical theory in Chapter 6, I take the important differences among its proponents to be those between the so-called New Keynesian, Walrasian and Austrian sub-groups. I recognise that many Austrians consider their approach to the study of the economy to be at odds with the general Neoclassical approach but, as I will make clear, while they may diverge from the latter in certain respects, they share most of its fundamental principles, particularly when explaining price. When considering the Post Keynesian theory of price in Chapter 7, I take the important differences to be those between the so-called fundamentalist Keynesians and Kaleckians. In keeping with the views of many in the Post Keynesian school, I see the Sraffian theory as falling outside of the orbit of this school and, therefore, analyse it separately in Chapter 8. The analysis in Chapter 8 is limited to the work of Piero Sraffa, and in particular his *Production of Commodities by Means of Commodities* (1960), since, not surprisingly, it is this work that is generally regarded as representing the very core of the Sraffian theory of price. I consider the critical appraisal of Sraffa's work as quite possibly the most important among the critical appraisals of the modern theories of price undertaken in the present study. This is because, on the one hand, this appraisal, more than the other appraisals, serves to highlight certain key elements of Marx's theory of price, and, on the other hand, Sraffa's explanation of price is seen as representing a major advance over that of Marx, even by certain sympathisers of Marx's work. I end, in Chapter 9, by drawing together what I consider to be the important and defining aspects of Marx's theory of price, locating this theory in terms of the spectrum of theories of price, ranging from those on the demand side to those on the supply side and, finally, suggesting why the discussion of Marx's theory of price has a significance beyond simply shedding further light on it at the present historical juncture.

2
Marx's Theory of Price in the Simple Circulation of Commodities

2.1 Why Marx begins with the simple circulation of commodities

Marx's purpose in *Capital* is to study the dynamics of the capitalist system; the laws of motion that govern, and tendencies that characterise, it. To understand these dynamics he considers it necessary to understand the movement of capital as a process of value expansion or wealth augmentation. At the very heart of this process is the circulation of commodities (including services) and formation of prices. Marx takes the circulation of commodities to be the exchange of commodities for money and money for other commodities. He depicts this as C-M-C', where C-C' represents both a change in the form of the commodity and, as is implied by the commodity as capital, an increase in value. He sees the circulation of commodities as facilitated by the circulation of money as capital. He depicts the latter as M-C-M', where M-M' represents an increase in the value of money. Marx argues, that to understand the fundamental nature of this circulation of commodities and accompanying formation of prices in capitalism, one must first abstract from capital; from commodities and money as capital.[1] One must begin with the simple circulation of commodities (C-M-C') and money (M-C-M), where C-C' represents only a change in form of the commodity and M-M signifies that there is no increase in the money worth of the commodity in the process of circulation.

2.2 Understanding the simple commodity circulation process

There are a number of aspects of the simple commodity circulation process analysed by Marx at the beginning of Volume 1 of *Capital* which warrant highlighting as a precursor to the exposition of his general theory of price in this setting. Firstly, because simple commodity circulation is intended to capture the essence of the circulation process in capitalism as a mode of production, it must be seen as presupposing the **production and reproduction** of commodities. Accordingly, it is implicit that the proceeds of the sale of commodities will be used at least in part for the purchase of commodity inputs and subsistence products to enable the renewal of production. Production, in turn, must be seen as social production (production founded on a division of labour), and exchange as mediating the division of labour and facilitating the reproduction of the individual commodity alongside all commodities. Most importantly, this means that it is entirely incorrect to see the exchange process in the simple circulation of commodities as the exchange between individuals 'naturally endowed' with products in the manner, say, of Neoclassical (or even Classical) economics.[2] In his *A Contribution to the Critique of Political Economy* Marx says:

> Individuals producing in society, and hence the socially determined production of individuals, is of course the point of departure. The solitary and isolated hunter or fisherman, who serves Adam Smith and Ricardo as a starting point, is one of the unimaginative fantasies of eighteenth-century romances á la Robinson Crusoe;... (1970, p. 188)

Marx was adamant that seeing exchange as divorced from production leads to a serious misunderstanding of price and an erroneous explanation of its magnitude. As will be elaborated on below, it leads to a failure to see the essential purpose of price as facilitating the reproduction of the commodity, and its magnitude as intrinsically linked to the conditions pertaining to this reproduction, i.e., as linked to the **value** or relative worth of the commodity.

Second, for Marx, the simple circulation of commodities is not the direct exchange of products, or barter, but rather the exchange of products mediated by **money**, with exchange taking place on the basis of money prices. It is a process in which commodities come into circulation with money prices and money comes into circulation representing exchangeable worth. As far as the theory of price is concerned, this means that it is incorrect to see commodities as acquiring money prices, and money acquiring exchangeable worth, as a result of their quantitative commensuration with one another in the process of exchange. It also means, incidentally, that Marx cannot be seen as subscribing to the traditional quantity theory of money (TQM) explanation of money prices since at the heart of this theory is the notion that commodities come into circulation without money prices and money without value.

Third, for Marx, the simple circulation of commodities needs to be understood as essentially the exchange of products by isolated producers working in relative ignorance of underling and ongoing changes in economy-wide conditions of production and the exchange value of money. These individuals need to be seen as pursuing their own interests (i.e., seeking to appropriate part of the social product) irrespective of the consequences their actions might have for the reproduction of the system as a whole, and yet dependent on one another and the continuing reproduction of the system for the reproduction of their individual commodities and means of sustenance. Marx says in this regard:

> Exchange and division of labour reciprocally condition one another. Since everyone works for himself but his product is nothing for him, each must of course exchange, not only in order to take part in the general productive capacity but also in order to transform his own product into his own subsistence. (1973, p. 158)

This means, as we will see, that for Marx actual exchange ratios between commodities are unlikely to correspond, for the most part, to those ratios facilitating balance in the economic system, although of necessity they will have to correspond to such ratios, at least periodically, if one is to assume continuity of the system.

2.3   Understanding price in simple commodity production

The exchange value or exchangeable worth of a commodity is the amount of another commodity it **commands** in the process of exchange. Produced goods acquire symbols of exchange value or exchangeable worth, i.e., they acquire **a price form**, when exchange becomes a widespread, generalised and recurrent activity, as opposed to an isolated, one-off, individual act. When exchange becomes widespread, generalised and recurrent, the symbol depicting general exchangeable worth becomes money, and the exchange values of commodities acquire a money form – they acquire **a money price form**.[3] The money price form is a general exchange value form. It is a symbol of the general worth of a commodity in the process of exchange. It indicates how much of all other commodities any one commodity will exchange with. Widespread and generalised exchange of commodities only becomes possible when all those individuals exchanging products use the same symbol or indicator of relative worth of these products in the exchange process, i.e., when they use money. Money, as the reflector of general exchangeable worth, emerges with the development of generalised and repetitive exchanges, as well as facilitating this development.[4] At the same time the price form becomes the money price form. The money price form is the characteristic price form of commodities when commodity exchange becomes generalised and repetitive.

Although Marx is not so explicit on the matter, it would appear that he saw prices as serving the fundamental **purpose** of facilitating economic reproduction in all economic systems founded on an extensive division of labour mediated by exchange. Prices do this by enabling individual producers to command parts of the social product (*viz.*, material inputs and consumption goods) which permit them to reproduce their individual commodities alongside the reproduction of all other commodities in accordance with social demand. That is, by exchanging their products according to given price ratios, producers are able to command the necessary generalised exchangeable worth in terms of money which allows them to purchase the requisite material inputs and consumption goods, and ultimately direct and indirect labour time, to recommence production.[5]

It is because prices serve this purpose in commodity production systems that they are of necessity **fundamentally linked to the values of commodities** and can only be really understood on the basis of these values. The characteristic features of an economic system founded on a division of labour are that goods are produced for society at large and not the direct consumption of the individual producer, and the productive resources used in the production of all goods in the system count as part of the total productive resources available to society for this production. These features result in the goods produced in such a system (not one necessarily mediated by exchange) having social usefulness – they are useful for society at large and not the producer of the goods *per se* – and social worth – they have worth or value in relation to one another. The notion of social usefulness needs no comment. Social worth, or value, does.

For Marx **value** refers to the objective worth of a commodity as distinct from its subjective worth or utility. This objective worth represents the relative (social) productive resources required to produce the good. The productive resources comprise produced material inputs and labour time. Labour time refers to the expenditure of labour by human beings in the process of production over a given period of time. Marx sees labour time as representing the ultimate productive resource in all systems characterised by a division of labour. This is because he sees production founded on a division of labour as social production, involving human beings, who through their cooperative efforts produce goods and services which are demanded by society as a whole. As long as society is founded on a division of labour, the products of labour will have value in relation to one another; their production will require a certain amount of society's labour.[6] This labour will be both direct – pertaining to the immediate process of production – and indirect – pertaining to the processes of production of the inputs. The indirect labour, incidentally, is not past labour, but part of the current expenditure of social labour which needs to be devoted to the replacement of inputs used up in the production of commodities. When exchange comes to mediate the division of labour, it was noted above, produced goods acquire exchangeable worth, or symbols of this exchangeable worth (prices), in relation to one another. This exchangeable worth, or price, is distinct from the value or intrinsic worth of the product, yet is necessarily related to it in a very fundamental sense. It is distinct in the sense that it, price, represents the productive resources, or direct and indirect labour time, **commanded** by the commodity in the process of exchange, while the value of the commodity represents the productive resources, or direct and indirect labour time, that needs to be **expended** in its production. Since price should facilitate the reproduction of the individual commodity in the course of the reproduction of all required commodities if the system is to continue, it is of necessity linked to value. It cannot logically be otherwise. Selling goods at certain prices enables producers to command the produced inputs (material inputs and consumption goods) which permit them to expend the necessary productive resources (material inputs and labour time) in the reproduction of commodities. In doing so, it allows them to command the necessary direct and indirect labour time to produce the required social product. Moreover, by implication, not only are prices related to values, they are obviously formed in the context of the same process – the reproduction of the economic system – and at the same time. As will be argued below (see Chapter 5), this interpretation of Marx's theory of price is opposed to those interpretations which see value as formed independently of, and prior to, the formation of prices of production.

This is not to say, however, that Marx sees actual prices as corresponding to values and/or those prices which permit a balanced reproduction of the system. For him, in fact, the price form of necessity gives rise to the possibility of a quantitative divergence between actual exchange ratios and those which permit the balanced reproduction of the system (see Marx, 1976, p. 197). Marx is most certainly not an equilibrium theorist.

2.4   The magnitudes of reproduction prices

Why start with reproduction prices?

When explaining the determinants of the magnitudes of prices, Marx focuses in the first instance on the prices which permit the repro-duction of the individual commodity as part of the balanced repro-duction of the economic system as a whole. Such prices are usually referred to as **equilibrium prices**, but should perhaps more appro-priately be regarded as **reproduction prices**.[7] Reproduction prices for Marx are averages of actual prices of a given type of commodity. The justification for starting with reproduction prices is that actual prices must tend towards these, at least fleetingly, if the system under invest-igation is to be seen as continuing. Although Marx is not explicit about this when analysing prices in simple circulation, it would seem that for him it is the explanation of the magnitudes of reproduction prices that constitutes the logical point of departure for the explanation of the magnitudes of actual prices since the latter can only be meaningfully understood as divergences from these. Marx states:

> The exchange or sale of commodities at their value is the rational, **natural law of the equilibrium** between them; this is the basis on which divergences have to be explained, and not the converse, i.e., **the law of equilibrium** should not be derived from contemplating the divergences. (1981, p. 289; emphasis added)

It also warrants noting that, although Marx recognises reproduction prices are averages of actual money prices, he abstracts from money in the first instance when explaining the determinants of reproduction prices. That is, he explains reproduction prices as **relative prices** in the first instance. He does this because he sees the worth of a commodity in general as having meaning most fundamentally in relative terms i.e., in relation to another commodity. Moreover, if price is seen as facilitating the reproduction of the commodity, what is important is the amount of inputs (including labour) the commodity is able to command. This means that it is the exchangeable worth of the com-modity in relation to that of the inputs required for its reproduction that matters. Of course, since it is money that actually mediates exchanges and enables the seller of the commodity to purchase the requisite inputs to renew production, money needs to be brought into the picture to complete the analysis. But it is only done so after the explanation of reproduction prices as relative prices.

Relative reproduction prices

Since the fundamental purpose of prices is to facilitate the repro-duction of commodities in the context of the reproduction of the econ-omic system as a whole, the magnitude of price should be linked to the conditions governing the production of commodities. Accordingly, for Marx, the major determinants of the magnitudes of reproduction prices of commodities in all commodity production systems are the relative magnitudes of their values. From the definition of value given above, this means that, for Marx, the magnitudes of reproduction prices in the simple circulation of commodities are primarily determined by the direct and indirect labour time that needs to be expended to pro-duce various commodities in the context of a balanced reproduction of the system.

Marx refers to the labour required for the reproduction of the commodity as socially necessary labour to convey the notion that what matters for the determination of price is not the actual past labour embodied in the individual commodity, but rather the labour required to produce a standard commodity of a given type, including the inputs required for this production at the time of the sale of the commodity:

> The value of a commodity is certainly determined by the quantity of labour contained in it, but this quantity is itself socially determined. If the amount of labour time socially necessary for the production of any commodity alters – and a given weight of cotton represents more labour time after a bad harvest than a good one – this reacts back on all the old commodities of the same type, because they are only individuals of the same species, and their value at any given time is measured by the labour socially necessary to produce them, i.e., by the labour time necessary under the social conditions exist-ing at the time. (1976, p. 318)

Marx sees the clearest manifestation of the link between prices and values to be evidenced by respective changes in their magnitudes. He observes that, for the most part, and over the long run, changes in prices are driven by changes in the magnitudes of values, and the latter, in turn, by changes in the physical productivity of labour. This physical productivity is in respect of both the immediate process of production and the production of the material inputs into this process.

This is all well known, but a number of aspects of this explanation warrant further elaboration and emphasis since they have a bearing on a host of debates surrounding the explanation.

First, although Marx sees value as the fundamental determinant of reproduction price, he does not see this determination as either direct or mechanical. Marx is clear that when producers set prices they do not directly compute prices in terms of values or relative labour times (see 1973, pp. 167–8). **Labour time is not the measure of the exchange values of commodities**. Rather, for Marx, when producers compute prices in a way which permits the reproduction of their commodities (using money as the basis for this computation), they effectively do so on the basis of values. That is to say, when producers compute prices to facilitate reproduction, they do so with a view to acquiring the necessary inputs to reproduce their commodities. These inputs are the material inputs used in the production of the commodity and the consumption goods needed to sustain themselves.[8] When producers compute prices in this way, they are estimating the worth of their commodities in relation to these inputs. Money is used as the standard for this estimation. The estimation of the required inputs comes from an assessment by producers of the technical requirements of production. It comes from an assessment of the resources that need to be expended in the production of the commodity. Estimation of the material inputs required to produce the commodity comes from an assessment of the amount and type of material needed in the production of the commodity. And, estimation of the consumption goods required to sustain the direct producer during the production of the commodity is based on an assessment of the amount of direct labour time required to produce the commodity. As argued above, for Marx, assessing the quantity of resources required to produce a commodity in economies characterised by a division of labour is in effect assessing the amount of direct and indirect labour time required to produce it. So, when producers set prices with a view to acquiring the necessary inputs to reproduce their commodities, they are in effect setting prices on the basis of values. Therefore, in all commodity-producing systems **prices must reflect values** if (balanced) reproduction is to take place, and value is necessary for the explanation of the quantitative determination of price as well as an understanding of it. This is not to say, however, that

producers have in mind the values of their commodities when setting actual prices. I will return to this point below in the discussion of
how actual prices are formed, and how and why they fluctuate around
reproduction prices.

A second point to be made in connection with Marx's explanation
of the magnitude of reproduction price is something of a repetition
of the point made earlier regarding the distinction between value and
price. It is that **value should not be confused with reproduction
price**, even though in the absence of a surplus product the two are
equal in magnitude to one another. Value refers to the direct and indirect labour time that needs to be expended in production, while reproduction price refers to the direct and indirect labour time that needs to
be commanded in the process of exchange to ensure the reproduction
of the individual commodity in accordance with the balanced reproduction of all other commodities. This distinction between value and
reproduction price assumes a considerable importance for Marx in his
explanation of the nature and magnitude of price.

Third, the required resources, or direct and indirect labour time, which
determines the magnitude of value, pertain to the conditions of production at the time of production and sale of the commodity (and
assumed repurchase of inputs), and not the resources actually expended
in its production. This means, that what is important for the determination of price is **current** and not **historic** resource cost. Marx's theory
of price is most definitely not a 'temporal', historic cost, explanation of
price as is sometimes claimed.

Fourth, for Marx, the value transferred to the commodity from the
commodity inputs required for its production is the value of these
inputs and not their exchange values or prices. That is, the value transferred from inputs is given by the direct and indirect labour time
required to produce the inputs and not the labour time they command
in the process of exchange, irrespective of whether this is the current
or historic labour time commanded. The point being made here is central to the debates about Marx's alleged failure to transform the value
of inputs into prices of production, and is also fundamental to the distinction which will be drawn below between Marx's and Sraffa's explanations of price. It must be acknowledged, however, that the written
word of Marx on this issue is unclear. It is even possible to find textual
evidence in his writings which suggests that for him the value transferred is the exchange value or money value of the inputs.[9] In spite of
this, I would argue that the logic of Marx's analysis suggests the value
transferred from the inputs to the value of the commodity is given by

the labour time required to reproduce the inputs. In fact, to see the value of inputs transferred to the value of the commodity as represented by the (reproduction) prices of these inputs, i.e., by the labour time commanded, is to abandon value and tautologically explain the prices of outputs by, among other things, the prices of inputs as outputs.

Finally, and related to this, Marx assumes the value transferred to the commodity outputs from the commodity inputs is not systematically above or below the value of these inputs. In making this assumption he was particularly concerned to oppose the view that some commodities, either by their nature or the particular manner in which they are used, transfer more or less value to the commodities they help produce than they themselves contain or represent. Crucially, this translates into his opposition to the idea that in surplus product systems the surplus can be seen as the result of buying cheap and selling dear. For Marx, as will be further expanded on below, it is only labour that can transfer more value to the commodity than it contains or represents in terms of the value of the wage goods required for its sustenance. In contrast with non-labour commodity inputs, there is no logical difficulty in conceiving of the fact that the value of the labour input (the value of the wages paid to labour) is less than the value this input transfers to the commodity it helps to produce.

Money reproduction prices

As noted above, Marx initially abstracts from money when explaining reproduction prices because what matters in the first instance in this explanation is the relative worth of the produced commodities, particularly their worth in relation to the commodity inputs they command in the process of their exchange. To repeat, reproduction prices of commodities are those prices which enable the producer to command the necessary inputs to reproduce the commodity in the context of the balanced reproduction of all commodities for which there is social demand. Hence, although prices are denominated in terms of money, and although commodities exchange for money and not for other commodities, what matters as far as the reproduction of the commodity is concerned is ultimately whether the price of the commodity allows the producer to command the commodity inputs needed to reproduce it. Since money can be argued to mediate the exchange of commodities even when considering the simple circulation of commodities, and since prices are actually money prices, money needs to be explicitly brought into the analysis of price to complete the picture. It is, in fact, the amount of money that the commodity commands which determines whether the required commodity inputs can be obtained. So when Marx brings money into the analysis, he is explaining in the first instance the money magnitudes of reproduction prices and, by extension, the money price level assuming the system is in balance. This means that the money prices he explains in the first instance are not actual money prices, but rather what may be called **money reproduction prices**.

An understanding of how precisely money facilitates the simple circulation of commodities and how money prices are determined requires some consideration of the form of money and the functions it performs. A misunderstanding of these, it will be shown later when considering other theories of money prices, causes a fundamental misunderstanding of the value of money and money prices.

For most of his analysis of prices in the simple circulation of commodities, Marx assumes money to be a commodity, i.e., gold. This is because he sees money emerging out of the process of generalised exchange as the most widely traded commodity with the requisite characteristics (*viz.*, durability, transportability, homogeneity, and divisibility) to fulfill the necessary functions of money. To the extent that he considers other money forms in this analysis, it is as tokens of money in the process of circulation (see below). He does not bring into consideration other more advanced forms of money, such as state-issued paper, since he considers this would presuppose an analysis which he has yet to develop, namely the credit and banking system under capitalism (see Marx, 1976, p. 224). As will become clearer from what follows, the implication of seeing money as a commodity is that its value, and therefore in the final instance the money prices of all commodities money circulates, will necessarily be linked to the physical resources required for its production.

As for the functions money performs in the process of simple circulation, Marx sees these as measure of value, medium of circulation, means of payment and hoard. Marx sees the measure of value function of money as its primary and defining function. As measure of value, Marx argues that money converts the exchangeable values of commodities into a common standard and regulates their exchanges with one another. In fact, because of this, it seems entirely more appropriate to refer to this function as the **measure of exchange value** function, especially because, as was noted above, Marx sees the measure of the value of a commodity as labour time. The exchangeable value which money confers on commodities allows producers of these commodities to command the requisite inputs to reproduce them – the commodities. To be able to confer exchangeable worth on commodities, money must represent exchangeable worth in general; it must represent exchangeable worth in relation to commodities. It comes to represent exchangeable worth in relation to all commodities by mediating their exchange, with the magnitude of this exchangeable worth, i.e., the exchange value or price of money, given by the average exchangeable worth of the commodities money circulates over a given period of time.[10] Of course, when money is a produced commodity, this exchangeable worth is ultimately determined by the relative resources required to produce it. That is, the labour time commanded by money in exchange when money is a commodity is ultimately determined by the labour time required for its production. Which also means that when money is a commodity, a long-term fall in its price, and a corresponding rise in the aggregate money price of all commodities, would only be possible if the direct and indirect labour cost of producing money were to fall relative to the direct and indirect labour cost of producing all other commodities (see Marx, 1970, p. 67, p. 106). This is not to say, however, that the latter could not be induced by a prior fall in the exchange value of money. A fall in the exchange value of money could, for example, result in less productive gold producers leaving the industry, or an expansion in the scale of gold production giving rise to a reduction in costs, both of which would impact on the value of money. It needs noting in this context that, while there can most certainly be a disjuncture between the exchange and intrinsic values of money, this should not be construed as implying a fundamental inconsistency between the two, as some interpreters of Marx have suggested.[11]

A number of additional points need to be made with respect to the preceding which arguably further aid understanding of Marx's explanation of the determinants of money price magnitudes. To begin with, Marx's conceptualisation of money as measure of exchange value implies that commodities and money should be seen as coming into circulation with money prices and a definite magnitude of exchangeable worth, respectively. Money functions as measure when producers set the prices of their commodities in terms of money before these enter circulation, and when they set their prices they do so on the basis of an assumed given magnitude of exchangeable worth for money. Moreover, money as measure of exchange value should not be confused with money as *numéraire*. As measure of exchange value, money does not reduce commodities to equivalence, while as *numéraire* it does. As measure, money represents the worth of commodities to one another. It is able to do this because commodities are intrinsically comparable as products of social labour; products produced in the framework of a division of labour where each labour input counts as an aliquot quantity of total social labour. As *numéraire*, in contrast, money reduces commodities which are not inherently comparable to equivalence. Lastly, although Marx recognises that as measure the exchange value of money should be stable, for him it does not have to be, and indeed cannot be, **invariable** (see 1970, pp. 67–8; 1976, p. 192). To argue that money's exchange value should be invariable is, for Marx, to misunderstand the essential nature and purpose of money as measure. It is to confuse money with labour time. Money, as the measure of the exchangeable worth of commodities, establishes their command over all other commodities, while labour time, as the measure of their intrinsic worth, establishes the amount of social labour time which is required to be spent in their production. The nature of money as measure of exchangeable worth of commodities means that its own worth in terms of the labour time it commands can and will change, and will do so as a result of the very same forces giving rise to changes in the values (and therefore exchange values) of commodities. The nature and extent of these changes in the value and exchange value of money will also naturally depend on the institutional setting of money – whether, for example, money is a commodity or intrinsically valueless pieces of paper. Although Marx argues money can be variable in its exchangeable worth when functioning as the measure of the exchange values of commodities, it does not mean he sees this variability as having no bearing on money's performance of this function. Marx is clear that, while variability in the exchange value of money *per se* does not significantly impair the performance of its measure of exchange value function, an excessive variability in its exchange value would.

Turning now to money as **medium of circulation**, Marx sees this function as facilitating the transfer of ownership of commodities between individuals at a given point in time. It facilitates 'spot transactions' to use modern parlance. However, it facilitates this transfer of ownership in the context of repeated purchases and sales of the commodity. As medium of circulation, the money acquired by the seller of commodities is not to hold for itself, as abstract wealth, but rather to purchase other commodities and thereby reproduce the commodities that were sold. It is for this reason that Marx refers to the function as its medium of 'circulation' and not medium of 'exchange' (see 1970, pp. 95–6). The medium of circulation function of money presupposes the measure of exchange value function. Money, as medium of circulation, circulates commodities with given money prices. Money is used by commodity producers as a measure of exchange value to set the prices of their commodities before the commodities are put into circulation and circulated by money. In the performance of its function as medium of circulation it is the quantity, not substance, of money that matters. Therefore, in the performance of this function money does not have to be physically present and can be replaced by lesser value tokens of itself.[12] Marx puts it as follows:

> [I]n this process which continually makes money pass from hand to hand, it only needs to lead a symbolic existence. Its functional existence so to speak absorbs its material existence. Since it is a transiently objectified reflection of the prices of commodities, it serves only as a symbol of itself, and can therefore be replaced by another symbol. (1976, p. 226)

An important implication of Marx's analysis of money's function as medium of circulation for his explanation of the magnitudes of money prices is that it allows for the possibility of a disjuncture between the amount of money in circulation and the money prices of commodities to be circulated. Since money can be replaced by lesser value, or valueless, tokens of itself in the performance of its function as medium of circulation, money prices could rise above levels suggested by the amount of money in circulation. Marx, in fact, argues that an important consequence of the replacement of money in circulation by less valuable tokens of itself is that there could be an **excess** of these tokens in the sense that more of them could be pushed into circulation than is warranted by the demand for them given their nominal exchange ratio with the commodity money they represent drafts on. He contends that, if this were to happen, the tokens would simply depreciate in value; they would represent a lesser amount of the money commodity than their face value would suggest.

> If the paper money exceeds its proper limit, i.e., the amount in gold coins of the same denomination which could have been in circulation, then, quite apart from the danger of becoming universally discredited, it will still represent within the world of commodities only that quantity of gold which is fixed by its immanent laws. No greater quantity is capable of being represented. (Marx, 1976, p. 225)

This is not to say that the increase in tokens of money would cause the money prices of commodities to rise, at least not over the long run. These prices would continue to reflect the relative worth of commodities in terms of the money commodity. Over the short run, the debasement of the tokens as a result of an excessive amount of them in circulation could most certainly cause a rise in money prices, but this rise would be reversed as soon as the convertibility of the tokens came to be in doubt. In a commodity money economy the likelihood of such doubts arising is far greater than with state-issued paper money since the quantity of actual money available is inherently more limited.

With the development of credit, money also appears in the process of circulation as a **means of payment**, to settle debt obligations. Some of these obligations are debts contracted in respect of the transfer of commodities from one person to another. The transfer of commodities in this case is facilitated by credit and not money. For Marx, however, **credit is not money**. Money serves to measure the exchange values of commodities and debt obligations at the point of transfer. It then enters the circulation process at a later stage to settle the debt obligations as a means of payment. The appearance of credit points to a further disjuncture between the amount of money in circulation and the level of money prices of commodities which are in circulation. On the one hand, part of the commodities in circulation at any point in time may be circulated by credit and not money, and, on the other hand, part of the money in circulation at any point in time may be to settle debts in respect of commodities which have long since departed the process of circulation (see Marx, 1976, p. 234).

Marx argues that money functions as **hoard** when it is held for itself, as the general form of value, and when it is held to service the circulation process. He contends that the former function of hoard disappears with the development of capitalism since in capitalism the hoarding of money as abstract wealth actually leads to a loss of wealth. In capitalism, wealth accumulation is the accumulation of capital, even if it assumes a money form (see Marx, 1970, p. 147; 1978, p. 423). This implies, incidentally, that Marx would have denied that money functions as a **store of value** in advanced capitalism in the manner suggested by, for example, the Post Keynesian approach. I will return to this issue again below when discussing the Post Keynesian approach (see Chapter 7). Accordingly, for Marx, the hoarding function of money is for the most part to service the circulation process. Such hoards are reserves of means of purchase and, with the development of the credit system, means of payment. These hoards are not to be confused with reserve funds of coin 'which form a constituent element of the total amount of money always in circulation' (Marx, 1970, p. 137). In its hoarding function, as in its measure of exchange value function, the actual presence of money is not required. Hence, from the early stages of capitalist commodity production and the development of the banking system, actual hoards of money come to be replaced by accounting entries – i.e., money comes to exist as money of account.

The view of the determination of the value of money and the level of money prices which emerges from Marx's analysis of money and the functions it performs in the simple circulation of commodities causes him to reject the TQM. The TQM held that the price of money (which is frequently referred to in expositions of the TQM as its 'value') and the level of money prices are determined by the quantitative relation of money and commodities in circulation (in actual exchange).[13] Marx's critical comments on the TQM are to be found in several of his works including *A Contribution to the Critique of Political Economy*, *Theories of Surplus Value* and *Capital*. Quite evidently, they are far from representing a coherent critique of the TQM. However, from these comments, and his explanation of money prices, one can deduce that Marx's opposition to the TQM was because it failed to see that: a) commodities and money come into circulation with money prices and value, respectively (see Marx, 1976, p. 220); b) tokens of money and credit may also facilitate the circulation of commodities disrupting the quantitative link between the amount of money in circulation and the money prices of commodities being circulated (see Marx, 1976, pp. 225–7, p. 237; 1981, pp. 653–5); c) an excess of money in circulation could filter into hoards unless the excess was constituted by tokens of money, in which case they would depreciate in value over the long run (see Marx, 1973, pp. 121–2; 1981, pp. 655–60);[14] and d) changes in the average money price level could be due to changes in the general level of labour productivity of all commodities.

2.5   Actual prices

Actual prices and reproduction prices

Although Marx begins his explanation of the determinants of price by focusing in the first instance on prices which enable the balanced reproduction of the system, and although he sees reproduction prices as averages of actual prices, he is at pains to emphasise that the latter would only rarely correspond to the former. It bears repeating that, although Marx most certainly conceives of reproduction or equilibrium prices, he is not an equilibrium theorist; he does not see actual prices as normally corresponding to, or inexorably tending towards their equilibrium levels. For Marx, actual prices will continuously deviate from reproduction prices in commodity producing systems because of the very nature of such systems and the way in which prices are formed. Moreover, in all such systems, the divergences of actual prices from those which permit balance can and will be quite significant and protracted, even occasioning ruptures in the systems. Marx does not, however, elaborate on why and how actual prices tend to fluctuate around reproduction prices in the course of his discussion of the determinants of price in simple commodity circulation, except to note in passing (admittedly when discussing reproduction prices in capitalism – see below) that the divergences are explained by **supply and demand imbalances**. It is most likely he felt that such a discussion would require a more detailed analysis of how prices are formed and, therefore, a more in-depth study of the actual production system than is possible or warranted in the study of simple commodity circulation. Against the backdrop of Marx's analytical legacy some elaboration of these issues at the present juncture may nevertheless prove instructive.

To begin with, it would seem from the preceding that the divergences of actual prices from reproduction prices can be broken down into two components; a relative and an absolute or money component. The relative component refers to the divergence of actual relative prices of commodities from those which would ensure the balanced reproduction of all commodities (excluding money) in the system. The money component refers to the divergence of the actual price of money (its exchange ratio with all other commodities) from that price which would ensure its reproduction in the context of the balanced reproduction of the system, or, alternatively, the divergence of the money price level of all commodities from the money price level which would ensure their balanced reproduction. Since the divergence of actual from the reproduction prices of commodities corresponds to a general imbalance in supply and demand, and since the former can be decomposed in the manner suggested above, it would seem that one could similarly decompose the general imbalance in supply and demand in a way which corresponds to this decomposition of the divergences of actual from reproduction prices. That is to say, relative price divergences can be seen as corresponding to supply and demand imbalances of commodities in relation to one another, and the divergence of the price of money can be seen as corresponding to supply and demand imbalances for money in relation to all other commodities. These decompositions can then be used to ascertain the possibility and causes of divergences between actual and reproduction prices, as well as adjustments of these divergences.

Possibility of divergences

Marx sees the possibility of the divergence of actual prices from reproduction prices, and, therefore, imbalance in the system, as arising from the very nature of commodity producing systems. The key feature of these systems which give rise to such a possibility is the separation of production from distribution, exchange and consumption. The consequence of this separation is that the supply of commodities is divorced from the demand for them. This is because, with the separation of production from distribution, exchange and consumption, the supply of commodities, including the money commodity, is not directly based on the actual demand for them, and the demand for commodities, including the money commodity, is not directly based on, or even necessarily proportionate to, the proceeds obtained from the supply or sale of commodities.

The possibility of a divergence between actual and reproduction prices is developed in simple circulation by the appearance of money, tokens of money, and credit. Money reinforces the possibility of a divergence between actual and reproduction prices by permitting one party in the process of exchange to sell or buy a good without simultaneously having to buy or sell another good. It means there does not have to be continuous balance between supply and demand, and actual relative prices need not at all times correspond to those relative prices which facilitate reproduction, and/or the exchange value of money need not correspond to its intrinsic exchangeable worth – that worth which facilitates the balanced reproduction of the system. In fact, it is the appearance of money that causes the imbalance between supply and demand to become widespread. To the extent that tokens of money replace money in the performance of its function as circulating media, they can be seen as further exacerbating these divergences; those which arise from not having to immediately buy or sell a good when selling or buying another. Credit exacerbates the divergences of actual relative prices from reproduction relative prices as well as the actual money price level from the reproduction money price level because it enables the sellers of goods to acquire goods without having sold and the buyer of goods to buy without having the requisite income. I will elaborate on this point in Chapter 3 (Section 7).

Sources of divergences

From the logic of Marx's analysis, if not his written words, one can deduce that for him the mere possibility of divergences of actual from reproduction prices does not explain their occurrence, extent, frequency and duration. For such an explanation one would need to delve into the specificities of the commodity production system under investigation. Although Marx's focus is capitalism, he does never-theless make a number of references during this analysis to sources of possible divergences of actual from reproduction prices in pre-capitalist commodity producing systems. Since these economies are typically based on agriculture, he sees the imbalances in respect of the supply and demand for commodities *vis-à-vis* each other as stemming from the conditions affecting the production of these commodities. Major divergences in actual agricultural commodity prices from their relative reproduction price levels would be the result of, for example, poor harvests, wars and even the expansion of trade within and between countries. The very same forces would also explain divergences in the price of money from its reproduction level, since they would most likely result in major changes (increases) in the demand for money in relation to other commodities – agricultural commodities.

It warrants noting here that while Marx certainly recognised the pos-sibility of price computational errors on the part of buyers and sellers of products, including producers, he appears to have not accorded such errors any significance in his explanation of the sources of divergences of actual from reproduction prices. Although, to the best of my know-ledge, he left no written indication as to why he chose not to accord them any significance, it seems to me that it was because he did not want to explain the sources of price divergences, like the magnitudes of the reproduction prices themselves, in terms of subjective factors.

The price adjustment process

Marx recognises that when there is an imbalance between supply and demand, not only would there be divergences of actual from repro-duction prices, there would also be forces at work pushing the two together. These reversals in price divergences would accompany, and give rise to, tendencies towards balance in supply and demand. To the extent that the 'reverse movement' in actual prices of commodities *vis-à-vis* each other imply changes in the conditions of production, there would tend to be a movement of reproduction prices and values of commodities accompanying this reverse movement in actual prices, possibly in the same direction as the actual prices, and in the same way there might be movements in reproduction prices and values accompanying the initial divergence. The same holds for the diver-gence of the price of money (in terms of all commodities) and associ-ated money prices of commodities from those magnitudes of the two which facilitate the balanced reproduction of the system. There would be reversals in these divergences which would in all probability be accompanied by changes in the conditions of production of money and, therefore, the value and reproduction price of money.

While accepting that there would be tendencies pushing prices back towards their reproduction levels following their movement apart, Marx rejects the notion that these would cause actual prices to coincide with reproduction prices, except fleetingly. This is because he saw the impulses disturbing the balance between supply and demand as recurrent, even in pre-capitalist systems. In such systems these impulses typically come from changes in the conditions of supply, especially the ever-changing configurations of supply of goods within, and outside of, community boundaries. In capitalism, as will be discussed below, these impulses are continuous and come from technological changes, the expansion of credit and competition between capitalists.

2.6 A digression on social and abstract labour

In his analysis of prices in the context of the simple circulation of commodities, Marx dwells at length on labour; the labour which gives rise to, and is the measure of, value. He sees this labour as 'social' and 'abstract' or general labour. As soon as individual labour is performed within a division of labour such that the commodity is produced alongside a mass of similar commodities to satisfy social (and not individual) need, the products of labour acquire worth in relation to one another, and the labour expended in the production of a good acquires the character of social labour. The labour expended in the production of a good is social labour in the sense that it is henceforth part of a mass of interlinked labour which, as a totality, reproduces the material base (the required mass of commodities and services) of the system (see Marx, 1981, pp. 777–8). For Marx, it is not the exchange process that transforms the labour expended on the commodity into social labour. Rather, when exchange mediates a division of labour, the exchange of products confirms that labour expended in the production of commodities is social in nature, that it is part of total labour.

Where exchange does have a transformative role is with respect to the actual, concrete, social labour performed; the specific type of labour. When the division of labour comes to be mediated by exchange and commodities begin to assume a comparable form as money prices, the concrete, social labour expended in the production of these commodities begins to count as general and qualitatively equal, or **abstract**, labour (see Marx, 1976, p. 142). Marx notes that the expenditure of labour as general or abstract labour becomes a visible reality under capitalism with the increasing mobility of labour between diverse productive activities and the de-skilling which accompanies technological progress.[15] Hence, for Marx, the substance of value in an exchange-based production system is not labour *per se* but social and abstract labour. Unless the labour expended in the context of a division of labour is seen as representing labour which is part of total labour and qualitatively equal to one another, the resulting commodity or service cannot be seen as representing value or comparable worth. The money price form of the commodity does precisely this. It shows the resources, and ultimately labour, that needs to be expended in the production of the commodities to be qualitatively equal and comparable.

The preceding can be put another way. When there is a division of labour, all individual productive activities become interlinked and count as part of a whole. They acquire a social dimension as opposed to a mere individual and isolated dimension. The labour expended in the production of all goods required by the system counts as social or interlinked labour. When the division of labour comes to be mediated by exchange, the fruits of the productive activities of labour have to be compared with one another for exchange-based reproduction of the system to take place. Comparison of the productive activities of labour for this purpose means comparing the productive resources required for the reproduction of the goods in question. In the final instance, since goods are typically produced by other produced goods and labour, this means comparing the labour expended in the production of goods, labour being the common denominator. Accordingly, the labour actually expended becomes comparable as qualitatively equivalent labour. The exchange process causes the actual concrete (social) labour expended to be compared as general labour.[16]

A vital implication of this interpretation of Marx's conceptualisation of labour is it denies that for Marx (individual and concrete) labour becomes social and abstract **in the process of exchange** in opposition to the interpretation of this conceptualisation by an important school of Marxist thinking – the 'value-form' school – which takes as its point of departure the work of I.I. Rubin (1972). What is being argued here is that, for Marx, labour expended in the production of goods becomes in essence social labour and goods acquire worth in relation to one another once production is organised on the basis of an extensive division of labour. When exchange comes to mediate the division of labour, the products of labour manifest themselves as representatives of social labour through the acquisition of the price form; they become commodities. And, when money comes to facilitate exchange, i.e., when the exchange of products is not direct, the labour expended in the reproduction of commodities also comes to show itself as representing general or abstract labour in as much as the price form becomes the money price form. The labour expended in the reproduction of commodities is able to show itself as general labour time because it comes to acquire a real existence in capitalism – capitalism being a mode of production in which labour moves increasingly freely between different activities. Seeing labour as becoming social and abstract in the process of exchange in the manner of the value-form approach may well have contributed to what is argued below to be the mistaken trajectory of many modern sympathetic interpretations of Marx's theory of price, interpretations which equate prices of production with value and see the measure of prices of production/value as both money and labour time, or even quite simply money (see, for example, Arthur, 2005, 2006).

3
Marx's Theory of Price – Capitalist Commodity Production

3.1   Understanding prices in capitalism

Prices in capitalism, as in commodity production systems in general, are symbols of the relative worth of commodities (and the production activities that give rise to them) which assume a money form. The particular money form they assume is not only a commodity money form but also, and typically, one of intrinsically valueless paper – state-issued paper money. For Marx, the purpose of prices in capitalism, as in all commodity production systems, is to facilitate the reproduction of individual commodities in the context of the reproduction of the economic system. In capitalism the reproduction of the system also implies its expansion. Capitalism is a commodity production system characterised by the existence of a surplus product which assumes an exchange value or money form and is appropriated by producers in relation to the exchangeable worth of inputs advanced to undertake production. The inputs advanced are **capital**, and include outlays on labour power. The surplus product permits an expansion of the system by enabling an expansion of inputs used in production (and encouraging technological change). Prices facilitate expanded reproduction by enabling producers to command, on the one hand, the necessary inputs to reproduce the existing volume of commodities and, on the other hand, additional inputs to produce additional commodities. Provided there is a physical surplus produced in the system as a whole, there can potentially be an expansion in the scale of production of at least one sector. The norm will be the expansion of many sectors, but also the decline of some. The extent to which one sector will expand in relation to another will depend on the magnitude of the surplus a sector manages to command in relation to the inputs required to produce the commodity. The extent to which the economy as a whole will grow depends on the extent to which the productive sectors are able to generate and appropriate a surplus product.

As in commodity production in general, so in capitalism, producers act in isolation from one another in pursuit of their own interests, yet are dependent on each other for the reproduction of their commodities. In capitalism producers seek, through the prices of their products, to maximise profits – i.e., to appropriate as large a part of the exchangeable worth of the total surplus produced as possible. Price formation and profit maximisation take place in the context of competition between producers within and between industries. Competition between producers in the same industry, or intra-industry competition, causes average producers in the industry concerned (those producing the bulk of commodities) to adopt similar prices for a standard product. It forces on average producers of a standard product an average unit cost by forcing on them a standard technique, scale of production and level of capacity utilisation (see Marx, 1969b, p. 207, p. 209; 1976, p. 436). Competition between producers in different industries, or inter-industry competition, causes producers of standard products in all industries to appropriate an economy-wide average rate of profit, allowing for differences in risk, turnover time, and the like (see Marx, 1981, p. 312). An average rate of profit is forced on producers of the standard product in all industries by the actual and potential migration of capital. Since appropriation of an average profit gives rise to the reallocation of the surplus resources expended by producers in different sectors such that the average producer in each sector appropriates a profit in proportion to the exchange value of capital advanced, prices will typically deviate from values. However, since prices facilitate the reproduction of commodities, they will necessarily continue to be fundamentally determined by values – provided that the system continues to reproduce itself.

It needs stressing that Marx sees **competition as a process**, one in which individual firms and industries attempt to appropriate as high a profit as possible in the course of the expanded reproduction of their products. Specifically, he sees it as a process involving tendencies and counter-tendencies, and giving rise to phenomena usually identified with monopoly. For example, while the tendency emanating from the intra-industry competitive process is towards standardisation – a standard price for a standard product based on a certain average unit costs of production – the same process gives rise to divergences. It gives rise, *inter alia*, to: actual and perceived product differentiation allowing for price differentiation; a lowering of average unit costs by some producers through the adoption of new technologies and techniques of production, an expansion of scale and the geographic relocation of production, etc. The excess profits earned by individual firms will attract others to copy the products and technologies of those making the excess profits. The result may well be a new product standard corresponding to a new average unit cost-price, or even a new industry or sub-industry founded an entirely new product or sub-product (e.g., the emergence of personal computers as an entirely new sector in the computer industry, the subsequent differentiation of personal computers into desktops and notebooks, and the further differentiation of the latter in terms of processing power, screen size, hard disk capacity size, etc.). The inter-industry competitive process similarly involves both tendencies and counter-tendencies; the tendency for capital to migrate and an average rate of profit to be imposed on all sectors, and the counter-tendency for impediments to this migration and resulting profit differences between sectors over and above those warranted by differences in risk, turnover time, and the like.

As noted in Chapter 1, although Marx's analysis of the dynamics of the capitalist system is premised on the existence of competitive processes, he accepts that there can be monopoly sectors in such a competitive setting. For Marx, a monopoly sector is one where the producers accounting for the bulk of the production of a certain type of product appropriate an excess profit, or monopoly (absolute) **rent**, over a considerable period of time. The excess profit appropriated by the producers in the monopoly sector implies a lower average rate of profit appropriated by the competitive part of the economy. Notwithstanding his view of the tendency of capital towards concentration and centralisation, it would seem that Marx considered monopolies to be, for the most part, both limited in scope and fleeting in nature in a competitive capitalist system. The competitive process itself, and the institutional apparatus built up around the process, would ensure this. This is not to say that he considered it impossible for the entire capitalist system to come to be dominated by monopolies. He most certainly accepted such an outcome to be entirely within the realm of possibility, but suggested that it would require a very different analysis of the economic system than he provides in *Capital* (see Marx, 1981, p. 368).

3.2   Marx's approach to explaining the magnitudes of prices in capitalism

Marx builds his explanation of the magnitude of price in capitalism throughout his analysis of capitalism in all three volumes of *Capital*. This explanation can be divided into two distinct parts. The first corresponds to his explanation of the magnitude of price in the context of an individual capitalist (or capital-in-general) and pertains to Volumes 1 and 2, while the second expands on this explanation in the context of competition between many capitalists and is to be found in Volume 3. The explanation of the magnitude of price in the first part crucially abstracts from the distribution of the surplus product between producers, while that in the second part takes this into account and then expands on this explanation to also take into account the further distribution of the surplus product between productive and non-productive capital (especially interest-bearing capital[1]), industry and agriculture, and monopoly and non-monopoly productive sectors. The explanation of price in both parts abstract in the first instance from the money form of price. However, because the first part looks at only capital-in-general, it is not concerned with explaining relative price magnitudes so much as explaining their nature – the constituent parts of price and how these are to be understood. Nevertheless, it needs emphasising that the first part provides the indispensable foundations for Marx's explanation of relative price magnitudes in the context of competition between capitals.

The explanation of the magnitude of price in the context of capital-in-general begins in Volume 1 from Chapter 4 onwards with the analysis of the capitalist commodity production process, and then, in Volume 2, moves on to a consideration of the capitalist commodity circulation process. Throughout this explanation, Marx assumes the price of the commodity to be equal to its value since there is no question of a re-distribution of the surplus product between capitals. Accordingly, Marx's focus in his analysis of price in Volumes 1 and 2 is the value of the commodity. Starting with the analysis of production in Volume 1, Marx shows that the value of a commodity is determined by the technical conditions of its (re)production; the inputs (measured by labour time) and direct labour time required for its production. There is a fundamental presumption that the time expended by workers in the production of a good is in excess of the (direct and indirect) labour time required to produce the wage goods needed to sustain them for the duration of the production of the commodity. This is because, for Marx, the essence of the capital–labour relation is the payment of workers a wage of a lesser value than the value of the commodities they produce. Marx refers to the value of the capital outlaid on the material inputs into production as 'constant capital' (C) to emphasise the fact that the commodities purchased with this capital only transfer the value they represent (the labour time required for their production) to the value of the output, and not any additional value. He sees the labour expended in production by workers as covering the value of the wages advanced by the capitalist, i.e., the labour time needed to produce the wage goods consumed by the workers, and an excess over this. He refers to the capital advanced to pay wages as 'variable capital' (V) to emphasise the fact that this capital results in an expansion of value, i.e., an expenditure of labour time over and above that needed to produce the wage goods consumed by workers – surplus value (S). Since the price of the product is equal to the value of the product when capital is seen as capital-in-general, it may be depicted as:

$$W = C + V + S$$

where w is the price of the product, c and v are the values of constant and variable capital transferred to the price of the product, and s the surplus value transferred to the price of the product.

In the analysis of the circulation of the commodity at the beginning of Volume 2, Marx seeks to show that, with the exception of transport costs, no value is added to the commodity in the process of its sale. Marx does, however, acknowledge that in so far as the circulation process conditions production it can have a bearing on the magnitude of value. If, for example, turnover time is more rapid, labour will produce more goods in a given time period resulting in a fall in the values of the goods.

As is well known, Marx devotes the last part of Volume 2 to a consideration of the simple and expanded reproduction of the economic system, but still assuming away competition between individual capitals. In this analysis he does not develop the explanation of price further, but shows that even if the commodity is sold at value, and abstracting from changes in values as a result of continuous technical change, it is unlikely that reproduction will be balanced and smooth. The reasons he gives are a) the unlikelihood of means of production and consumption (and luxury) goods being produced and exchanged in proportions required for balance – the familiar problem of disproportionality – and b) the possibility and necessity of hoarding of money, in large part due to the need to finance fixed capital outlays.

Having explained the formation and determination of the value of the commodity in the context of the circulation of capital-in-general in Volumes 1 and 2 of *Capital*, Marx proceeds in Volume 3 to show how this value assumes the price form in capitalism in the context of competition between capitals. As should be evident from what has been said above, Marx sees the latter as a process in flux; one in which there are tendencies and counter-tendencies, moving the system towards and away from competitive norms, *viz.*, uniform prices for standard products and average rates of profits. Most importantly, this means that Marx's method and analysis does not preclude, and, indeed, even demands, consideration be given to divergences from these competitive norms in the course of the study of the competitive process.[2]

3.3   The magnitudes of 'prices of production'

Relative prices of production

When Marx moves to the explanation of price magnitudes formed in the process of competition between individual capitals in Volume 3, his focus continues to be those prices which permit a balanced reproduction of the system – prices I have referred to above as reproduction prices when discussing price magnitudes in simple commodity production. He refers to such prices in capitalism as '**prices of production**'. To be clear, prices of production are the prices which would need to prevail if the commodity is to be reproduced such that there is a balanced, expanded, reproduction of the system as a whole. They are, in other words, reproduction prices under capitalism. As reproduction prices, they must, in the final instance, reflect values, since they must, in the final instance, reflect the technical requirements of production. Marx argues, '…it is values that stand behind the prices of production and ultimately determine them' (1981, p. 311). Moreover, as reproduction prices, they must, for reasons given above, also be formed alongside, and at the same time as, values. The difficulty with recognising the relation between the two in capitalism is that prices of production typically deviate from value magnitudes for most commodities. However, for Marx, the relation becomes clearer once it is recognised that the link between prices of production and values is mediated by **cost-price**, and also when considering **changes** in prices of production.

The price of production comprises a cost-price component and an average rate of profit. The cost-price component of the price of production of a commodity refers to that part of the selling price which enables the average producer to command the commodity inputs and labour power needed to reproduce the commodity (i.e., c+v).[3] The commodity inputs are the material inputs used in the production of the commodity, while the labour power commanded can be equated with the consumption goods that need to be provided to sustain the workers. The average rate of profit (r) is the value of the total surplus product appropriated by a sector in relation to the value of the total commodity inputs used to produce the required quantity of the commodity, including wage goods. Marx calls the value of the surplus product appropriated by producers in a given sector **profit** to distinguish it from the **surplus value** produced by the sector. The basic rule under capitalism is that producers appropriate aliquot shares of value of the total surplus produced in the system in proportion to the values of the outlays advanced by them for production. This means the profit appropriated by them is proportionate to the cost-price. The price of production can then be depicted as:

$$p = (c + v) (1 + r)$$

where, p = price of production and r = the average rate of profit (S/C + V).

As is well known, for Marx, the formation of the economy-wide average rate of profit means that there is a divergence of the surplus value or profit appropriated by the average producers in an industry from the surplus value generated by them. There is a transfer of surplus value between sectors. This is because, assuming similar rates of exploitation (S/V) between sectors, if the average producers in each sector appropriate only the surpluses produced in their own sectors, the rates of profit they appropriate would differ. With similar rates of exploitation across sectors, the tendency would be for sectors with a higher value of material inputs to labour power (C/V) to have lower rates of profit. Since such a situation could not endure with, on the one hand, a variety of techniques of production being employed to produce a multitude of products and, on the other hand, the possibility of a migration of capital to high profit sectors, there must necessarily be a tendency for a transfer of surplus from low to high C/V sectors with the formation of prices of production.[4]

Marx sees prices of production being formed in the context of competition between producers both within and between sectors. He takes competition between producers, or 'capitals', as the norm for explaining prices, because it captures the essence of the functioning of the capitalist system, and not because he sees capitalism as perfectly competitive. As noted above, competition within a sector results in producers of a similar product adopting a standard price for an average sample of the product. The standard price will be set by producers producing the bulk of products. These prices will be based on standard cost-prices. Marx assumes that these cost-prices will correspond to average technologies, but does not preclude the possibility that they will correspond to more or less efficient technologies. This is because for him the average technology underlying average cost-price is the technology used to produce the bulk of the commodities of a given type. The average producer in an industry will appropriate an industry average rate of profit. It is the rate appropriated by the producers producing the bulk of commodities. The appropriation of an average profit by the average producer also does not preclude the possibility of some producers in an industry obtaining higher or lower rates of profit than the average. Differences in technologies within the industry will almost certainly guarantee such differences in individual intra-industry rates of profit as a result of differences in costs.

As also noted earlier, competition between sectors imposes on the average producer in a given sector an economy-wide average profit. It causes the average profit appropriated by the average producer in each sector to be equalised allowing for such factors as risk and turnover time. Average producers in more risky sectors, or those where turnover time is longer than the average, would require higher average rates of profit as compensation. The tendency towards equalised profit rates between sectors is ensured by the mobility of capital between sectors.[5] It is, in fact, the assumed mobility of capital that justifies the assumption of an economy-wide average rate of profit in the analysis of prices of production.[6] This does not, however, preclude the possibility of divergences in average rates of profit appropriated by different industries beyond those justified by the needs of reproduction (e.g., as a result of greater risk-taking, exceptionally long turnover times, and changes in the structure of demand). For Marx not only are such divergences possible, they are likely. However, and to repeat, for him, it is not from the divergences that one begins one's analysis.

What the above means is that prices of production are proportionate to and, therefore, fundamentally determined by, cost-prices for a given structure of profit rates. Marx sees the link between price of production and cost-prices as evidenced by the close correspondence between changes in them. Changes in the rate of profit could most certainly impact on prices of production but, for Marx, this impact would depend on the organic composition of capital and, more importantly, is likely to be less consequential than the impact of changes in cost-prices (see below).

This raises the question of what determines cost-prices. For Marx they are fundamentally determined by values – the physical requirements of production as measured by labour time. Again, the link is evidenced by respective changes in the two. Changes in cost-prices are directly linked to changes in values. This is because the inputs required to produce commodities are linked to the direct and indirect labour time that needs to be expended in the process of producing them. Thus, a change in unit non-labour, material, input costs (as measured by labour time) is to be explained by a corresponding change in the non-labour, material inputs (as measured by labour time) required for the production of the commodity. And, similarly, for Marx, a change in unit labour costs is mostly to be explained by a corresponding change in the direct labour time required for the production of the commodity – the productivity of labour. Marx certainly recognises that changes in unit wage costs, and therefore prices of production, could result from changes in the wage rate, but argues that the latter are likely to be less significant for changes in unit wage costs than labour productivity changes, and, in any case, that changes in wage rates are themselves considerably influenced by productivity changes in wages goods sectors. It is pertinent to note in this regard his comment on Ricardo's views on the sources of changes in prices of production:

> ...Again Ricardo comes to the one point with which he is really concerned in his investigation. These variations in the cost-prices [prices of production] of commodities resulting from a rise or fall in wages are insignificant compared with those variations in the same cost-prices which are brought about by changes in the values of commodities, that is changes in the quantity of labour employed in their production.... One can therefore, by and large, 'abstract' from this and, accordingly, the law of value remains virtually correct.... (1969b, pp. 193–4).

Although Marx considered the rate of profit as less important for the explanation of price of production than cost-price because he saw the rate of profit as relatively stable over the long run, he nevertheless sought to emphasise the fact that changes in the rate of profit are also, for the most part, to be explained by changes in value – the value of wage goods. A rise or fall in the value of wage goods would imply a rise or fall in the value of labour power and a corresponding fall or rise in the rate of profit. Moreover, although Marx accepted that in certain sectors and at certain junctures individual firms could, for a variety of reasons, command profit rates well in excess of the average, he also denied, for reasons given above, that different rates of profit within and between industries should be the point of departure for analysing price formation in capitalism. I will return to this point when discussing the Post Keynesian approach.

For Marx, it is not simply that values can be shown to be the primary determinants of prices of production in capitalism, but also, and perhaps more importantly, there can be no understanding of the latter without an understanding of the former. Neither cost-price nor profit, the two components of price of production, can be entirely understood without an understanding of value. '....If one did not take the definition of value as the basis, the *average profit*, and therefore also the cost-prices [prices of production], would be purely imaginary and untenable....' (Marx, 1969b, p. 190). Let us consider cost-price first. The cost-price in *Capital*, it will be recalled, refers to that part of the selling price which permits the average producer to command either directly (as with material inputs) or indirectly (as with wage goods) the necessary commodity inputs to reproduce the commodity. The required direct and indirect commodity inputs **commanded** by the individual producer, in turn, depends fundamentally on the conditions of production of the commodity; the direct and indirect commodities and, therefore, the indirect and direct labour time **required for** the production of the commodity, i.e., the values of the inputs. Thus, there can be no understanding of the relative material input costs of production of a commodity without an understanding of the relative material inputs (as measured by labour time) required for its production, and there can be no real understanding of unit wage costs without a corresponding appreciation of the direct unit labour inputs required.

Similarly, for Marx, profit cannot be understood without an understanding of value. The rate of profit applied to cost-price in the computation of the selling price in any given sector is related to the general, economy-wide, rate of profit. The latter is given by the ratio of the value of the surplus product to the value of the (input and consumption) goods required to produce the surplus product. It will be recalled that Marx refers to the value of the surplus product as 'profit' when it pertains to that part of the surplus product appropriated by the **individual** average producer. The surplus product, for Marx, arises from workers producing more goods than they are able to command with their wages. Moreover, since material inputs only transfer the value they contain to the value of the produced commodities, the value of the surplus product must of necessity come from the labour input. To repeat, the value of the surplus product is the difference in the value imparted to goods by the performance of labour in the immediate process of production and the value of the wage goods needed to sustain this labour. This means that profit too can only be understood by reference to value.

Marx's transformation procedure

No presentation of Marx's explanation of the determination of prices of production under capitalism would be complete without some discussion of his 'transformation procedure'. Marx introduced this procedure in Volume 3 of *Capital* to show that, notwithstanding the formation of a general rate of profit and the quantitative divergence of prices of production from values, prices of production are still fundamentally determined by value, as also evidenced by the fact that changes in prices of production are fundamentally determined by labour productivity changes. More specifically, the transformation procedure in Marx is a set of numerical examples designed to show that with competition between capitals of different sectors and the formation of a general rate of profit there would, as noted above, be a redistribution of surplus value between sectors in accordance with the value ratios of material inputs to labour power, i.e., the organic composition of capital (C/V),[7] such that the average producer in each sector appropriates an average rate of profit. Since the formation of the general rate of profit and prices of production only involves a redistribution of surplus value, the total value appropriated in the form of prices remains unchanged as does the total amount of surplus value in the form of profit – which is simply redistributed surplus value.

Critics have seen fault with Marx's transformation procedure for a number of reasons, but, to repeat, mostly because of an alleged failure on his part to transform input values into prices of production. However, as should be apparent from what has been said above, had Marx done this he would not have been able to show what he was attempting to show since, among other things, it would result in a divergence between the value and price of production rates of profit, a change in the real wage, and the need to abandon one of his two aggregate identities – values/prices and surplus values/profits.[8] Indeed, as should also be evident from what was said above, and will be further elaborated on below, it would have been entirely illogical for Marx to have transformed the values of inputs into prices of production when what he was seeking to do was to 'explain' the prices of production.[9] To transform both inputs and outputs into prices of production is to explain prices in terms of prices – prices in the transformation procedure being modified values. I will return to this issue again below when discussing the traditional and modern 'solutions' to what is perceived to be Marx's transformation problem in Chapter 5.

Supply and demand

Although Marx sees supply and demand to be in balance in the course of his explanation of prices of production, he explicitly denies that this balance *per se* could explain the magnitude of reproduction prices. He argues that when supply and demand balance, they explain nothing. When they balance, it is only costs of (re)production that explain the magnitudes of prices, i.e., it is only the conditions of supply that explain the magnitudes of prices:

> It [Classical Political Economy] soon recognised that changes in the relation between demand and supply explained nothing, with regard to the price of labour or any other commodity, except those changes themselves, i.e., the oscillations of market price above or below a certain mean. If demand and supply balance, the oscillation of prices ceases, all other circumstances remaining the same. But then demand and supply also cease to explain anything. The price of labour, at the moment when demand and supply are in equilibrium, is its natural price, determined independently of the relation of demand and supply. It was therefore found that the natural price was the object which actually had to be analysed. Or a longer period of oscillation in the market price was taken, for example a year, and the oscillations were found to cancel each other out, leaving a mean average quantity, a constant magnitude. This naturally had to be determined otherwise than by its own mutually compensatory variations.... As with other commodities, this value [Marx is referring to the value of labour power] was then further determined by the cost of production. (Marx, 1976, p. 678)

This is not to say that for Marx the **level of demand** has no bearing on the magnitude of price of production. It most certainly can and does, but only through its impact on the average conditions of production – the relative direct and indirect physical (labour) costs required to produce a commodity. Hence, the importance of focusing in the first instance on the conditions of production (supply) when explaining the magnitudes of prices of production.

It is sometimes argued that one reason why Marx considered the level of demand as irrelevant for the explanation of the magnitude of price of production is that he tacitly assumed **constant returns** to scale. But, Marx assumed no such thing. If he assumed anything, it was a tendency towards increasing returns in capitalism. The reason for this assumption is because he saw the expansion of output in capitalism as driven by competition between producers to maximise profits through a reduction in costs and underpinned by both continuous (labour) cost- saving revolutions in technology and expansions in the average operating size of business enterprises. This contrasts with the increasing costs/ decreasing returns to scale assumption of Neoclassical economics which underlies the entire edifice of its long-run price theory – *viz.*, the upward sloping long-run supply curve. Empirical evidence, as well as simple observation, appears to have vindicated Marx in this respect.[10]

Money prices of production

As with simple commodity circulation, money needs to be brought explicitly into the analysis to complete the picture of prices in capitalism – the prices which facilitate the balanced (expanded) reproduction of the capitalist system. The inclusion of money permits an explanation of money prices of production and the aggregate money price level when expanded reproduction is balanced. As with simple circulation, this explanation too requires an elaboration of the forms and functions of money.

The forms of money which need consideration are commodity money and state-issued, inconvertible paper money.[11] Although it has to be said that Marx assumes for the most part money to be commodity money when extending his analysis of price in capitalism, there is ample evidence from his writings to suggest that he did not see this as the only, or even the characteristic, form of money in this mode of production. Not only does he argue that money can be replaced by tokens of itself in the process of circulation when money is a commodity, he explicitly notes on a number of occasions money can actually be intrinsically valueless bits of paper issued by the state (see for example Marx, 1970, p. 116; 1973, pp. 121–2).[12]

The functions performed by money in capitalism are essentially the same as those performed by it in simple circulation, although there are some differences of note regarding the way in which money performs these functions. Indeed, it would seem that for Marx these differences arise from the above-mentioned changes in the form of money as well as the development of the banking and credit system in capitalism. The change in money's form refers to the shift in it from being a produced commodity which is intrinsically valuable to being intrinsically valueless pieces of paper issued by the state; a shift from an entity which requires the expenditure of social labour time to one which requires relatively little expenditure of social labour time. With this change in its form, money is more easily replaced by substitutes of itself. As a consequence, actual money facilitating circulation tends to be reduced to a minimum. At the same time, with the development of the banking and credit system, what effectively functions as money is expanded considerably. Money and tokens of money which facilitate circulation are augmented by commercial bank liabilities and accounting entries. These liabilities must in the final instance be supported by a certain quantity of state-issued paper money, which is not simply the amount which conforms to legal requirements. This is most in evidence in periods of crises, when it becomes apparent that without the requisite increase in the cash base of the system the entire edifice supporting the circulation of commodities is likely to come crashing down.

In capitalism, as in simple commodity production, as long as money is a commodity, its exchangeable worth over the long run is given by the reproduction price of the commodity that serves as money and, ultimately, its relative value. Changes in the money price level of all commodities are due to relative changes in labour productivity in the money commodity producing sector. As in the case of commodity money in simple commodity production, money prices of all commodities would only rise over the long run if labour productivity in the money commodity sector were to rise, and fall if labour productivity in the sector were to fall. There can be divergences of the exchange value of money from its value for reasons other than differences in the organic composition of capital of the money producing sector, and these divergences can have an impact on the long-term price of money for reasons given above in the discussion of commodity money in simple circulation. The replacement of commodity money in the performance of its functions by tokens of itself and bank liabilities could cause the exchangeable worth of money (the labour time it represents in exchange) to fall below its intrinsic value (as determined by the labour time required for its production). The resulting excessive increases in money prices are typically redressed when tokens of money cease to be acceptable as media of circulation, credit contracts, and money is demanded for itself – as in a crisis. But they can also be redressed by changes in the conditions of supply of the money commodity. The point will be elaborated on below in the discussion of the price adjustment process.

When money becomes state-issued inconvertible paper, it ceases to have any intrinsic value, i.e., value which stems from requiring social labour to be expended in its production, but does nevertheless continue to represent a given magnitude of value (and social labour time) in the performance of its functions as money. This magnitude is given by the quantitative relation of money which is required to circulate commodities and the value of the commodities to be circulated over a given **period of time**. It is the average value of commodities which money circulates over a given period of time. The quantity of money refers to the amount of state-issued paper money (so-called high-powered money) and bank liabilities which facilitate the circulation of commodities over a given period of time.[13] Although the value of money is given by its exchange relation to commodities when money is state-issued inconvertible paper, this value still needs to be distinguished from the exchange value or price of money. The exchange value of money is given by the exchange value of commodities commanded by money at any given moment or point in time. Moreover, although it, state-issued paper money, is not a produced commodity as such, it can and should be conceived of as having an equilibrium price in the sense of one which permits the balanced reproduction of all commodities in the system. This equilibrium price can be regarded as the value of money. Unlike commodity money, however, there is no necessity for this value to correspond to any particular level. Indeed, the reproduction price of money can correspond to an array of price levels. Or, to put it another way, balanced economic growth in a paper money world is consistent with an array of different money price levels. Which level will prevail in any particular period will depend on a host of different socio-economic factors, including cyclical ones.

It would be a mistake to conclude from this, as some commentators on Marx's analysis of money have, that, with the shift to intrinsically valueless paper issued by the state, Marx's explanation of the money price level and changes in it is effectively the same as the so-called modern quantity theory of money (MQM).[14] I will expand on this in Chapter 6, when considering the MQM in greater detail. However, here it needs noting that while Marx most certainly acknowledges there can be an excess of money and substitutes of money in relation to the demand for these emanating from the needs of the circulation of commodities, the logic of his analysis suggests he would deny that the excess automatically and immediately translates into a higher money price level of commodities in the manner of the MQM. This is because the transmission from the quantity of money which facilitates circulation to money prices is for Marx entirely more complex than that perceived by the MQM, and of necessity gives rise to a divergence of the exchange value of money from its value. The point will also be elaborated on below in the section discussing money price adjustment.

3.4   Changes in prices of production

Relative prices of production

To repeat what has been said above, Marx argues that there are just **two** possible causes of **changes** in the relative price of production of a commodity; a change in the value of the commodity concerned and a change in the general rate of profit (1981, p. 307). He argues that changes in the value of the commodity may be 'because more or less labour is required for its actual reproduction, whether because of a change in the productivity of the labour that produces the commodity in its final form, or in that of the labour producing those commodities that go towards producing it' (Marx, 1981, p. 308). Taking the example of cotton he argues further that, 'The price of production of cotton yarn may fall either because raw cotton is produced more cheaply, or because the work of spinning has become more productive as a result of better machinery' (*Ibid.*). The impact of changes in the general rate of profit on prices of production will depend on the average organic composition of capital (C/V) of the sector concerned in relation to the economy average. A rise in the general rate of profit will cause prices of production of goods produced with above average organic compositions to rise and those produced with below average organic compositions to fall. But, having noted the two possible causes of changes in the relative prices of production of a commodity, Marx goes on to argue that the more fundamental of the two causes is the change in the value of the commodity, i.e., the change in the productivity of labour in the immediate process of producing it and/or the production of its inputs. This is because for him changes in the general rate of profit tend to be more long-term and of a lesser magnitude (see Marx, 1969b, p. 194), and also because these changes are for the most part also the result of changes in the productivity of labour – the productivity of labour in the wages goods industries (see Marx, 1976, p. 659, p. 661).

What needs further emphasis or adding here is the following. When Marx argues that the source of changes in the exchange value (price of production) of a commodity can be a change in the values of inputs, he means values and not, as is frequently argued, the prices of production or exchange values of these inputs. That is, he means the direct and indirect **labour required for their production** and not the **labour commanded** in exchange. Again, as noted above when discussing the magnitude of price, it has to be acknowledged that there are instances where Marx appears to confuse the two. Secondly, the price of production that is being analysed is the price of a **standard commodity** of a certain type. The standard commodity reflects the average (in the sense of 'normal') labour time required to produce the bulk of the commodity in accordance with social demand. Most importantly, this means that the price of the (standard) commodity will not change if the individual values of commodities of this type produced by any one firm change, unless the firm happens to produce the bulk of the commodities satisfying demand. Lastly, although it was noted above that for Marx prices of production cannot be explained by the balance of supply and demand, it does not mean that their interaction has no role to play in the explanation of changes in these prices. In fact, for Marx, imbalances can most certainly have a bearing on changes in the magnitudes of prices of production, but only through their impact on labour productivity and, ultimately, costs. For example, an excess demand for a given product could cause profits in a sector to rise above the economy average (in the context of a rise in market prices above prices of production) attracting new producers to the sector who might bring with them more advanced technologies and better production methods, thereby reducing average costs. Or, the excess demand may allow existing producers to expand the scale of their production thereby also reducing costs.

Money prices of production

To also repeat what was said above, Marx sees the sources of changes in money price magnitudes as dependent on the form of money; whether it is a commodity or inconvertible state-issued paper money. When money is a commodity, changes in the money price level will for him result from changes in the reproduction price of money and, ultimately, its value as given by the requirements of production of the money commodity. That is, when money is a produced commodity changes in the money price level will ultimately be due to changes in the labour productivity of the money commodity producing sector in relation to the average changes in labour productivity in all other commodity producing sectors. As also noted above, money prices of all commodities would only rise over the long run in a commodity money setting if the relative labour productivity of the money commodity producing sector falls relative to the average for all other commodity producing sectors. When money is state-issued paper, changes in the money price level can result additionally, i.e., in addition to changes in the average levels of labour productivity of all commodity producing sectors, from changes in the average quantity of money that circulates a given amount of commodities over a given period. In fact, with state-issued paper money, the tendency is for there to be continuous increases in the quantity of money in relation to commodities over time. This is because, with the development of the payments and credit system, there is a tendency for periodic surges in the use of near-money substitutes, including credit, to circulate commodities, whose inflated money prices are then partially or wholly validated through the issue of money by the monetary authorities when the need arises.

What needs emphasising, or adding, in respect of the above is the following. First, changes in the average quantity of money circulating commodities is neither entirely **endogenous**, in the sense of wholly responding to demand for it, or **exogenous**, in the sense of being entirely independent of demand, say because it is controlled by government. It is not exogenous since money, especially state-issued paper money, is readily substitutable by all manner of near-money substitutes at certain junctures, and it is not entirely endogenous in that many of these substitutes cease to be acceptable as money at other junctures, especially when the authorities choose not to validate the notional claims on money these substitutes represent. Second, it needs stressing that, for Marx, changes in the money price level at any given point in time need not reflect changes in the value or intrinsic price of money,[15] whether money is a commodity or state-issued paper. When money is state-issued paper, money prices will typically rise above that level which reflects the intrinsic price of money during the upswing phase of the business cycle, and either fall or continue to rise in the downswing phase as the price of money moves back towards its intrinsic level (see below, in the discussion of the adjustment process, for an elaboration of these movements in money prices over the course of the business cycle). Third, Marx denies that a rise in money prices, and implied fall in the value of money, would typically be brought about by a rise in money wages. Actually, he was quite explicit that for the most part increases in money wages would tend to follow increases in the level of money prices, suggesting profit increases for producers of commodities in periods of inflation (Marx, 1978, pp. 415, 486). To see increases in money wages as preceding increases in money prices means seeing the value of money as determined by the money wage bargain – something Marx fiercely opposed in his discussions of Adam Smith's theory of price (see Chapter 4). Having said this, it is reasonable to suppose that Marx would not have denied that there could only be a sustained increase in money prices in a state-issued paper money system when money wages, or some other means of sustaining the purchasing power of a large section of the population, rises along with money prices. One should also add here, that Marx would similarly have rejected the notion that increases in the money price level are the result of increases in the average money mark-up by producers. This is because such a view would imply seeing firms in general as having the power to raise money mark-up levels, and therefore profits, at will. If this were the case, one would have to ask, as Marx does, why firms do not do this all the time (1978, p. 414).

3.5   Prices of production with non-producible inputs

Marx, like most Classical economists, assumes in the first instance that all inputs are producible and then, later in his analysis, relaxes this assumption to take into account non-produced inputs. In doing so he modifies his explanation of prices of production, particularly in those sectors using significant amounts of non-produced inputs such as agriculture and raw materials. For Marx, prices of production in these sectors are still determined by producers using average techniques of production, but now also those using these techniques in conjunction with the worst quality of non-produced inputs. However, the prices of production in these sectors are not reproduction prices, since the latter will include a margin over and above the average rate of profit; a margin which will accrue to the owners of the non-produced inputs. This margin is rent, or to be more precise, **absolute rent**. Absolute rent, for Marx, is the minimum return required by owners of non-produced inputs for use of these inputs by producers. It is a return accruing to the owner of the non-produced input for temporarily parting with this input. The magnitude of absolute rent will depend on a host of factors including the strength of demand for the commodity, the degree of competition between owners of the non-produced input, and the like. The rent accruing to the owners of non-produced inputs can, for Marx, also be in excess of this absolute rent. This would be the case where the quality of the non-produced inputs is superior to the worst quality of these inputs, and/or where producers using the non-produced inputs are using more efficient techniques of production. In both these cases, the costs of production of producers of a given type of good would be below those of producers using average techniques of production and the worst quality of non-produced inputs, giving rise to a excess profit over and above the absolute rent and the possibility for the appropriation of a part of this excess profit in the form of additional rent, **differential rent** (which Marx refers to as differential rents 1 and 2, respectively), by the owners of the non-produced inputs.[16] That is to say, for Marx, differential rent, unlike absolute rent, has no bearing on the magnitudes of the reproduction prices of commodities produced using non-produced inputs.

The non-produced input which Marx pays most attention to is, unsurprisingly, land, and the commodities produced using the non-produced input, agricultural commodities. He sees the prices of production of agricultural commodities as given by their prices on the poorest quality of land. Although it is not always clear from what Marx writes, it can be argued that for him these prices are determined by the average techniques of production used on the poorest quality lands.[17] Building on what was said above, the prices of production are not the reproduction prices of commodities produced on the poorest quality of land, but systematically below these prices. That is, the reproduction prices of agricultural commodities include a surplus above the average rate of profit. This surplus is given by the magnitude of absolute rent. Factors influencing the magnitude of absolute rent will include the level of imports of the agricultural commodity in question and the degree of intensive cultivation. Marx argues that the pre-condition for the existence of absolute rent in agriculture is that the organic composition of capital is below the economy average and, related to this, the 'limit' for the market price to exceed the price of production of the agricultural commodity produced on the worst land, is the value of the commodity. He suggests that it is only by seeing agricultural commodity prices in this way that value can be regarded as determining prices of production of commodities produced in the agricultural sector in the same way as it can be seen as determining prices of production in manufacturing. It has to be said, however, that Marx provides no rationale for why seeing value as determining the prices of production of agricultural commodities requires seeing the organic composition of capital of the agricultural goods sector as below the economy average and/or the value of agricultural commodities setting a limit for the market prices of these commodities.[18] Seeing market prices in agriculture as systematically in excess of both prices of production and values, simply implies admitting to the possibility of a transfer of additional surplus value (in addition to what might be implied by the relative organic composition of capital) to the agricultural sector from other sectors. It does not mean having to accept these prices can no longer be regarded as determined by values.

It needs emphasising that Marx, like Ricardo, but in opposition to Smith, denies that differential rent has any bearing on the regulating prices of agricultural commodities. This is because, for Marx, differential rent arises from the difference between market prices of agricultural commodities and the costs of **individual** agricultural producers. As such, it cannot have a bearing on the prices of agricultural commodities (see 1969b, p. 316). The prices of agricultural commodities are based on average costs of producers producing on the poorest quality lands.

In keeping with his explanations of changes in prices of production in general, Marx puts considerable emphasis on changes in labour productivity, especially labour productivity increases, when explaining changes in the magnitudes of prices of agricultural commodities. He sees the direct impact of productivity increases on agricultural commodity prices as occurring when these increases take place in production on the worst lands, and the indirect impact when they are concentrated on better lands, giving rise to a displacement of production on the worst lands. Marx accepts that it is possible for productivity to decline and prices to rise as a result of more capital being invested in a limited amount of land, but considers this to be unlikely (see 1981, p. 819).

Two other factors which Marx considers to also have a bearing on changes in agricultural commodity prices are a shift in cultivation to different quality lands and changes in conditions governing the magnitude of absolute rent. In his discussion of shift in cultivation to different quality lands, Marx is at pains to deny that the historic tendency is for the shift to be onto increasingly poor lands resulting in a rise in agricultural commodity prices (see 1969b, p. 335). For him, better lands could be brought into cultivation and, to the extent that this results in an increase in output which displaces production on poorer quality lands, prices of agricultural commodities could fall. That is, in opposition to Ricardo, Marx considers it possible, and even likely, for an extensive development of agriculture to be accompanied by a fall in agricultural commodity prices. Marx similarly seeks to deny that an increase in demand for agricultural commodities automatically translates into higher prices for these commodities. He argues that if the increase in demand encourages a greater investment in more fertile lands, production on poorer quality lands could be displaced resulting in a fall in prices as a result of better quality lands becoming the worst quality lands on which the prices of agricultural commodities are set (see Marx, 1981, p. 819). Finally, Marx sees the changes in the conditions governing the magnitude of absolute rent as largely resulting from institutional changes (e.g., changes in the degree of liberalisation of agricultural commodity imports), that by their nature would only take place slowly, over long periods of time, and, therefore, would not be as important in explaining changes in agricultural commodity prices as productivity changes, or even shifts in cultivation to different qualities of land.

3.6   Monopoly prices

As has already been noted in the introductory chapter, since Marx's focus is on prices in the context of a competitive environment, he did not leave behind anything that could be reasonably construed as a coherent theory of monopoly price. What he in fact left was a theory of rent and indications of how this could aid an understanding of monopoly price. What follows will be an attempt to develop this understanding in the framework of his analysis of price in a competitive environment.

Within the framework of a competitive environment, a monopoly price (of a manufactured product) can be defined as one which is systematically above the price of production and, correspondingly, where the mark-up for the producer(s) producing the bulk of the commodities in the sector continuously exceeds the economy-wide average rate of profit for reasons other than those pertaining to differences in required growth (i.e., growth which is required by structural shifts in demand), turnover time, and risk. It is not a price pertaining to a differentiated product, where the producer of a differentiated product is able to charge a higher price than for the standard product and appropriate an above average rate of profit. Nor, as intimated above, is it necessary for a monopoly sector to be one comprising a single producer. It can also comprise several producers, although the presumption here is that the producers act in collusion with one another in setting prices. Monopoly prices can be argued to arise and coexist alongside competitively determined prices of production because of natural and artificial barriers to the free movement of capital into and out of an industry. An example of a natural barrier is the exclusive ownership of an indispensable natural input by a producer, e.g., oil reserves in the case of the production of oil. A patent preventing the copying of a certain product or method of production would be an example of an artificial barrier.

As with competitive prices of production, the proximate determinants of monopoly prices, or more accurately monopoly reproduction prices, are the average costs of production and mark-ups on those costs. Unlike competitive prices of production, the mark-up in the case of monopolists is systematically in excess of the average rate of profit. Marx refers to the excess profit of the monopolist as rent – absolute rent. But, and this is important, the average rate of profit remains a point of reference for the mark-up by the monopolist, provided that the monopolist is seen as operating in a largely competitive environment. That is to say, the monopolist will aim to appropriate a rate of profit in excess of the average rate in the competitive part of the economy, at least over the long-run. Marx sees the extent to which the mark-up is in excess of the average rate of profit as depending on the 'the buyers' needs and ability to pay' (1981, p. 910), and gives the example of a vineyard producing extraordinary wines in relatively small quantities. Some commentators, even those sympathetic to Marx, have taken this to mean that in a monopoly setting he considers price is no longer to be explained by value. However, in the context of what was said earlier regarding Marx's concept of value and the determination of prices of production, it can justifiably be argued that he regards, and indeed must regard, the magnitude of monopoly price too as fundamentally determined by value. Specifically, since monopoly prices also comprise cost-price and profit components, since cost-prices can be argued to vary more than the rate of profits of monopolists over the long term, and since cost-prices are fundamentally determined by values, value must of necessity be seen as the major determinant of price even in monopolistic industries. Moreover, it can also be argued that the profit appropriated by monopolists, as in the case of competitive firms, cannot be understood without an understanding of value. Here, it is not simply that profit *per se* cannot be explained without reference to value, but also that the excess profit of the monopoly industry arises from a **transfer of surplus value** from the competitive part of the economic system to monopoly industries.[19] Marx makes this point in the following passage:

> A monopoly price for certain commodities simply transfers a portion of the profit made by the other commodity producers to the commodities with the monopoly price. Indirectly, there is a local disturbance in the distribution of surplus-value among the various spheres of production, but leaves unaffected the limits of the surplus-value itself.... The limits within which the monopoly price affects the normal regulation of commodity prices are firmly determined and can be precisely calculated. (1981, p. 1001)

3.7   Market prices

Prices of production are averages, not centres of gravity, of actual prices in capitalism.[20] Marx refers to these actual prices as **market prices**. He sees them being formed in capitalism in the course of the production and reproduction of commodities against a backdrop of competition between producers within and between sectors. As in the case of simple commodity circulation, Marx sees actual prices typically deviating from reproduction prices, but he also sees important differences between capitalism and simple commodity circulation in this regard. These differences pertain to the possibility, nature, causes and adjustment of the divergences between actual and reproduction prices.

Possibility of divergences

For Marx while the possibility of a divergence of market prices from prices of production in capitalism is, as in simple commodity production, fundamentally due to the separation of production from distribution, exchange, and consumption, this possibility is further developed under capitalism. It is developed by the accumulation process, the development of the financial system, and the emergence of various substitutes for money stemming from the development of the financial system – particularly the substitutes arising from the development of the payments and credit system.

The accumulation process in capitalism is premised on production for profit. It reinforces and develops further the inherent separations of production from exchange and consumption which are characteristic of all commodity production systems. Production in capitalism, as in all commodity producing systems, is not for exchange *per se*, but for exchange which yields a surplus to the producer – a surplus of exchangeable value in relation to the exchangeable value outlaid to commence production. It is this surplus that is the basis for the accumulation process – the expansion in the value of capital. At the same time, the development of the financial system creates a pool of interest-bearing capital which contributes to a massive expansion of credit, driving the supply of commodities beyond its revenue base and the supply of what performs the functions of money beyond the money base of the system. Credit doesn't simply permit a renewal of production without the sale of what has already been produced, it permits the expansion of production well beyond what is associated with normal levels of revenues. Also, credit doesn't simply enable the consumer of goods to maintain consumption in the context of delayed income flows, it also permits an expansion of consumption beyond normal income levels. And, credit doesn't simply substitute money in the circulation of commodities, it causes this circulation to expand well beyond what is sustainable by the monetary base. The further development of money substitutes accompanying the development of the financial system under capitalism takes the form of, on the one hand, a variety of credit-based payments instruments such as bills of exchange and credit cards which arise out of the development of the credit system, as well as, and on the other hand, direct–debit payments instruments such as cheques and debit cards which arise out of the development of the payments system itself (i.e., the commercial banking system). An excessive expansion of money substitutes refers to the expansion of these substitutes in relation to the money base on which they rest. This expansion too enhances the possibility of a divergence between the actual and intrinsic price of money – its exchange value and value.

Nature of divergences

Marx sees divergences of market prices from prices of production of commodities as typically following a **cyclical pattern** in capitalism, with a certain level of synchronisation between sectors.[21] The divergences between market prices and prices of production tend to be at their height in the boom and overexertion periods – on the eve of a rupture in the system.[22] In a boom, market prices are typically above reproduction prices, while in the over-exertion phase, on the eve of a crisis, they are typically below the latter. In the boom phase market prices would tend to be above prices of production because of a corresponding tendency for an excess demand for all commodities. The excess demand causes the mass of commodities produced to represent in the market a greater mass of labour time than is actually required for their production. This gives rise to either a fall in the price of money (a rise in the money price level), and therefore the labour time commanded by the money revenue of producers, or an increase in the amount of labour time expended in the production of the goods (i.e., and increase in supply of goods involving more labour time). In the over-exertion period, when there is an overproduction of commodities in many if not most sectors of the economy, the mass of the commodities produced represents in the market less labour time than is required for their production. Some of the labour expended in the production of the commodities is superfluous. Reflecting this, there would be a fall in market prices below their prices of production and/or some of the commodities produced would remain unsold. The fall in the market prices below their prices of production during this phase means that the labour time commanded by the commodities is less than the labour time which would be commanded if the commodities sold at market prices corresponding to prices of production. Synchronisation of the divergences of market prices from prices of production between sectors is the result of competition and flows of capital. These serve to transmit disturbances in one or several sectors to all others (see Marx, 1969b, pp. 523–4).

Causes of divergences

Following from his view of the nature of the divergences of market prices from prices of production, Marx, quite naturally, sees the fundamental cause of these divergences as the same as that driving the business cycle; technological change and competition between producers. Technological change and competition give rise to divergences of market prices from prices of production over the course of the cycle by increasing, on the one hand, the scale and efficiency of production, and, on the other hand, the range and quality of the products. Increases in the scale and efficiency of production induce costs of large numbers of producers to fall, while increases in the range and quality of products encourages price buoyancy in the face of these cost reductions. Competition between producers in different sectors, and a resulting migration of capital between sectors, transmits the price disturbances throughout the economy, causing them to be increasingly widespread. These divergences are further driven by the workings of the financial system and the expanded use of tokens of money or money substitutes. The extent and duration of the divergences will depend on the extent of general overproduction in the system.

The price adjustment process

The price adjustment process in capitalism, as in simple commodity circulation, involves movements in (market and reproduction) prices of both commodities and money. Let us consider the adjustment process with regard to commodities first. When the supply of, and demand for, commodities in relation to one another are not in balance, market prices will move away from their prices of production. However, the movement in market prices away from prices of production may be accompanied by a movement of the latter in the same direction as the former, depending on the source and the extent of the imbalance. For example, if the source of the imbalance is rapid technological change, causing the supply of the product in question to greatly exceed demand, the prices of production would most likely fall along with the fall in market price, although by a lesser magnitude. The imbalance in supply and demand, and corresponding divergence of market price from price of production, would then induce countervailing movements in supply and demand, and a reversal in the magnitude of the divergence. This reversal would result from a reversal of the market price movement and, quite possibly, a further (but not necessarily reverse) movement in prices of production. Continuing with the preceding example, the reversal could result from a rise in the market price and possibly a continuing fall in the price of production. Much would depend on the nature of the initial increase in supply. The end result of the initial imbalance would then be higher levels of supply and demand corresponding to a lower price of production. Alternatively, and less likely for Marx, it could result in lower levels of supply and demand corresponding to a higher price of production, as more efficient producers are driven out of the sector in the course of the adjustment process.

If the initial imbalance is the result of an excessive increase in demand, a similar price adjustment process would operate, but in reverse. The market price would rise above the price of production, but, in this case, quite possibly along with an increase in the price of production. Again, much would depend on the nature and possible extent of the increase in demand, as well as capacity levels in individual industries. The excess demand, and corresponding divergence of market price from the price of production, would then give rise to countervailing movements in demand and supply, causing a reverse downward movement in market prices back towards prices of production and, quite possibly, a downward movement of prices of production – as new entrants into the industry adopt more efficient techniques of production – below pre-disturbance levels.

Marx implicitly, and to some extent explicitly, conceived of a similar adjustment process operating with respect to the price of money, although he recognised that the mechanics of the process would depend on the form of money; whether money is a commodity or state-issued paper. In both cases, and as with the relative prices of commodities, the adjustment of supply and demand imbalances will involve changes in both the market and long-term average or intrinsic price of money, with the latter being given by the price of production of the commodity which serves as money in the case of commodity money, and the stock relation of commodities to money over a given period of time in the case of state-issued paper money. Since the price of money is given by its exchange relation to all commodities (whatever the form of money), imbalances in the supply of, and demand for, money will necessarily be mirrored by imbalances in the demand for, and supply of, all commodities. And, divergences of the price of money from its long-term average will be mirrored by divergences of the aggregate money price level of all commodities from its long-term average.

Let us now consider the price adjustment process in the event of such an imbalance when money is commodity money, say gold. An excess of gold is taken to mean there is too much gold as media of circulation in relation to the goods produced at existing gold money prices. Or what is the same thing, that there is an excess demand for goods produced at existing gold money prices. In such a situation, the price of gold will fall below its price of production, and the average gold prices of commodities will rise above their long-term average levels. To the extent that the bulk of gold is henceforth produced by relatively more efficient gold producers, there could also be a fall in the price of production of gold along with a fall in its market price. The fall in the price of gold and rise in gold prices of commodities will then elicit countervailing tendencies in the supply of, and demand for, gold in relation to all other commodities. There will be a **relative** contraction in the supply of gold involving an **absolute** contraction in gold supply, and/or an expansion in the supply of all other commodities. Marx, in fact, believed that rising gold prices would most likely stimulate the output of commodities (in the upswing phase of the business cycle) due to the impact of this rise on the value of labour power and through this the average rate of profit.[23] This is because, as noted above, for Marx, a rise in the money prices of commodities will tend to reduce the value of labour power because of a lagged response of money wage demands by labour to the rise in money prices. Workers do not, and cannot, typically strike wage bargains in relation to future price rises – they cannot bargain for a certain real wage, although they can, and usually do, fight to maintain living standards. As a consequence of the contraction of gold supply and expansion of output of commodities, the relative price of gold will move back to its price of production level, although this level itself could have risen or fallen in the process of adjustment. At the same time average gold prices of commodities will fall back towards their pre-adjustment level with, again, the extent of the fall depending on the corresponding movement in the price of production of gold.

The imbalance in the supply of, and demand for, money, and corresponding imbalance of the supply of, and demand for, all commodities in relation to money, is accentuated with the appearance of tokens of money, bank liabilities, and credit. The appearance of these causes some of the functions performed by money in respect of the circulation of commodities to be performed by money surrogates. The more these surrogates perform the functions of money, the greater will be the disjuncture between the supply of, and demand for, actual money, and the more the actual price of money will deviate from its reproduction or intrinsic level. Thus, when money is gold, when the process of reproduction is proceeding relatively smoothly, and when credit and tokens of gold replace gold in circulation, the demand for gold to meet circulating (including hoard) requirements will be well below its supply such that the price of gold (the price reflecting the actual balance of supply and demand for gold as money) will fall below its intrinsic price (the price permitting the balanced reproduction of the system and reflecting the relative labour requirements of gold production). There will be a corresponding upward pressure on gold money prices of commodities and a contraction in gold production. When the reproduction of commodities is interrupted and credit disappears, the underlying demand for money will make itself felt such that the price of money will rise sharply and the money prices of commodities will fall correspondingly. The value of tokens of money will fall to the extent that there is an excess of these in relation to the demand for gold in the process of circulation. In other words, credit and tokens of money will serve to aggravate imbalances and amplify the resulting aggregate price adjustments in the context of commodity money.

With the shift to state-issued paper money, the adjustment process in terms of the price of money and the aggregate price level is further transformed. Most obviously, with the appearance of this form of money, the tendency is for the adjustment process to take place during a sustained increase in the aggregate price level and a corresponding fall in the average price of money. Consider again an initial situation of an excess supply of money (in this case state issued paper money and bank liabilities which facilitate the circulation of commodities) and a corresponding excess demand for commodities at existing money prices. In this situation both the actual and intrinsic price of money will fall, but not necessarily by the same extent. It is quite possible that the actual price of money will fall by less than its intrinsic price because money is demanded more as a medium of circulation and not for itself. **When money is demanded as a medium of circulation, its value is taken as given.** The fall in the price of money means that the aggregate money price level will rise. This fall in the price of money will not, unlike the case of commodity money, result in a contraction in its supply, even if the fall in price of money exceeds the fall in its intrinsic level. However, as in the case of commodity money, the rise in the money prices of goods may well induce an expansion in supply of all commodities in so far as it implies a fall in the value of labour power and a corresponding increase in the general rate of profit. The increase in the supply of goods would eliminate the excess demand for them in relation to money, at least to the extent that this increase in supply of goods represents an expansion in the average amount of commodities produced in relation to the money which circulates them. Balance in the supply of, and demand for, money *vis-à-vis* commodities would be restored as a result of an increase in the aggregate money price level because of the implied fall in the price of money. Indeed, to the extent that the price of money does not initially fall by the full magnitude of the implied fall in the intrinsic price of money resulting from the initial excess of money supply, the countervailing increase in aggregate commodity production is likely to be accompanied by a continuing increase in the money price level, even without any new increases in money supply.

The expansion of bank liabilities (and credit) will also accentuate the imbalance between the supply of, and demand for, money when money is state-issued paper money. However, the resulting price adjustment in this case will not involve an amplification of the the price **cycle** but could result in a significant increase in the money price level. This is because, when the demand for money moves towards actual cash (or even cash and near cash), as in a situation of interruptions to the process of reproduction, money prices of commodities would only fall appreciably if the supply of cash did not accommodate the expanded demand for it. But, if the supply of cash accommodated the expanded demand for it, the money price level would rise during the adjustment. In short, the expansion of credit and bank liabilities under a state-issued paper money system gives rise to the possibility of more extensive and protracted increases in money prices in the adjustment process.

Since the divergences of market prices from prices of production follow the business cycle, the price adjustment process needs also to be explained in the context of the **business cycle**. At the beginning of the cycle, **just after the trough**, the supply of, and demand for, commodities as a whole can be argued to be relatively in balance. Or, to be more precise, the supply of, and demand for, commodities is more in balance at this stage than at any other stage over the cycle. As the upswing progresses, sectoral imbalances increase, and there is some tendency towards an excessive demand for commodities. The excess demand for commodities in turn implies an excess supply of money, causing money prices to rise and the price of money to fall (see Marx, 1978, p. 486). When money is a commodity the fall in its market price will tend to be greater than the fall in its price of production, even though there may be a sizeable fall in the latter as less efficient gold production is eliminated. When money is state-issued paper money, the fall in the market price of money will most likely be proportionate to the fall in its intrinsic price. Whether money is a commodity or state-issued paper money, the rise in money prices will typically coincide with and, for reasons noted above, reinforce tendencies giving rise to an expansion of production, especially towards the end of the upswing, in the **over-exertion phase**.[24] This expansion in production could reduce the excess demand for commodities, and possibly give rise to an excess supply or 'overproduction' of them. Overproduction of commodities means that most commodities are sold at prices which do not yield a satisfactory return to the producer, and an increasing number are not saleable at all. The elimination of excess demand and tendency towards overproduction may not cause money prices of commodities to fall, even in the case of commodity money. This is because there will be a tendency in the over-exertion phase for an expansion in the supply of **money substitutes** circulating commodities as part and parcel of an expansion in the credit system accompanying the expansion in production. In the case of paper money, there may also be an expansion in the supply of money to support the expansion in the credit system.

Towards the **peak** of the cycle, with increasing interruptions to reproduction of commodities, the demand for money surges. At this stage substitutes for money become less acceptable, particularly since money is now demanded to hold and not simply as a medium of circulation and means of payment (see Marx, 1981, pp. 648–9). When money is a commodity, the result of the surge in demand for it is an increase in its price, well above its price of production, and a corresponding fall in the money prices of commodities. When money is state-issued paper, the increase in demand for it can be accommodated by an immediate increase in its supply. Whether money prices fall or continue to rise in a state-issued paper money setting will depend on the extent of the accommodation. The more accommodation of the demand for money there is, the less likely that prices will fall, but the more likely it is that the economic downturn will be protracted and/or the recovery less forceful. An excessive accommodation could result in continuing or even rising inflation in the context of a protracted but gradual contraction in production – the phenomenon of stagflation. Very little accommodation would most likely result in a fall in money prices and a considerable (and possibly unnecessarily damaging) contraction in production.

Balance will typically be restored towards the end of the downswing with an elimination of the excess production of commodities and corresponding excess supply of money. The forces which would tend to restore balance would be mostly a destruction of capital (i.e., elimination of some supply) and some expansion in aggregate demand (use of production revenues which have been taken out of circulation). Accompanying this, would be a fall in the demand for money and, in the case of state-issued paper money, a rise in its supply. It needs stressing that, for Marx, balance in cyclical terms requires also balance in respect of a number of other factors, including; the rate of profit in relation to its long-term average, the price of labour power in relation to its value, the amount of debt contracted by consumers and producers in relation to historic levels, the level of interest rates in relation to the long-term average rate of profit, the rate of inflation in relation to its long-term average, etc. But to fully appreciate what is meant by this one needs a more detailed analysis of the cycle, something which is beyond the scope of the present work.

4
Marx on Smith and Ricardo

Marx saw the Classical economists as, to one degree or another, trying to understand the inner workings of the capitalist system, in contrast with those economists he termed as 'vulgar', the ancestors of the present-day Neoclassical economists, who he dismissed as being little more than apologists for the capitalist system. There is in fact little doubt that he owed a considerable intellectual debt to the Classics, particularly Adam Smith and David Ricardo, who he regarded as easily the best among them. Since Marx devoted so much attention to the critical appraisal of these two Classical economists in particular, frequently using his criticisms of their works to benchmark his own contributions to economic thought, the present chapter will focus on this appraisal with a view to clarifying further his own distinctive theory of price.

4.1   Adam Smith

Marx sees Smith's positive contributions to the theory of price as beginning with his recognition that the pre-condition for commodities having worth or value is the existence of **a social division of labour**. Marx even sees Ricardo as being less clear than Smith on this issue (see 1969a, p. 76). However, he is critical of Smith's view that exchange is a necessary pre-condition for the division of labour. Eric Roll, the well known British economic historian, comments:

> It is logically demonstrable that a certain social organization...can have a technology using division of labour without exchange. And communities of this type can be shown to have existed. Adam Smith was guilty of making the characteristics of the society of his own day valid for all time. (1973, p. 155)

Marx suggests it is because of this that Smith failed to see value as antecedent to, and independent of, exchange value or price. For Marx, it is only once there is a division of labour that the products of labour come to acquire worth in relation to one another in the process of exchange, and not the other way around.

Marx considers a second, and possibly more important, contribution of Smith to the theory of price to be his view that labour is the source of (exchange) value or price, and his corresponding explanation of the magnitude of price in terms of labour time. But Marx is also critical of Smith on this score. On the one hand, he is critical of Smith for not recognising that the labour which gives rise to price is social labour and not individual labour *per se*. For Marx, as soon as economic activity is organised on the basis of a division of labour, the performance of individual labour counts as social labour – part of the whole. On the other hand, he criticises Smith for arguing that exchange value or price is only determined by labour time in 'early and rude' states of society, and not recognising that it is determined by labour time in all commodity producing societies, including capitalism. In fact, for Marx, the labour theory of value is actually not relevant for the explanation of price in precisely early and rude states of society. This is because these societies basically comprise self-sufficient communities exchanging their surplus produce at prices determined by all manner of random factors. Commenting on Smith's mistaken view of the applicability and non-applicability of the labour theory of value to different social organisations, Marx says:

> This means...that the law which applies to commodities *qua* commodities, no longer applies to them once they are regarded as capital or products of capital.... Thus the law of value is supposed to be valid for a type of production which produces no commodities...and not to be valid for a type of production which is based on the product as a commodity. (1972, p. 74)

Lastly, Marx has praise for several aspects of Smith's theory of rent, including; his view that rent in general accrues to the owner of land (and other non-reproducible inputs) for use of this land (1969b, p. 343), his conception of rent as comprising both absolute (or general) and differential components, and his view of differential rent as arising from differences in market and individual values of agricultural commodities due to differences in land fertilities (*Ibid.*, p. 356). Marx nevertheless criticises Smith for not seeing rent arising from the monopoly ownership of land (and non-produced means of production), for theorising rent as an original revenue component of the price of the commodity, and for arguing that the prices of agricultural commodities are regulated by the prices of commodities set by producers using the **most** fertile lands. For Marx, Smith recognises that the existence of rent depends on whether or not landed property can assert itself economically, but fails to recognise that this implies the market prices of agricultural commodities will generally be above their prices of production.

Perhaps Smith's biggest failing as far as Marx is concerned is his confusion of **values** with **prices** of commodities, and his resulting explanation of the magnitudes of prices in terms of their revenue components, *viz.*, wages, profits and rent. For Marx, there are two important problems with this explanation. One is that it required Smith to see the input component of prices of production as also reducible to their revenue components, and the inputs into these inputs likewise reducible to their revenue components, and so on *ad infinitum*. Marx criticised this reduction as implying that all the produce of a country is in principle consumable (1969a, pp. 100–2), and costs are reducible to embodied historic costs. A second problem for Marx with Smith's explanation of the magnitude of price is that it requires him to see the revenue components of price, *viz.*, profit, wages and rent, as independent of one another as well as antecedent to the formation of prices of commodities (1969a, p. 94, p. 96; 1969b, pp. 218–19). In the case of agricultural commodities, for example, it causes Smith to incorrectly see the prices of these as given by the prices of the commodities produced on the most fertile land; land yielding a positive rent. For Marx, not only are the revenue components of prices interdependent, they are formed in the process of the formation of prices, *viz.*, in the process of the reproduction of commodities. Marx concludes that in explaining the magnitudes of prices in terms of their revenue components Smith is reflecting the views of the individual capitalist who takes the cost components of price, including the rate of profit, as given, and the price which reflects these as the ideal or natural price – which is then regarded as the value of the commodity (*Ibid.*).

Marx also contends that Smith's move towards a cost/revenue explanation of the magnitude of price causes him to abandon the notion of the labour time required for the production of the good as measure of its worth, and instead adopt as measure the quantity of labour that can be bought with a given amount of wage goods. That is, it causes Smith to adopt wage goods, or the real wage, as the measure of worth of commodities (1969a, pp. 70–1). This, however, raises the question of how and why the relative worth of commodities is reducible to bundles of wage goods. And, since Smith does not draw a distinction between value and price, it also begs the question how the real wage can be seen as regulating the exchange ratios between commodities and what this means for the role of money. In fact, for Marx, Smith's adoption of the real wage as measure of value in the context of the collapse of value into exchange value, leads him to a distorted view of money. It causes him, by implication, to see money as the standard of the real wage whose value is determined by the exchange ratio of the bundle of wage goods with money. As will be seen below, this implicit view of money and the determination of its value in Smith's work has a certain resonance with the Post Keynesian approach.

4.2   Ricardo

There can be little doubt that Marx considered Ricardo to be a cut above Smith and the other Classical economists, and that he drew considerably more from Ricardo's work in his own study of the capitalist system than from any other Classical economist, including Smith. His writings are in fact littered with praise for Ricardo's work. In his *A Contribution to the Critique of Political Economy*, for example, Marx says of Ricardo:

> Although encompassed by this bourgeois horizon, Ricardo analyses bourgeois economy, whose deeper layers differ essentially from its surface appearance, with such theoretical acumen that Lord Brougham could say of him: "Mr. Ricardo seemed as if he had dropped from another planet". (1970, pp. 60–1)

He praises Ricardo for looking beyond the level of appearances of capitalism and understanding its deeper layers. He lauds Ricardo for having 'a notion' that there is a difference between the magnitudes of prices of production and the magnitudes of values of commodities (Marx, 1972, p. 71), as well as for seeing more clearly than other Classical economists that prices express the relation of the productive activity of producers to one another (*Ibid.*, p. 181). He commends Ricardo for his contention that the impact of changes in **wage rates** on prices are insignificant compared to the impact of changes in values, as well as, and in opposition to Adam Smith, that changes in the aggregate **wage share** would not cause the aggregate price level to rise but, instead, aggregate profits to fall, with some prices rising and others falling as a result of differing capital to labour ratios (Marx, 1969b, p. 195, pp. 199–200).

This praise notwithstanding, Marx was also extremely critical of Ricardo's economic analysis, and in particular his theory of price. To begin with, even though he praises Ricardo for his method of analysis, i.e., for looking beyond the level of appearances, he also criticises him for not adequately investigating the links between the inner essence and the surface appearances of economic phenomena. Marx points to Ricardo's attempts to explain the magnitude of the price of production directly in terms of labour time as one of the clearest manifestations of this weakness (a point I will return to again shortly):

> Ricardo's method is as follows: He begins with the determination of the magnitude of the value of the commodity by labour-time and then *examines* whether the other economic relations and categories *contradict* this determination of value or to what extent they modify it. The historical justification of this method of procedure, its scientific necessity in the history of economics, are evident at first sight, but so is, at the same time, its scientific inadequacy. This inadequacy not only shows itself in the method of presentation (in a formal sense) but leads to erroneous results because it omits some essential links and *directly* seeks to prove the congruity of the economic categories with one another. (1969b, pp. 164–5)

Marx also criticises Ricardo for focusing narrowly on the determination of the magnitudes of prices and the impact of changes in the wages share on changes in these magnitudes, and, thereby, failing to investigate the price form in any depth (1969a, p. 205). It is this failure which for Marx caused Ricardo to **confuse value and price**, and arrive at an erroneous explanation of the magnitude of price and money in capitalism. According to Marx, having first defined value as the price of the commodity when it is determined by labour time, and then distinguished this from cost-price or price of production, Ricardo mistakenly proceeds to identify the two; value and price of production (1969b, p. 211). For Marx, this confusion causes Ricardo to wrongly see labour time as the **direct regulator** of price and, ultimately, to arrive at a correspondingly erroneous theory of money. Marx acknowledges that Ricardo most certainly recognises that in capitalism prices deviate from values as a result of differing capital to labour ratios, but argues that he, Ricardo, fails to explain these divergences, suggesting, without any substantiation, that the divergences are only minor. Actually, once Ricardo collapses value into price, he has little choice other than to see labour times as directly determining prices if he wants to continue adhering to the labour theory.

Having praised Ricardo for arguing that the impact of changes in relative wage rates on relative prices are insignificant compared to the impact
on the latter of changes in values,[1] Marx criticises Ricardo for failing to
explain the origin of changes in the wage share, and why such changes
are likely to be of a lesser significance for relative price changes over the
long run than changes in the productivity of labour. For Marx, Ricardo
does not see that changes in the wage share are also the result of productivity changes in the wage goods sector, and that the significance of
such changes are likely to be relatively less consequential for prices than
productivity changes because changes in the wage share (and attendant
changes in the general rate of profit) tend to respond fairly sluggishly to
changes in productivity in the wages goods sector.

Marx has, similarly, both praise and criticism for Ricardo's explanation
of prices in the context of non-produced inputs, particularly land. Thus,
while Marx praises Ricardo for seeing, in opposition to Smith, that prices
of agricultural commodities are set by producers producing on lands of the
poorest quality (those yielding zero differential rent), he criticises Ricardo
for failing, unlike Smith, to acknowledge the existence of absolute rent
and, like other Classical political economists, for conceiving of differential
rent as only arising from differences in the quality of land (and non-
produced inputs in general). Specifically, Marx criticises Ricardo for failing
to see that the magnitudes of relative prices of agricultural commodities
are not given by their prices of production, but by their prices of production modified by a factor allowing for absolute rent. For Marx, what
Ricardo does not appreciate is that differential rent can only exist because
of the monopoly ownership of land, meaning that absolute rent is a
pre-condition of differential rent.[2] Moreover, for Marx, Ricardo is also
unable to conceive of differential rent as arising from differences in capital
advanced in the production of agricultural commodities because of his
failure, unlike Smith, to distinguish between individual and market value.

In contrast with his attitude towards Ricardo's explanations of the
magnitude of price and changes in it, Marx is unreservedly critical of
Ricardo's search for an **invariable standard** of prices. The invariable
standard Ricardo sought was a commodity whose price in terms of labour
time does not change with changes in the wage share. Ricardo believed
such a commodity would help him to show that a change in the wage
share does not impact on the aggregate price level but primarily on the
rate of profit with, as noted above, some prices rising and others falling. The direction of price change of any particular commodity would
depend on the ratio of capital to labour used in its production. Ricardo
recognised that the invariable standard commodity he sought to help

him show this would have to be one produced with a capital to labour ratio which approximated the economy average. The labour time commanded by such a commodity, i.e., its relative price, would, as a consequence, not change in response to a change in the wage share. Ricardo also recognised, however, that finding such a commodity would be difficult. In the end, in the third edition of his *Principles*, he settled on the money commodity as the closest approximation to the invariable standard he sought, assuming it to be 'produced with such proportions of the two kinds of capital as approach nearest to the average quantity employed in the production of most commodities' (Sraffa, 1981, p. 45). Marx sees Ricardo's search for an invariable standard as futile and, more importantly, misguided – the result of his focus on the magnitude of price and his confusion of value and price.

Ricardo's search is futile for Marx in that, even if one could identify a commodity which is produced using an economy-wide average capital-labour ratio, it is unlikely that over time it would continue to be produced under such conditions, i.e., with an economy-wide average technology. At the very least, one would need to assume away technological change for this to be the case.[3] Ricardo's search for an invariable standard is in any case misguided because what he is seeking in the final instance is a measure or regulator of the exchangeable worth of all commodities. This measure is, and can only be, money. Marx argues that Ricardo does not seem to realise that in order to show what he wishes to show with his invariable standard, it is only necessary that the exchange values of all commodities change in equal degree in relation to the chosen standard, and not that the exchange value of the standard is invariable. The standard that all exchange values of commodities change in equal degree in relation to is money and not just any commodity. The relative worth of money in circulation is its average exchange ratio with all commodities. Hence, whatever impact a change in the wage share has on the exchange values of all commodities including money, the exchangeable worth of commodities in relation to one another will remain the same when expressed in money. Marx makes this point explicitly when discussing Ricardo's quest for an invariable measure in Part 2 of his *Theories of Surplus Value*:

> When gold rises or falls in value, from whatever causes, then it does so to the same extent for all commodities which are reckoned in gold. Since it thus represents a relatively unchangeable medium despite its changeability, it is not at all clear how any relative combination of

fixed and circulating capital in gold, compared with commodities, can bring about a difference. But this is due to Ricardo's *false assumption* that money, in so far as it serves as a medium of circulation, exchanges as a commodity for commodities. Commodities are assessed in gold before it circulates them. (1969b, p. 200)

For Marx Ricardo's mistaken quest for an invariable standard, like his mistaken explanation of the magnitudes of prices, stems from his failure to distinguish between value and price, and the eventual collapse of the former into the latter. Marx puts it as follows:

> The problem of an 'invariable measure of value' was simply a spurious name for the quest for the concept, the nature, of *value* itself, the definition of which could not be another value, and consequently could not be subject to variations as value. This was *labour-time, social labour*, as it presents itself specifically in commodity production. A quantity of labour has no value, is not a commodity, but is that which transforms commodities into values, it is their *common substance*; as manifestations of it commodities are *qualitatively equal* and only *quantitatively different*. They [appear] as expressions of definite quantities of social labour-time. (1972, pp. 134–5; square brackets in text)

For Marx, labour time is an invariable measure of the value and not exchange value of a commodity. The measure of the exchange value of a commodity is money, but money is variable in both its value and exchange value.

As noted earlier, Ricardo's failure to distinguish between value and price causes him to misunderstand **money** and, consequently, **money prices**. It causes him to adopt what was referred to above as the traditional quantity theory of money. To repeat what was said earlier, this theory considers the level of prices and the value of money to be determined by the relation of the quantity of money to the quantity of goods and services in the process of circulation. It needs remarking, Ricardo does not begin with a quantity theory of the aggregate price level, but ends up with one when he comes to discuss the flow of money between countries in the context of his theory of trade.[4] Ricardo's confusion of value and price causes him to see labour time as the measure of price, i.e., the regulator of worth in exchange. Since he is aware that money is actually the medium of circulation, money ends up being for Ricardo effectively **a standard of labour time** which facilitates exchange according to labour time. That is, he tacitly assumes that commodities come into circulation with relative labour time prices and then acquire money prices in proportion to these as a result of the quantitative relation of money to commodities. How and why commodities should come into circulation with prices directly corresponding to labour times is not explained. For Marx, commodities come into circulation with money prices. Money acts as the measure of prices or exchange values of commodities. The value of money in circulation and the magnitudes of money prices of commodities are determined before money and commodities enter circulation.

And, lastly, although Marx did not explicitly criticise Ricardo's view of the link between prices of production and actual prices, it is readily apparent that their perceptions of this link are very different. Ricardo sees prices of production as **centres of gravity** of actual prices, while Marx sees them as averages of actual prices. Seeing prices of production as centres of gravity in the manner of Ricardo would suggest they have a separate existence from actual prices, begging the question of how they come to be formed. Seeing prices of production as averages of actual prices in the manner of Marx means that there is no need to explain how they come to be formed separately from actual prices, and, indeed, suggests they can only be understood in the context of the formation of the latter.

5
Marxist Interpretations of Marx's Theory of Price

Since the publication of *Capital*, there have been a great many interpretations of Marx's theory of price, both sympathetic and hostile. My
concern in this chapter is with the sympathetic interpretations over
the last 50 years or so which, because of their sympathetic nature and
not the self-descriptors used by the interpreters themselves, I refer to as
'Marxist'. For analytical convenience I cluster them into two categories;
traditional and modern interpretations. It can be argued, without much
fear of contradiction, that most attention has been accorded by these
interpretations, particularly the modern ones, to Marx's alleged 'transformation problem'. This is quite understandable given that it has been
seen by all and sundry as the major theoretical defect in his work. My
purpose in reviewing these sympathetic interpretations of Marx's price
theory is not to assess their relative merits and demerits *per se,* but to
bring out and further expand on my own interpretation of this theory.

5.1   Traditional interpretation

The traditional interpretation (TI) of Marx's price theory is taken here
to be that which prevailed in the post-World War II period up to the
mid-1970s, and along the lines of those interpretations provided
by such authors as P. Sweezy, M. Dobb and R. Meek. In essence, the TI
view was that Marx's explanation of price is not pivotal to his major
project – exposing the true nature of exploitation under capitalism
– and could, and should, be abandoned. There appear to have been
two major reasons for this negative attitude towards Marx's theory
of price. One was the acceptance of the Böhm-Bawerk criticism of
Marx's transformation procedure and, related to this, the fact that most
defences of Marx seemed to suggest either that some crucial element of

his theory needed to be sacrificed or that value was entirely irrelevant to the computation of price. A second reason was, as noted in Chapter 1, the widespread view among Marxists at the time that competitive capitalism had given way to 'monopoly capitalism' and that Marx's explanation of price could in any case only be deemed to be fully valid with respect to the former. Although for both these reasons the consensus among TI adherents was that Marx's theory of price should be abandoned, there was no similar agreement as to what might replace it. Some, such as Meek, appeared to favour adopting Sraffa's theory of price (Meek, 1977, p. 132), while others, who came to be known as 'the monopoly capitalist school', and identified with the writings of Sweezy, Baran and those associated with the *Monthly Review* journal, favoured developing an explicitly monopoly capitalist theory of price. Although some members of this school, most notably Sweezy, saw no real problem with even including bits of orthodox Neoclassical price theory in extending Marx's theory of price to take into account monopolies, many of the school went on to embrace, and even contribute to, what is now known as the Post Keynesian theory of price.

Marx's 'transformation problem'

It was argued above that, in his transformation procedure in Volume 3 of *Capital,* Marx wanted to show that although (reproduction) prices are no longer proportional to values with the appearance of a surplus and the formation of a general rate of profit in capitalism, they are still fundamentally determined by values. As noted above, it is this procedure that has been the focus of most of the attacks on Marx's theory of price. It is generally agreed that Böhm-Bawerk's criticism of this procedure was seminal. Although Böhm-Bawerk actually criticised Marx's theory of price on a number of grounds, what has attracted most attention over the years is his contention that Marx failed to also **transform input values into prices of production** in his transformation schema, and because of this did not show that values explained prices in capitalism. TI adherents largely accepted these and related criticisms of Marx's transformation procedure and, initially at least, adopted one or another of a variety of 'solutions' which appeared to throw a life line to the concept of value. The best known of these solutions are those identified with Bortkiewicz (1975)[1907], Winternitz (1948) and Seton (1957). The solutions were typically presented in the form of a series of production equations linking quantities and prices of outputs with the quantities (reckoned in terms of embodied labour times) and prices of inputs and an average rate of profit. Since this gave rise to more unknowns than equations, it required either one price be set equal to unity (the Bortkiewicz approach) or the addition of an extra equation (the Seton approach). The extra equation was typically one of Marx's two aggregate equivalences; aggregate prices and values or aggregate surplus value and profit. The Bortkiewicz approach implied that aggregate values do not equal aggregate prices and, therefore, value does not explain price, while the Seton approach gave one the choice of which aggregate equivalent to maintain and, therefore, the choice of whether value is more relevant for the explanation of price or profit. In the final instance, most TI adherents saw Marx's theory of value as more important for the explanation of profit, and suggested price would be better explained by other theories. Sweezy reflected this line of thinking:

> In so far as the problems which are posed for solution are concerned with the behavior of the disparate elements of the economic system (prices of individual commodities, profits of particular capitalists, the combination of productive factors in the individual firm, et cetera) there seems to be no doubt that value calculation is of little assistance. Orthodox economists have been working intensively on problems of this sort for the last half century and more. They have developed a kind of price theory which is more useful in this sphere than anything to be found in Marx or his followers.

> One might be tempted to go farther and concede that from the formal point of view it is possible to dispense with value calculation even in the analysis of the behavior of the system as a whole. There is, however, a weighty reason for believing that this would be a mistaken view.... As long as we retain value calculation, there can be no obscuring of the origin and nature of profits as a deduction from the product of total social labor. (1968, p. 129)

From the perspective of the interpretation of Marx's price theory advanced in Chapters 2 and 3, it can be argued that the TI approach misunderstands the purpose and nature of Marx's transformation procedure, and that this in turn stems from a misreading of his theory of price. To begin with, there appears to be no real recognition by TI adherents that what Marx is trying to do with this procedure is to **explain** prices and not simply **compute** their magnitudes. While Marx certainly recognises prices can be computed in terms of costs and the rate of profit, this computation does not constitute an explanation of prices or an understanding of their fundamental determinants. For this explanation – for the explanation of both costs and profits – value is indispensable. Furthermore, there appears to be no appreciation by the TI of the fact that Marx's transformation procedure does not require the transformation of input values. The Böhm-Bawerk criticism of Marx on this point was simply accepted.[1] It is easy with hindsight to see why and how the TI mistakenly made this concession to Marx's transformation procedure critics. For the TI, Marx is seen as defining value as labour time (i.e., as its measure) and equating the magnitude of value with the magnitude of reproduction price in his analysis of price in the simple circulation of commodities. As a consequence, the magnitude of value becomes the magnitude of reproduction price denominated in terms of labour time. Value is in effect reduced to price, reproduction price, and the latter measured in terms of labour time. The implicit assumption is that it is labour time (and not money) that regulates exchange in the simple circulation of commodities. When it is then recognised that in capitalism the magnitudes of reproduction prices no longer equal values, the values are 'transformed into' or replaced by reproduction prices denominated in terms of labour. The reproduction prices are, in effect, seen as values – modified values. With this transformation, it makes no sense for the reproduction prices of some commodities (outputs) to be seen as modified value ratios while those of others (inputs) remain as value ratios. All prices of all commodities need to be 'transformed' into modified value ratios. Apart from contradicting Marx's theory of price as outlined earlier, this begs the well-known Sraffian questions to Marxists; why begin with commodities exchanging according to value ratios in the first place, and why denominate prices of production in terms of labour time?[2]

It should also be evident that all the proposed TI solutions to Marx's alleged transformation problem are necessarily flawed from the standpoint of the interpretation of his price theory presented in this study. It is not simply that the solutions incorrectly presume the need to transform input values into prices, but more fundamentally that they cause value to disappear from the explanation of price. Consequently, Marx is interpreted as tautologically explaining the price of outputs by the price of inputs (and rate of profit). Of course, most TI adherents did not recognise that this was the logical consequence of the various solutions they proposed.[3] They did not see this because they equated labour time with value and saw all prices and the magnitude of profit denominated in terms of labour times.

The TI misunderstanding of Marx's theory of price is also reflected in the fact that the proposed 'solutions' consider it possible and meaningful to drop one or another of Marx's so-called aggregate equivalence postulates. There appears to be no recognition that, for Marx, the equivalence of aggregate profits and surplus value implies the equivalence of aggregate prices and values, and the latter equivalence in turn implies the former. This is in turn because there appears to be no recognition that what Marx sought to show with his numerical examples is that the **aggregate labour time commanded** in exchange by all commodities after a redistribution of the surplus labour expended in their production (as a result of the formation of the general rate of profit) remains the same and necessarily equivalent to the **aggregate labour time expended** in their production prior to this redistribution.

Monopoly capitalism

Although the TI accorded the monopoly capitalism argument less attention than the transformation problem, this argument did serve to reinforce in many the view that Marx's theory of price should be abandoned. The basic contention was that the capitalist system which Marx analysed, the competitive capitalist system, was no longer the dominant form of capitalism. It had been replaced by monopoly capitalism. Capital was no longer free to migrate between sectors and profit rates did not converge toward a system-wide average rate. One could add, although this was not something the TI explicitly did to my knowledge, that with this transition to monopoly capitalism prices are no longer formed within sectors as a result of the competitive averaging process depicted by Marx. The crucial problem, as many TI adherents saw it, was that the labour theory of value failed to explain the magnitudes of profit rates in different sectors in a monopoly setting. As such the concept of price of production and its determination by value was deemed to be invalid. Howard and King put forward the monopoly capitalism case against the labour theory of value as follows:

> It is clear that in the absence of free competition there is nothing which would enforce the law of value, since profit rates may differ between sectors permanently. The question of monopoly thus raised is independent of the transformation problem, and would persist even in the absence of the latter. (1975, p. 136)

Meek went further and argued that under monopoly it does not even seem reasonable to suppose that the main source of profit is surplus value and, therefore, that total profit can be assumed to be equal to total surplus value (see 1973, pp. 285–6, pp. 292–3).

Let us consider these arguments in turn. To begin with, it is worthwhile repeating Meek's own caution; that one should not exaggerate the extent to which the coming of monopoly capitalism has invalidated the traditional analyses based on the assumption of competition (*Ibid.*, pp. 286–7). More fundamentally, however, the TI appears to have missed the point that Marx sees competition as **a process and not an end state**, one involving tendencies and countertendencies towards, and away from, competitive norms. These norms are an average rate of profit and a common price for producers of the standard product in a given sector. In respect of these norms, the competitive process can, and most likely will, witness some firms within an industry appropriating above-average profits for varying periods of time without this having any consequences for the relative magnitudes of prices of production. This is the case where the firms appropriating the excess profits are not producing the bulk of commodities. The excess profit appropriated will be for fairly short periods of time as a result of, say, product differentiation and improved production techniques, and for somewhat longer periods of time as a result of, say, the exclusive ownership of a non-produced input or patent/copyright. Intra-industry competition will tend to eliminate these excess profits as a result of copying of both products and production techniques, and, where this is not possible, the development of alternative products and production technologies. The competitive process can also give rise to the appropriation of excess profits by firms in an industry where, in contrast, there are attendant consequences for the price of production. This will be the case where the firm or firms appropriating the excess profits are producing the bulk of commodities in the industry. Such excess profits become possible as a result of barriers to entry, and will last for varying periods of time depending on such factors as the nature of the sector, the institutional setting, and state policies towards the sector. Marx regards such sectors as monopolistic and their prices as monopoly prices, but considers their existence as not only consistent with, but also the product of, the competitive process in capitalism. This is not to say that he denied the possibility of monopoly engulfing all sectors such that the fires of competitive capitalism would be entirely extinguished. Not only did he accept this to be a possibility, but, as noted above, he argued that in these circumstances much of his analysis would be irrelevant.

What the preceding should suggest to the reader is that Marx's theory of price (and general analysis of capitalism) is fully capable of being extended to take into account monopoly tendencies in a competitive capitalist setting, unless, of course, monopolies come to dominate all, or most, sectors in the economy, and there is no tendency for the formation of an economy-wide average rate of profit. Marx himself points to his rent theory as the requisite vehicle for this task. It is this theory that informs much of the discussion of the competitive process in his work. It is this theory that provides the basis for understanding the implications for price of the distinction between monopoly profits appropriated by a few firms in a given sector and those appropriated by firms producing the bulk of products – the average firms. When individual firms appropriate an excess profit, it is akin to the appropriation of differential rent and has no bearing on the price of production. When the average firm appropriates an excess profit – an excess in relation to the economy-wide rate of profit – it is akin to the appropriation of absolute rent and has a bearing on the price of production.

Given that Marx's theory of rent is an integral part of his theory of price, this also means that the existence of monopoly cannot be said, as the TI suggests, to invalidate his concept of price of production or its explanation by value. Marx certainly acknowledges that the appropriation of monopoly profits by the average firm would cause prices to deviate further from values than is already implied by the formation of the general rate of profit in the context of different organic compositions of capital (1981, pp. 896–7). He even appears at times to explicitly deny that the magnitude of monopoly price is primarily determined by value (*Ibid.*, p. 898, pp. 910–11). However, to repeat what was said in Chapter 3, the logic of Marx's analysis suggests that monopoly price is for the most part determined by value and could not be understood without reference to it. It is primarily determined by value in the sense that changes in these prices too are mostly determined by changes in costs and the latter, in turn, mostly by changes in value. Although the rate of profit pertaining to a monopoly sector deviates from the economy-wide average, as was argued above, there is no reason to suppose that the monopoly rate is particularly volatile or would vary more than costs over the long run. In any case, both the costs and profits of the monopoly sector can only be fully understood with reference to value. Of particular note is the importance of value for understanding the profit appropriated by firms in the monopoly sector as resulting from a transfer of value to it from other sectors.[4]

5.2 Modern interpretations

Among the many modern interpretations of Marx's theory of price, two have attracted the most attention from his supporters and critics alike. They are, as noted in Chapter 1, the New Interpretation (NI) and Temporal Single System Interpretation (TSSI). Both interpretations see themselves as rescuing Marx's value analysis by looking at his transformation procedure differently to the TI. Crucially, both see the purpose of Marx's value theory, and therefore the significance of his transformation procedure, as, on the one hand, demonstrating how profits are related to the performance of surplus labour, and, on the other hand, showing that the performance of labour in general assumes a money form under capitalism. Both attempt to reinterpret, and expand on, Marx's transformation procedure in a way that maintains his two fundamental equalities referred to above, but both, it will be argued below, suffer from the same fundamental flaw, one which they share with the TI: **a confusion of value and price.**

The New Interpretation

The origins of the NI may be traced to the early 1980s,[5] and can be argued to have focused most of its attention since its inception on what is perceived to be Marx's transformation problem. For the NI, Marx's theory of price is essentially intended as explaining **the money form of price** and the magnitude of aggregate money prices while unmasking the process of exploitation, which is argued to be the real focus of Marx's economics. The NI denies that Marx was interested in explaining individual prices, either in general or more specifically in his transformation procedure.[6] Like the TI, the NI accepts that Marx's transformation procedure as set down in *Capital* is both **incomplete** and **defective**. It is seen as incomplete in that it fails to transform input values into prices of production, and it is regarded as defective in that, if input values are transformed into prices of production, the dual equalities do not hold, the value and price rates of profit are no longer equal to one another, and the real wage changes.[7] The NI proposes a solution to this problem which addresses these inconsistencies, but denies that value can be said to **determine** prices of production of individual commodities. The solution proposed assumes first and foremost that the equivalence of aggregate values and prices pertains to commodities comprising the **net** and not **gross** product.[8] Different reasons are given by NI adherents for choosing the net over the gross product, but the most common appears to be that it avoids double counting when it comes to surplus labour time performed and profits. A **constant of proportionality** between labour time and money is introduced to obtain equivalence between the labour and money values of the net product. Equality of aggregate surplus value and profits is then derived by means of the further assumptions that workers bargain over the wage share and that this share is represented by the exchange value (prices) of wage goods. Aggregate surplus value is seen as the inverse of the wage share for a given net product. The constant of proportionality is then applied to the magnitude of aggregate surplus value to get its equivalent in a money form – the magnitude of aggregate profit.[9]

Although the NI appeared to promise a great deal to those Marxists who perceived a number of problems with the TI, particularly in the face of Sraffian criticisms of Marx and TI attempts to 'rescue' him from these, it will be argued in what follows that the NI represents quite possibly an even more distorted vision of Marx's theory of price than that of the TI. The essential problem is that the NI interprets Marx's transformation procedure as seeking to explain the **money forms** of value and surplus value; to demonstrate a link between value and surplus value by 'explaining' the link between their money forms – price of production and profit. While Marx certainly pays considerable attention to explaining the money form of value and surplus value, this is not his purpose in his transformation procedure. To repeat, this purpose is to show that value continues to be the fundamental determinant of the reproduction prices of individual commodities in spite of the fact that with competition and the formation of a general rate of profit the magnitudes of reproduction prices deviate from values. The money form does not aid this explanation and, therefore, is for the most part abstracted from in Marx's transformation procedure. Paying heed to the money form in the transformation procedure might even confuse matters in that it could give the impression that Marx is seeking to explain actual (market) prices instead of reproduction prices in this procedure. Since actual prices have a money form and reproduction prices are averages of actual prices, it cannot be denied that reproduction prices are in principle money prices; average money prices. However, the money form is not immediately relevant for explaining either the relative magnitudes of reproduction prices or changes in these magnitudes. Moreover, the explanation of the money form of prices for Marx requires a prior explanation of the exchange relation between commodities, their relative worth. It is for this reason, incidentally, that he seeks to explain the exchange values or relative prices of commodities before explicitly considering their money form in his analysis of prices in simple commodity circulation at the beginning of Volume 1 of *Capital*.

In keeping with its interpretation of Marx's transformation procedure as fundamentally explaining the money form of value and surplus value, the NI appears to also incorrectly suggest that price and profit are to be distinguished from value and surplus value primarily because of their form. That is, the NI appears to suggest that the transformation from values to prices and surplus value to profit is primarily one of **form**. In fact, for Marx, such a change of form does not come into the transformation procedure picture. Rather, the distinction between the two is that between, on the one hand, gross and surplus resources (measured by labour time) **expended in** the production of commodities, and, on the other hand, gross and surplus resources (measured by labour time) **commanded by** the producer or owner of the commodity through its sale in the context of competition between producers and the formation of a general rate of profit. Value and surplus value refer to the resources expended in the production of goods, while price and profit refer to the resources commanded in the process of exchange. It bears repeating here that Marx pointedly does not refer to surplus value as profit in Volume 1 of *Capital* even though he acknowledges that surplus value is appropriated in a money form (M-M'). It is only in Volume 3 that he refers to surplus value as profit, explicitly remarking that he does this to indicate that the surplus value actually appropriated by the producer is not what is generated in the production of the individual commodity (Marx, 1981, pp. 268–9).

One final point to be made with regard to the NI understanding of Marx's transformation procedure is that it incorrectly sees Marx as being mostly concerned with the **aggregate** price level and not **individual** commodity prices, certainly not individual relative prices.[10] In fact, the NI incorrectly sees the demonstration of the equivalence between aggregate prices and values as separable from the explanation of individual prices. Hence, the assertion by one prominent NI adherent that Marx's transformation procedure is consistent with any theory of price (see Foley, 1982, p. 38). But this is a serious distortion of Marx's purpose in showing the equivalence of aggregate prices and values (and profit and surplus value) in his transformation procedure. This purpose is to reinforce his argument that, even with the redistribution of surplus value among producers in the process of exchange, value continues to be the most important determinant of reproduction prices of individual commodities. Equating aggregate prices and values in the absence of an explanation of individual prices in terms of values makes the former devoid of any real meaning.

As with the TI, so with the NI, there is a mistaken acceptance of the traditional criticism of Marx's transformation procedure; that he failed to transform input values into prices. And, as with the TI, the reason for the acceptance of this criticism appears to be a misunderstanding of Marx's concept of value and the distinction he draws between the magnitude of value of a commodity and its price of production. The NI, like the TI, defines value as labour time, and then, unlike the TI, equates labour time with money. The assumed equivalence of labour time and money, as I will elaborate on below, is required by the proposed NI solution to Marx's 'transformation problem'. Accordingly, value is not only reduced to its measure, labour time, but also to the measure of price, money. Foley, for example, states value is general exchangeability (see 1986, p. 13). But, as we know, for Marx, it is money that has general exchangeability. This misunderstanding of value is then compounded in the NI by a confusion of the magnitude of value and the magnitude of price (of production). Therefore, when prices of production of commodities are seen as deviating from their values, it seems only logical that the latter, including the value ratios of inputs, be transformed into, or **replaced** by, the former. Since, for the NI, the magnitude of price is measured interchangeably by both money and labour time, transformed input values can still be seen as 'determined' by labour time or value, creating the illusion that the essence of Marx's analysis remains intact, and justifying the conversion of input values into prices.

The NI confusion over Marx's concept of value, and in particular its misunderstanding of the distinction between value and price of production, also explains why some NI adherents accept that a further problem with Marx's transformation procedure is that it results in a deviation of the value of the goods purchased with the wage (the real wage) from the price of production of these goods.[11] For Marx, although there can most certainly be a deviation of value from the price of production of goods comprising the real wage, this divergence will have no consequences for an understanding of price determination. This is because, for him, the prices of production of wage goods, like the prices of production of all other goods, are determined by their values and not by the prices of production of the direct and indirect inputs into the production of these (wage goods) and other goods. Hence, when explaining the value of goods, what matters in respect of the wage component is the labour time required to produce the goods consumed by labour and not the labour time commanded by these goods. Labour time commanded could only be seen as being relevant if one accepted the need to transform input values, including the commodities required to sustain labour, into prices of production.

Given what is perceived to be their flawed understanding of Marx's transformation procedure, it should come as little surprise that the proposed NI solution to Marx's transformation procedure is also seen as problematic. Of course, the fact that the NI sees the need to provide a solution to what is considered by them to be Marx's transformation problem, is itself problematic. However, this aside, there are a number of other difficulties of note. To begin with, and in line with criticisms advanced by a number of other commentators, there does not appear to be any meaningful theoretical justification for the use of the **net** as opposed to the **gross** product as a basis for the proposed solution.[12] Indeed, it would appear that the choice of the net product is simply motivated by the desire of the NI to avoid the alleged problems which are seen as arising when input values are transformed into prices. But, perhaps the real problem with the choice of the net product is that it cements the disappearance of value from the explanation of price. This is because the money value of the net product is not **explained** by the total labour time required to produce the net product, or even the money equivalent of this labour time, but rather by the direct labour time required to produce the gross product, or rather the money equivalent of this direct labour time. Simply positing the equivalence of the money value of the net product and the direct labour time expended in the production of the gross product, and then defining value as direct labour time, is not the same as **explaining** individual money prices, or even the aggregate money prices of the net product, in terms of anything remotely resembling Marx's concept of value.

Another problem with the proposed NI solution is the assumed **constant of proportionality** between money and labour time. This constant is in effect a conversion factor which translates prices denominated in labour times into those denominated in money. There are a couple of theoretical difficulties with it which merit some attention. One is that it implies labour time is a measure of the exchange value of a commodity in the same way as money. That is, the constant tacitly assumes producers use labour times to compute the relative worth of their commodities in the same way they use money. Marx certainly sees a link between money and labour time, but he is careful to distinguish between the two. For him, money is used by producers to measure the relative worth of their commodities, and, in so doing, to allow them to exchange their commodities for productive resources in magnitudes which permit the reproduction of these commodities. Because of this, money must be perceived by producers as representing a certain magnitude of real resources. Since the ultimate productive resource is labour time, this perception is in turn about the (social) labour time represented by the commodities. That is to say, money represents labour time in the final instance and there is a quantitative link between the two, but money is not labour time and prices computed in terms of money only approximate their relative worth in terms of labour time. Of course, the real problem with the NI in this regard is that it posits a link between money and labour time without providing any explanation for it.[13]

The second theoretical problem with the NI constant of proportionality is that it implies the value of money is given by the ratio of the money value of the net product to the living labour required for the production of this net product, tacitly denying there is any meaningful distinction to be made between the value and exchange value of money, especially in the context of paper money. The reason for explaining the value of money in this way, and in particular for collapsing the value into the exchange value of money, appears to be quite simply the requirements of the NI 'solution' to the transformation problem. The value of money can certainly be understood in terms of the ratio of the money value of output to the labour time required to produce that output, but what matters is gross and not net output. It needs recognising in this context that the living labour employed in a given period produces a gross and not net product. Contrary to the NI view, this value will be equal to, and explained by, the labour time required to produce money when it is a commodity. It is an equality which is not dependent on any assumption of 'equal exchange' among commodities – i.e., exchange according to equal values. When money is intrinsically valueless paper, the value this paper represents will primarily depend on the quantity of it which circulates commodities over a given period, allowing for structural shifts in the velocity of circulation. The value of money so determined is necessarily qualitatively and quantitatively different from its exchange value (its worth at any given point in time). Inflation at a given point in time will not necessarily directly reflect the intrinsic value of money.

There are also problems with the NI understanding of the wage and its determination. The NI incorrectly argues that the value of the wage should be taken as its exchange value, and its determination the result of bargaining over the net product. That the NI sees a need to equate the value and exchange value of the wage is understandable given the expunging of value from its analysis, and requires no further comment. The view that the exchange value of wage goods is determined by the bargaining of workers over the net product does. Not only is this view of the determination of the wage inconsistent with Marx's own writings on the subject (i.e., for Marx wages are agreed prior to production taking place), it leads to very different **explanations** of profit and prices from that of Marx. It also undermines one of the most important elements of Marx's explanation for the inherent tendency towards technological change in capitalism – the advance of the wage prior to production.

A final problem with the proposed NI solution is that it appears to see the equivalence of aggregate surplus value and profit as contingent upon the equivalence of aggregate value and price. This is because the former equivalence requires the application of the constant of proportionality to surplus value to derive aggregate money profit, and the constant of proportionality is in turn derived from the postulated equivalence of aggregate value (living labour time required to produce the net product) and the money value of the net product. For Marx, the relationship between the two equivalences is in fact the opposite of that proposed by the NI. As noted in Chapter 3, what Marx seeks to show with his transformation procedure is that, while the formation of a general rate of profit gives rise to a transfer of surplus value between sectors, there is no net loss or gain of surplus value by all producers and, therefore, no net loss or gain of value as a result of the transfer. The deviation of value from price of production at the individual commodity level is simply due to a redistribution of surplus value. Since there is no change in the aggregate quantity of surplus value after its redistribution, aggregate surplus value equals aggregate profit (where profit is understood as the aggregate surplus value appropriated by producers after redistribution of the surplus has taken place) and, by implication, the aggregate value of commodities must equal aggregate prices of production (aggregate value commanded by the sellers of commodities after redistribution of the surplus has taken place).

The Temporal Single System Interpretation

The TSSI dates from the late 1980s and, like the NI, also initially focused much of its attention on the transformation problem. In a somewhat similar vein to the NI, the TSSI can be said to see Marx's main purpose in his transformation procedure as demonstrating that social wealth, in the form of the money value of commodities, is the product of labour, and the performance of surplus labour the source of money profit. Also like the NI, the TSSI appears to want to solve, or to be more precise,

interpret, Marx's transformation procedure in a way that upholds what is seen to be his aggregate 'duality' conditions. But, unlike the NI, it seeks to do this in a way that does not require assumptions to be made regarding the importance of the net as opposed to the gross product in value and price computations. Although the TSSI does not deny that Marx sought to explain individual prices in his transformation procedure, it does deny that these prices could be interpreted as in any sense equilibrium prices, or that Marx sought in this procedure to explain prices in terms of a separate system of labour times. Indeed, TSSI adherents see themselves as opposing all interpretations of Marx's theory of value which regard its purpose as one of computing actual or equilibrium prices in terms of a separate system of labour times through the solution of a set of simultaneous equations.[14] For the TSSI, what Marx seeks to do in his transformation procedure is to demonstrate the equivalence of, on the one hand, labour values and/or actual money prices of commodities after their production but **prior to** their exchange, and, on the other hand, labour values and/or money prices of commodities **after the process of exchange** and redistribution of surplus value between sectors to facilitate an equalisation of profit rates between them. That is, for the TSSI, Marx's transformation procedure is a sequential process which takes place in 'historical time', going from input values corresponding to output prices of a preceding period to output prices of the present period. It is for this reason, more than any other, that the TSSI sees no problem with Marx's alleged failure to transform inputs into prices of production.[15] If there is a problem with his procedure for the TSSI, it is that he did not complete it. Most TSSI adherents argue for completion of the process with the aid of an arbitrarily chosen 'monetary expression of labour time' (MELT) linking labour time and money in the manner of the NI constant of proportionality, and, at least for some proponents, a 'conversion factor' linking the value of money before and after exchange.[16] The job of the arbitrarily chosen constant is to translate the labour values of commodities produced but not exchanged into money prices, and *vice versa*, and that of the conversion factor to translate money prices and labour values of commodities prevailing before exchange into those prevailing after exchange.

The first thing to be said about the TSSI is that, like the TI and NI, it too misinterprets what Marx was trying to do with his transformation procedure. Like the NI, the TSSI appears to see this procedure as essentially an explanation by Marx of the money form of prices. The reasons why this is mistaken were given above in the discussion of the NI. A further problem with the TSSI interpretation is that, while it accepts Marx's transformation procedure was intended to explain individual prices, it denies these are reproduction prices in the sense that, if they prevailed, they would give rise to a balanced reproduction of the system. Instead, the TSSI sees the prices explained by Marx in his transformation procedure as 'disequilibrium money prices'.[17] Although it is not entirely clear what the TSSI means by disequilibrium money prices, it would seem that they see these to be what has been referred to above as actual prices. In their introduction to a seminal collection of writings by TSSI proponents, Freeman and Carchedi claim 'Carchedi, de Haan, Giussani and Freeman demonstrate that the central category of Marx's concept of price is not, as widely believed, the concept of price of production but of *market* price, the actual price goods are sold at' (1996b, p. xvii). But, as a number of other authors have commented, this is a misinterpretation of both the letter and method of Marx.[18] Marx most certainly seeks to explain actual prices in the final instance, and he most certainly conceives of such prices as deviating from those which give rise to the balanced reproduction of the system. But there can surely be no doubting that the prices he was explaining in his transformation procedure, the prices of production, are equilibrium prices – what is referred to above as reproduction prices in capitalism. In fact, one of Marx's intentions in his theory of price is precisely to show how and why the system moves continuously through recurrent cycles of divergences and (sometimes forceful) convergences of actual prices from those which correspond to the balanced reproduction of the system. To show these divergences and convergences, Marx needs in the first instance to conceive of prices which aid balanced reproduction. He needs to conceive of prices of production, and then show why and how actual prices deviate from these.[19]

The TSSI also incorrectly interprets Marx as conceiving of price and value in his transformation procedure as qualitatively equivalent to one another. TSSI adherents typically see themselves in this regard as opposing 'dualistic' interpretations of Marx and favouring instead 'single system' interpretations. However, as should be evident by now, a fundamental premise of Marx's entire theory of price is that value and price are qualitatively distinct from one another and that value is the fundamental determinant of price in all commodity production systems. That the TSSI fails to recognise this distinction is because it confuses the two. Kliman and McGlone state, for example, 'The temporal single-system interpretation of Marx's theory, in contrast, holds that the value of capital advanced depends on the prices, not the values, of the inputs...' (1999, p. 34). One reason for the confusion appears to be the interpretation of Marx, like that of the NI, as seeing both money and labour time as the measure of exchange value. Kliman argues, for example, that when exchange value is taken to be measured by labour time it constitutes the value of the commodity and when it is measured by money it constitutes price (see 2007, pp. 24–5). But for Marx money alone is the measure of exchange value or price. It alone is the yardstick used by producers to measure the worth of their commodities in exchange. Labour time is not, and cannot be, used for this purpose. There are not two different measures of price for Marx. This said, one can readily agree that Marx reduces exchange ratios to labour time ratios in his transformation procedure. However, his purpose in this reduction was to show the link between value and average price; to show that the resources **commanded** by the producer in the sale of the commodity are necessarily linked to the resources that need to be **expended** in the reproduction of the commodity if prices are to facilitate the (expanded) reproduction of the system.

A final point of note with regard to the TSSI interpretation of Marx's transformation procedure is that it incorrectly sees values and prices as **sequentially** related to one another. TSSI proponents pointedly oppose what they see as all **simultaneous** interpretations of Marx's transformation procedure. To quote Freeman '...the basic weakness of simultaneous models...[are that they] assume that input values are equal to the corresponding output values at the end of production. In fact they equal the output values of the *preceding* phase of production' (1996b, p. 227). One problem with such an interpretation is that it suggests Marx has a historical cost explanation of price. However, apart from the fact that it would contradict the logic of his analysis, there is considerable textual evidence to suggest this was certainly not the case.[20] I will not get into a discussion of this evidence here since it has been recently accepted by a number of TSSI proponents that Marx did not in fact have a historical cost explanation of price.[21] What these proponents fail to do, however, is explain why and how the 'sequential interpretation' does not imply a historical cost interpretation. A second, and perhaps more fundamental, problem with the sequential interpretation of Marx's transformation procedure proposed by the TSSI is that it suggests Marx is explaining output prices in terms of input prices in the manner of say the TI, except now the input prices are **lagged prices** – lagged output prices from a preceding time period. It should be clear that, once again, the source of the problem is the TSSI confusion of value with price of production. In this case the confusion is also value with price of production from a preceding period. Indeed, it is this confusion that permits the TSSI to argue that value determines price as much as price determines value.[22]

It is also this confusion of values with lagged prices of production that, somewhat paradoxically, leads the TSSI to **correctly** conclude that there is no need for a transformation of input values into contemporaneous prices of production. Obviously, if one interprets values to be prices of production from a preceding period, and one further interprets the transformation procedure as being sequential, then there is no reason to require values of inputs to be transformed into prices of production since the former are deemed to be prices of production, albeit from a preceding period. For Marx, in contrast, there is no need to transform the values of inputs into prices of production because values are qualitatively distinct from prices and transforming value magnitudes into price magnitudes in the explanation of prices would result in prices being tautologically explained by prices, albeit lagged prices.

Needless to say, there are also problems with the proposed completion of Marx's transformation procedure by the TSSI. One problem is that, like the NI, it sees the need to adopt a MELT to convert labour times into money values, and *vice versa*. The theoretical problems arising from the adoption of a MELT are much the same as with the NI constant of proportionality, since they are in effect the same thing. These problems were noted above and do not need repeating here. What perhaps needs some additional attention is the view on the part of certain of the TSSI adherents that the MELT does not need any explanation and can be any 'arbitrary constant'. Since the constant is in effect the value of money, these TSSI adherents are suggesting that it not important to explain the value of money when explaining money prices in terms of labour times.

A second problem with the proposed TSSI completion of Marx's transformation procedure is the adoption by certain adherents of a conversion factor linking money values before and after the exchange of commodities with money.[23] In fact, the conversion factor turns out to be **the implied change in the value of money** between the two instances. This suggests that the value of money is given in the process of exchange. Moreover, to the extent that this conversion factor can be used in conjunction with the MELT to link money prices with labour times, it effectively denies the possibility of any deviation of money prices from values. This is perhaps the ultimate misreading of Marx's transformation procedure and his theory of price.

6
The Neoclassical Theory of Price

6.1   Introduction

The origins of what, following Veblen (1900), has come to be referred to as the Neoclassical school of thought can be traced to the writings of Jevons, Menger and Walras in the latter part of the 19th century.[1] These writings, and those of their disciples, constituted a break with the hitherto dominant Classical school of economic thought as represented by Smith, Ricardo and Marx.[2] The focus on income distribution gave way to one on the allocation of scarce resources, and the attempt to understand the economic system in terms of objective laws relating to class-based production gave way to an attempt to understand it in terms of the **subjective** (marginal) decision making of individuals in the process of exchange and consumption. Not that income distribution was ignored by the new approach. Instead, it was 'explained' in the course of explaining the allocation of scarce resources and the maximisation of satisfaction by individuals. During the course of the 20th century the Neoclassical approach came to hold sway over the economics fraternity such that today, at the beginning of the second decade of the 21st century, in spite of the innumerable attacks on its methodological foundations, logical coherence, empirical validity and policy relevance, it is far and away the dominant approach to the study of the economic system. This is not to say that there is today one all-encompassing and universally accepted Neoclassical approach. Rather, what can plausibly be argued is that there are certain shared principles of members of this broad church which are manifest in their explanations of economic phenomena in general and price in particular.[3] In the critical assessment of the Neoclassical theory of price which follows, I will focus for the most part on these shared principles, but also pay heed to the divergent interpretations offered by what are arguably the three most important sub-groupings of the school: the

New Keynesians[4] (which is the modern incarnation of the old Neoclassical Synthesis approach), the Walrasians[5] and the Austrians.[6,7] It bears repeating that the primary purpose of this chapter is not to offer a critique of Neoclassical price theory *per se* but rather to elucidate further Marx's theory of price. Accordingly, a number of well-known and oft-repeated weaknesses and failings of the Neoclassical theory will not be touched upon.

As will become evident from what follows, from the perspective of Marx's approach, most of the problems with the Neoclassical textbook explanation of price can be argued to stem from its fundamental purpose; to show that 'market-determined' prices lead to an 'optimal', in the sense of welfare maximising, allocation of resources. This essentially ideological purpose in the study of prices follows, needless to say, directly from the more general ideological purpose of Neoclassical economics in the study of the economy; to sanitise and justify the capitalist system and changes in this system in accordance with the needs of the dominant classes. It causes Neoclassicals to adopt an ahistoric and subjective approach which analyses price from the point of view of the individual 'consumer' imbued with innate tastes. As has been noted by numerous critics of Neoclassical economics, it is for this reason that the approach pays little attention to production and production relations between classes, and instead focuses on exchange and exchange relations between isolated **individuals**.[8]

6.2 The exchange process

Since the Neoclassical explanation of price, like most explanations of price, is founded on a distinct conceptualisation of exchange, it is appropriate to begin with a consideration of this conceptualisation. Neoclassicals typically conceive of exchange in the first instance as the isolated, non-repetitive exchanges of commodities between individuals, as consumers, seeking to enhance their consumption satisfaction or utility.[9] The individual act of exchange is seen as resulting from different subjective valuations of commodities by individuals, who are assumed to be endowed with different sets of commodities. It is this conception of exchange that forms the basis for the Neoclassical understanding of generalised economy-wide exchange.[10] What is notably missing from this account of exchange is the **production/reproduction** of the commodity and **money**. Production and reproduction of the commodity are missing because it is assumed, at least in the first instance, that individuals are naturally endowed with goods and the purpose of exchange is simply the consumption satisfaction of the parties to the exchange. The extreme in this regard are the Austrians, who have traditionally considered production entirely irrelevant for understanding exchange. Money is missing because exchange is conceived of as essentially an act of barter, where the goods exchanged are to satisfy the consumption needs of those undertaking the exchanges. Of note here is the Walrasian approach, the logic of which denies any role for money whatsoever.[11] The notable exceptions among the Neoclassicals when it comes to seeing a role for money in the process of exchange are the Austrians, most of whom argue that exchange is fundamentally money-based.[12]

Even when production and money are brought into the analysis, it is for the most part in an inessential manner, i.e., one that does not affect or contradict the results of the analysis of exchange, which initially excludes them. When production is brought into the analysis of exchange, it is typically to explain the source of the individual's endowments. Producers of commodities – as parties to some of the exchanges – are seen as motivated in their production by the enhancement of their own consumption satisfaction. That is, producers are seen as producing and exchanging their commodities with consumers, and even each other, because of their desire to enhance their consumption satisfaction. They are, in effect, seen as consumers. There is no real recognition among Neoclassicals that even if this is the motivation of producers, rather than say the augmentation of their wealth, exchange involves the production and reproduction of commodities. There is no recognition that production underlies and conditions exchange, much as, albeit to a more limited extent, exchange underlies and conditions production. In the final instance, production is reduced to exchange – the exchange of inputs for consumer goods.[13] Moreover, even those Neoclassicals who accept that production is important in the analysis of exchange and distinct from the latter, still tend to see the former as subordinate to the latter.

Money is typically brought into the analysis of exchange to aid the explanation of how generalised exchange takes place. Generalised exchange is conceived of as the aggregation of individual acts of exchange. Individual acts of exchange are essentially acts of barter in which the commodities exchanged are measures of the worth of one another in terms of the preferences of the contracting parties. When money is brought into the picture to aid the explanation of how generalised exchange takes place, it is as *numéraire* and medium of exchange. As *numéraire* money reduces commodities as intrinsically incomparable objects of utility to equivalence in a way that reflects the relative preferences of individuals for the commodities, and as medium of exchange it facilitates the exchange of the equivalent commodities according to price ratios which reflect these relative preferences. Hence, the introduction of money does not influence the results of the Neoclassical analysis of exchange as barter. Money is, in effect, introduced into the analysis as a 'veil'. It is of note in this context that even though the logic of the Walrasian approach denies money any role, a number of adherents to this approach have sought to introduce it into their analyses with a view to enhancing the realism of these analyses. Prominent among them are the 'overlapping generations' and 'rational expectations' versions of the 'temporary equilibrium' models. Rogers (1989) provides a good review of these and other Walrasian attempts to introduce money into their analyses. He points out that although money is introduced as a store of value in overlapping generations models, any interest-bearing asset would dominate money in this function and, significantly, money is denied a medium of exchange function in these models (*Ibid.*, p. 47). He also finds that the 'rational expectations' hypothesis in models of the same name reduces these models to those of inessential sequence economies in which money is irrelevant (*Ibid.*, p. 49). It is also of note that even though Austrians, in contrast with most other Neoclassicals, see money as necessarily mediating exchanges from the outset, the way in which they bring money into the analysis also reduces it to a veil, albeit a 'fluttering veil'.[14] That is to say, they too see it as a *numéraire* and medium of exchange, whose introduction does not fundamentally alter the results of the analysis of exchange in the absence of money. In fact, for Austrians, money is deemed to only have a bearing on the exchange process when its value changes rapidly (when excessive quantities of money are being printed by the authorities).

As should be apparent from what was presented earlier, Marx too abstracts in the first instance from both production and money in his analysis of exchange. However, the manner of his abstraction is very different from that of the Neoclassicals. In Neoclassical analyses, abstraction is what may be called a partialisation of the phenomenon being studied; i.e., the study of important elements comprising the phenomenon being studied but without reference to the phenomenon as a whole. In Marx's work, abstraction is a process which seeks to capture the essence of the phenomenon as a whole. Thus, in Marx's analysis of exchange, both the production/reproduction of commodities and its mediation by money are presupposed. The exchange process for him is fundamentally premised on production and reproduction. It is seen from the outset as mediating an extensive division of labour between producers and involving the production and reproduction of commodities. The very nature of the exchange process and its purpose in a modern capitalist economy setting cannot be understood except in the context of the production and reproduction of commodities. It is because of this, as we have seen above, that

for Marx exchange ratios necessarily reflect the requirements of the production and reproduction of commodities. The exchange process, as a
generalised and repetitive process facilitating the production and reproduction of the commodity is also, for Marx, premised on the existence of
money as a measure of the exchangeable worth of commodities. Without
money as a measure of the exchangeable worth of commodities there can
be no such generalised and repetitive exchanges – no extensive division
of labour mediated by exchange. Exchange which is generalised and repetitive, and which mediates an extensive division of labour, is necessarily
money-based. Money has a considerable bearing on actual exchange and
is not simply a veil. Since Neoclassicals, in contrast, study exchange
in the first instance by abstracting from (in the sense of ignoring) production and money, when these two are brought into the picture, they
should not alter that picture. It is for this reason that Neoclassicals
can justifiably be argued as bringing production and money into their
analyses in what is effectively an **inessential** manner.

6.3   Understanding price

The pre-condition for the existence of prices

The problems with the Neoclassical explanation of price begin with its
view of the pre-condition for the existence of price. It is argued that this
pre-condition is **scarcity** – either of the goods or the resources used to
produce them. A frequent contention of Neoclassicals is that freely available goods don't have prices. Yet, while it can be accepted that freely
available goods don't have prices, it does not follow that those goods
which are limited in supply necessarily have prices. Rather, goods which
are not freely available come to acquire prices when they are produced in
the context of a division of labour for the purposes of exchange. It is production, as social production for exchange, which causes goods to have
prices and not their scarcity. In any case, as a number of commentators
have observed, the property of a commodity to be scarce is an *ex-post* and
not *ex-ante* property, since it is the price of a commodity that determines
whether it is scarce or not, and not the other way around.[15]

Formation of prices

For most Neoclassicals, prices are argued to be formed in the process of
exchange between those in possession of goods, i.e., traders, and taken
as given by producers of goods for their decision making in respect of
production levels which maximise profits. It is assumed that compet-

ition between producers as price takers ensures the adoption by them of identical prices for homogenous products which are produced using homogeneous technologies and permitting the appropriation of an economy-wide average rate of profit. It is tacitly denied that money has any role to play in the formation of prices.

The exceptions to this general Neoclassical line of thought on price formation are, once again, the Austrians and Walrasians. Austrians see product and price differentiation as the norm, and ascribe an important role to money in the formation of prices. Walrasians deny that prices are even formed in exchange. For Walrasians, as is well-known, prices are formed outside of exchange by an auctioneer – which could be interpreted as a central planning body.[16] Adherence to this bizarre construct is, of course, necessitated by theoretical expediency in the Walrasian economic universe. As has been amply demonstrated, if prices are seen as being formed in exchange, i.e., in the context of bargaining between individuals, there would be no reason to suppose that it would lead to a unique and stable set of prices with 'agreeable welfare implications',[17] at least not without highly dubious assumptions regarding the decision making of individuals and market structure, e.g., individuals with 'rational expectations' behaving in identical fashion and the existence of all spot and futures markets for all commodities and factor inputs.[18] Rizvi comments that recognition of this has caused a number of formerly erstwhile champions of general equilibrium theory to abandon the field (2007, p. 385).

There are several related problems with the preceding Neoclassical views of price formation from the perspective of Marx's analysis. Most immediately, and following from the analysis of the exchange process, it is apparent that there is no recognition by Neoclassicals of the role of the production and reproduction of commodities in the formation of price. Austrians, naturally enough, deny that production matters at all for price formation.[19] What matters for them is only what happens in the process of bargaining between traders as each tries to maximise their utility. For Walrasians, not only are prices formed outside of the exchange process they are also formed outside of the production process, by the imaginary auctioneer.

There is also no recognition of the role of competition between producers in the process of price formation. Indeed, as I will argue below, to the extent that prices are conceived of as being formed in the context of competition, the latter is seen as between those engaged in the process of exchange. As a result, there is no convincing explanation for how standard prices for standard products arise, except as the outcome of a process of arbitrage among large numbers of those engaged in exchange. There is no recognition, for instance, that standard prices for standard products arise in a competitive process among producers in which price divergences and product differentiations are the norm. Moreover, although Austrians, uniquely among Neoclassicals, conceive of price divergences and product differentiations in a competitive setting, these are not seen as resulting from a competitive process among producers, but rather the consequence of the uniqueness of each and every act of exchange. In fact, this view of the uniqueness of each and every act of exchange causes Austrians to typically deny the formation of standard prices for standard products, since each product is in any case not defined by its physical characteristics alone but also by the context of its exchange.

Also, following from their analysis of the exchange process, Neoclassicals fail to recognise the fundamental role played by money in the process of price formation. Because prices are seen by Neoclassicals as formed in a process of exchange (which is conceived of as an atomised process) in which individuals express their subjective preferences for commodities in relation to one another, the commodities being exchanged themselves effectively serve as measures of the exchangeable worth of one another. To the extent that money is brought into the analysis of price formation, it is, as noted above, as *numéraire*; the vehicle for reducing exchange ratios, and therefore relative preferences, to equivalence. Since the exchange ratios between commodities are seen as determined by relative preferences, their conversion to money is notional. Money as *numéraire* functions as a veil. It has no real role in the formation of relative prices. Needless to say, the extreme view in this regard is held by Walrasians, who, in keeping with their views of the process of exchange and the lack of importance of money in that process, see no role whatsoever for money in price formation. In the standard Walrasian system, prices are set by an auctioneer without the aid of money.[20] In augmented Walrasian models, money plays at most a notional role in price formation. Also needless to say, at the other extreme, are the Austrians, who appear to accord money a pivotal role in price formation. For Austrians, consumers and entrepreneurs use money for the purposes of economic calculation in disequilibrium situations. Consumers allegedly use money to order commodities in terms of their preferences, and entrepreneurs to compare returns on different configurations of inputs.[21] However, leaving aside the issue of why economic calculation using money is only required in disequilibrium situations, it cannot be argued that the use of money for economic calculation by the individual is the same thing as the use of money in the formation of prices. The use of money to order preferences by individuals, or compute returns on inputs by entrepreneurs, does not make it the measure of the exchangeable worth of commodities. It does not make it the general equivalent in the process of exchange and, therefore, that which regulates the actual exchange of commodities. This is because the use of money to set prices which directly or indirectly reflect preferences/utility would imply, given the heterogeneity of preferences/utility, that money in some way or another also reduces preferences/utility to equivalence.[22] But given the nature of preferences/utility, such a reduction would appear to be contradictory.

Form of prices

Although most Neoclassicals recognise prices are in actual fact **money** prices, the logic of their analyses denies the necessity for prices assuming such a form. This is because, as argued above, Neoclassical analyses are unable to show that money is integral to the exchange process or, related to this, that money is essential in the formation of prices. It will be recalled, commodity exchange is seen by Neoclassicals as an individualised, non-repetitive process which serves to enhance the consumption satisfaction of those engaged in it, with prices being formed as a result of bargaining between the contracting parties. When viewed in these terms, the exchange process has no need or theoretical rationale for a general equivalent – general exchangeable worth. Comparison of commodities is by each individual for the purposes of consumption satisfaction. Accordingly, as just noted above, the traded commodities themselves serve as measures of exchangeable worth. The extreme in terms of the denial of the money form of price are, not surprisingly, the Walrasians. Since money has no role to play in exchange and the formation of price in the Walrasian system, it cannot really be argued that price has of necessity a money form. At the other end of the Neoclassical spectrum are the Austrians, who, in keeping with their analyses of exchange and price formation, argue that price of necessity assumes a money form.[23] As noted above, it is claimed this necessity arises from the fact that consumers and entrepreneurs use money for economic calculation. Yet, as also noted above, it is unclear why the use of money for economic calculation by the individual or the entrepreneur should imply the use of money as measure, and, therefore, why price should necessarily assume a money form.

Purpose of prices

Neoclassicals see the purpose of prices as the **allocation of resources** (especially 'factor inputs') to maximise consumer satisfaction through the provision of **signals** for decision makers.[24] The decisions taken in response to price movements are those in respect of the quantities demanded and supplied. A distinction is made between temporary and permanent quantity changes. Temporary quantity changes are those that elicit further price changes, which in turn beget further quantity changes. Prices that give rise to temporary quantity changes are referred to as disequilibrium prices. It is argued that, for one reason or another, these prices do not reflect a balance between the quantities demanded and supplied. Prices that give rise to quantity changes and which do not beget further quantity changes are referred to as equilibrium prices. Equilibrium prices reflect a balance in the demand for, and supply of, the product. Walrasians typically assume that prices are always equilibrium prices, while Austrians assume that prices are always disequilibrium prices, although tending towards equilibrium.[25] Hence, for Walrasians the quantity responses of individuals and firms to prices are deemed to be permanent and determined prior to, or in the context of, the formation of the equilibrium prices. It is for this reason that prices in the Walrasian system are criticised by other Neoclassicals as having no real signalling purpose.[26] They are argued to merely reflect quantity decisions taken beforehand, i.e., before the exchange process. For Austrians, in contrast, the quantity decisions are transient, based on prices that do not reflect a fundamental balance between demand and supply. Resulting erroneous quantity decisions elicit further erroneous price and quantity decisions, albeit decisions which are assumed to somehow move the system towards equilibrium. Finally, for all Neoclassicals, the quantity demanded is argued to move inversely to price, while the quantity supplied is argued to move for the most part proportionately to price.

It should be readily apparent that the general Neoclassical view of the purpose of price is premised on the assumption that the exchange of commodities is always, at least in the final instance, for the purpose of consumption satisfaction, and is either between consumers themselves or involving producers who are aware of the spectrum of consumer preferences for their products. There is no recognition, and indeed cannot be any recognition, that the purpose of exchange and, therefore, price, is the reproduction of the commodity, and that it involves producers who have no knowledge of the ranking of consumer preferences, even those preferences of the consumers of the commodities they produce.

There is also no understanding among Neoclassicals, at least not formally speaking, that it is not prices that govern the allocation of resources but rather the incomes of producers and, in particular, the profits of productive capitalists.[27] If producers do not receive an adequate return, either to sustain them in a physiological sense or at a level comparable to other producers of similar products, they will move to other activities. Related to this, there is no reason to suppose that rising or falling prices will cause a corresponding increase or decrease in production. Such a mistaken supposition in Neoclassical thinking is based on the added mistaken assumption of increasing costs underlying the upward sloping supply curve (see below for an elaboration of this point).

Nature of prices

Relative prices

It is usually argued by Neoclassicals that relative prices reflect the relative (marginal) preferences of consumers for different commodities, and either the relative availability of commodities in exchange (as for Walrasians and Austrians) or the (marginal) costs of their production (as for New Keynesians). And it is probably fair to say that most Neoclassicals would subscribe to the view that relative prices are in the final instance fundamentally explained by the relative preferences of individuals.

The notion that prices reflect relative preferences or utility for Neoclassicals, follows logically from their views of the exchange process, price formation and the purpose of price. It is only by seeing the goods exchanged as in the first instance naturally bestowed on individuals, and prices formed in the process of exchange and serving to enhance consumer satisfaction, that prices can be seen as fundamentally reflecting utility/preferences. It goes without saying that, from the perspective of Marx's analysis outlined earlier, this misrepresents the very essence of the exchange process, the way in which prices are formed, and their purpose in commodity producing systems such as the modern capitalist system. Most importantly, the Neoclassical approach fails to recognise that the commodities being exchanged are produced and reproduced, and that prices are formed in the context of, and serve to facilitate, the latter – the production and reproduction of commodities. Even when Neoclassicals bring the production of commodities into the picture, it is in a manner that allows prices to be seen as still reflecting subjective preferences of individuals in respect of the consumption of commodities. As such, they fail to see prices as fundamentally reflecting the physical requirements of the reproduction of commodities.

There are also a number of other problems with the Neoclassical view of the nature of price which warrant remarking on. One is that it implies the satisfaction or utility different individuals derive from the consumption of commodities can somehow be seen as homogeneous when, by definition, it cannot. I will return to this point in the discussion of the Neoclassical explanation of the magnitude of price. A further problem pertains to the view espoused by certain Neoclassicals that prices reflect in part the relative availability or scarcity of a product. As I have already noted above, availability or scarcity is logically an *ex-post* and not *ex-ante* property of a commodity. This means that price should not so much be seen as reflecting availability/scarcity, as availability/scarcity should be seen as reflecting price. And, lastly, to argue that prices reflect marginal costs of producers as some Neoclassicals (most notably the New Keynesians) do would seem to deny that prices are formed in the process of exchange as a result of the subjective preferences of the parties to the exchange. Indeed, as Austrians have rightly suggested, it would appear to open the door to more objective theories of price, even though the marginal costs being referred to are argued to be the subjective opportunity cost valuations of producers.[28]

Money prices

To the extent that Neoclassicals accept prices assume a money form, it is argued they are separate from relative prices, in the sense that they have no bearing on the latter, simply mirroring these. That is, for Neoclassicals, money prices directly reflect relative prices.[29] It is further argued that the value of money and, therefore, the level of money prices, reflects, on the one hand, the preferences of individuals for money as a medium of exchange and, on the other hand, the relative availability of money.[30]

From the perspective of Marx's analysis of money price, the major drawback with the Neoclassical view of the nature of money prices is that it implies money is an economy-wide **standard of preferences** or utility. If the relative preferences for different commodities are seen as regulating their exchange ratios with one another, when money is accepted as mediating exchange and prices as having a money form, money prices can only be seen as directly reflecting the relative preferences for commodities, and money the common standard of preferences or utility. But the question is, as I have already noted above in the discussion of Neoclassical views of the formation of money prices, how money is supposed to reflect these inherently incomparable subjective preferences or utility. Needless to say, Neoclassicals are silent on this issue since it would require them to explain additionally the link between money and subjective preferences/utility, i.e., the link between money and what is assumed to regulate exchange.

The Neoclassical view of the nature of money price also incorrectly implies that the value of money reflects the relative availability of money as a medium of exchange. From the perspective of Marx's analysis, what this crucially overlooks is that money performs other functions in the circulation of commodities apart from that of medium of exchange (or circulation). These functions include those of settling debts and store of value (hoard). As will be elaborated on below, it is this myopia that in part explains the Neoclassical failure to provide a clear operational definition of money, and recognise the impossibility of constancy in either the transactions or income velocity of circulation of money.

6.4 Price constructs

Neoclassical explanations of the magnitudes of prices are founded on a number of price constructs. Therefore, before considering this explanation, it seems pertinent to look at these constructs.

Equilibrium prices

When explaining the magnitude of prices, Neoclassicals, once again with the possible exceptions of the Austrians, typically begin with an explanation of equilibrium price magnitudes. Moreover, even though Austrians do not usually begin their analyses of the magnitudes of prices with equilibrium prices, it is evident that the latter are implicit in these analyses.[31] Equilibrium prices are seen by Neoclassicals as the **centres of gravity** for actual prices, thus warranting the prior explanation of their magnitudes. A major point of divergence among Neoclassicals is whether equilibrium prices should be first analysed in terms of individual markets, then moving on to the economy as a whole – the so-called partial equilibrium approach – or they should be analysed from the outset in the framework of the economy as a whole – the general equilibrium approach. For the partial equilibrium approach, equilibrium prices are those prices which balance the supply of, and demand for, the individual product without reference to balance in respect of other products, while for the general equilibrium approach they are economy-wide prices which balance the supply of, and demand for, all commodities in the economy at large such that the aggregate excess demand for commodities sums to zero. At equilibrium prices, there is argued to be no tendency for changes in either prices or quantities. Many Neoclassicals have extended the definition of equilibrium prices in a general equilibrium setting to include the property of welfare maximisation. Where equilibrium prices can be argued to also maximise the collective satisfaction of all agents, the resulting allocation of commodities (and resources used to produce the commodities) is argued to be 'Pareto optimal'. Pareto optimality means that no other set of prices would improve collective satisfaction to this extent.[32]

From the perspective of Marx's analysis of price, it can be argued that the Neoclassical concept of equilibrium price is an artificial construct which fails to aid the explanation of the magnitude of price. This is because its existence is premised on a number of dubious assumptions, and no plausible explanation is provided as to how it is supposed to act as a centre of gravity for actual price. I will look at each of these two points in turn.

It has long been recognised, even by Neoclassical economists, that the existence of equilibrium prices in a Neoclassical framework depends on assuming away such factors as increasing returns and market power.[33] However, from the perspective of Marx's analysis of price outlined above, the major problem with the Neoclassical concept of equilibrium price, particularly in its Paretian garb, is, once again, that it crucially assumes the fundamental purpose of exchange is an improvement in the consumption satisfaction of the contracting parties. This is argued to be the purpose of those involved in exchange irrespective of whether the contracting parties are exchanging commodities for direct consumption or, as in the case of producers, consumption at a later date. It is only on the basis of this assumption that it can be plausibly argued that bargaining, and actual trading, eventually lead to a set of prices which yield the highest possible level of satisfaction for the contracting parties. Even adherents to the Austrian approach, who consider the attainment of equilibrium prices to be untenable because of perceived 'information problems' on the part of those involved in exchanges, nevertheless affirm the existence of tendencies towards such prices, i.e., equilibrium prices which maximise welfare.[34] If, however, exchange is seen as mediating a division of labour and facilitating the reproduction of commodities, then equilibrium prices can only be meaningfully conceived of as those which facilitate the balanced reproduction of commodities – which is a very different notion of equilibrium prices.

The Neoclassical argument that equilibrium prices are centres of gravity for actual prices presupposes that the individuals involved in the exchange of commodities are innately aware, or can become aware, of the preferences and endowments of other individuals. Thus, Rational Expectations general equilibrium economists simply assume omniscience on the part of individuals (or a single individual – the auctioneer), while Austrians argue that the requisite knowledge for taking traders towards equilibrium prices is acquired in the process of exchange, particularly exchange involving entrepreneurs.[35] What Austrians fail to explain is how individuals are supposed to acquire this information in the process of exchange, or how and why entrepreneurs come to possess the requisite knowledge for taking traders towards equilibrium, particularly in the context of 'shifting' conditions of equilibrium – which Austrians consider to be the norm.

None of the above is meant to deny the usefulness of the concept of equilibrium price as an analytical tool. Marx too conceives of equilibrium prices (what I have called reproduction prices), but the nature of this conceptualisation is very different from that of the Neoclassical approach noted above. For Marx equilibrium prices are those which facilitate the reproduction of commodities in the context of the balanced reproduction of the system. Equilibrium prices must exist, even fleetingly, if the system is seen as reproducing itself. The same cannot be said for Neoclassical equilibrium prices, since exchange is not conceptualised as mediating the reproduction of commodities. Perhaps most importantly, for Marx, equilibrium prices are not distinct from and, therefore, centres of gravity of, actual prices, but are the averages of these.

Long- and short-run prices

A second price construct found in Neoclassical analyses is that of short- and long-run (equilibrium) prices. This construct is mostly used by New Keynesians, and originates from the work of Alfred Marshall (see Marshall, 1920). As is well known, Marshall's distinction between the short and long run is founded on the relative fixity of factor inputs. The short run is argued to be that time period during which most factor inputs are fixed, and the long run that period when all factor inputs are variable.[36] In the course of his short run analysis, Marshall was particularly concerned to show a link between price and the productivity of inputs. However, as Sraffa demonstrated in his generally ignored 1926 article on the subject, Marshall's distinction between the short and the long run rests on the shaky ground of the definition of the industry adopted. For inputs to be seen as in any way fixed over the short run, the definition of an industry should be quite broad, e.g., agriculture. As Sraffa points out, the broader the definition of an industry, the less plausible the pivotal partial equilibrium assumption that changes in the variable factor will have no impact on prices in other sectors (see Sraffa, 1926).

Although Marx does not formally distinguish between the short and long run, it is certainly implicit in his work that the short run pertains to cyclical movements while the long run pertains to trend movements over many (business) cycles. In other words, to the extent that Marx makes such a distinction, in contrast with the Marshallian distinction, it has a basis in reality.

Competitive and monopoly prices

The third price construct used by Neoclassicals which warrants some attention is that of competitive (or 'perfectly' competitive[37]) price and its concomitant, monopoly price. Although there are considerable differences between Neoclassicals with respect to the precise definition of a competitive price, it can be said that there is broad agreement (with the possible exception of Austrians) that it is any price formed **in the process of exchange** where neither buyers nor sellers are able to exert any undue influence on the price, and where the latter allows firms to appropriate an average rate of profit selling a standard product and using a standard technology for its production. Austrians deviate from this view of the competitive price, seeing it instead as any price formed in a process of exchange devoid of government interference. They deny that such a price necessarily implies large numbers of buyers and sellers unable to influence outcomes, or homogeneous products and technologies, or even the appropriation of an average profit by all firms.[38]

From the perspective of Marx's analysis, the basic problem with the Neoclassical concept of competitive price is that it abstracts from, in the sense of disregards, the actual process of competition. For Neoclassicals, competitive prices are those which emerge in the process of exchange as a result of the unfettered activities of traders seeking to enhance, either directly or indirectly, their consumption satisfaction. They are not seen as formed in the context of the rivalrous productive activities of firms. For Neoclassicals, competitive firms are, in fact, price-takers and quantity setters. They adjust output levels for given price levels so as to maximise profits.

This failure of Neoclassicals to conceive of the essential nature of competition underlying price formation causes them to assume, without explanation, the existence of standard prices for standard products and, correspondingly, the adoption by producers of similar production technologies and, at least for the New Keynesians, the appropriation of an average rate of profit. It causes Neoclassicals, with the exception of Austrians, to mistakenly see non-competitive prices as those formed in the context of product and technology differences, barriers to entry and different rates of profit between and within industries. For Marx, in contrast, as has been argued above, these phenomena are fundamental characteristics of the competitive process in capitalism. Prices in a competitive setting are formed and reformed in the context of differences in technologies, a myriad of barriers to entry in various industries, and considerable differences in intra- and inter-industry profit rates. Moreover, while Austrians criticise the general Neoclassical conceptualisation of competitive price, arguing that it is founded on a static and not dynamic view of competition, they remain wedded to the notion that the competitive process refers fundamentally to the unfettered interaction of **traders** seeking, at least in the final instance, to maximise satisfaction. For Austrians a competitive environment is simply one in which there are a large number of traders.[39] For them too, and perhaps even more so than for other Neoclassicals, production and competition between producers in pursuit of profit has no bearing whatsoever on price formation.

If the Neoclassical concept of competitive price is found to be artificial, then it should come as little surprise that the same holds for the complimentary concept of monopoly price. This concept is used in conjunction with that of competitive (or perfectly competitive) price, mostly by the New Keynesians, to highlight the alleged welfare and efficiency advantages of competitive industries. Non-competitive industries, whether they are characterised by the existence of a single firm (a pure monopoly industry) or more than one firm (oligopolistic or monopolistically competitive industries), are to be distinguished from (perfectly) competitive industries by the fact that, in the former case, firms face downwardly sloping demand curves and, for the most part, appropriate above-average profit rates – the exception being monopolistically competitive firms over the long run. The condition for the existence of above-average profits is argued to be some form of barriers to entry to the industry. This is why in 'monopolistically competitive' industries, where there are no barriers to entry, excess profits are deemed to be competed away over the long run.

The major problem with the Neoclassical conceptualisation of monopoly price from the perspective of Marx's analysis is that, as with competitive price, it is assumed to be formed in the process of exchange, between the monopolist and the buyers of the product. Monopolists, like competitive firms, are assumed not to set prices as such but rather output levels. Prices are seen, as with competition, as arising out of the process of exchange, in this case the process of bargaining between the monopolist(s) and consumers. Monopolists are seen as setting output levels with references to these prices so as to maximise profits. Of course, since the monopolist is the sole supplier of the goods in question, setting output levels effectively means setting price, at least in the Neoclassical conception of things. However, this roundabout conceptualisation of price-setting assumes monopolists have a comprehensive knowledge of market demand (i.e., the relative demand of consumers for their product at each and every price), that they take this demand as given, that they have U-shaped average unit cost curves much like their competitive counterparts, and are aware, and take decisions on the basis, of unit marginal (opportunity) costs. In fact, firms, even monopolists, rarely have this sort of knowledge of market demand, nor do they take demand as given, or necessarily face U-shaped cost curves, or consider marginal unit costs when taking production decisions.

Relative and money prices

The last of the artificial Neoclassical price constructs which warrant attention is that drawn between **relative and money prices**. Neoclassicals, with the possible exception of Walrasians (who are unable to admit to the existence of money let alone money price), assume that money prices are separate from, but related to, relative prices; that they reflect relative prices, at least in the final instance. As was argued earlier, this assumption is in turn premised on the view that money is 'a veil'. It is a view of money that denies prices are always only money prices. It denies that the relative worth of a commodity is always expressed in terms of money when the economic system in which commodities are produced is founded on a division of labour mediated by exchange. More fundamentally, it assumes that it is not money which governs exchange but something else, individual preferences or utility, and that money somehow reflects the latter. This brings us back to the earlier discussion of how subjective preferences are supposed to govern exchange ratios and, additionally, how money is supposed to reflect these inherently incomparable subjective preferences or utility. Although Austrians, uniquely among Neoclassicals, see prices as money prices, and argue that money is not a veil in the sense that it is unable to affect the structure of relative prices,[40] they too contend that it is subjective preferences or utility which ultimately governs the exchange of commodities, and that money fundamentally reflects these subjective preferences or utility, even if somewhat imprecisely, without any explanation as to how.

Of course Marx too distinguishes between relative and money prices, but only in the sense of distinguishing between actual prices and those which facilitate the reproduction of the system. For him money always mediates and conditions exchanges. Producers use money to compute the relative worth of their commodities, but in doing so money prices reflect the intrinsic, relative objective, worth of commodities in terms of the material resources, and ultimately labour time, required to produce them.

6.5   The magnitude of equilibrium relative price

The standard point of departure for most Neoclassical explanations of the magnitudes of equilibrium relative prices of products in a competitive market setting is that they are determined by demand and supply. However, with prices seen as formed in the process of exchange, and exchange conceived of in terms of bargaining between individuals with a view to maximisation of their individual consumption satisfaction (and without any reference to production), it would seem that the fundamental, if not sole, determinant of the magnitude of price for Neoclassicals should be the relative preferences of those involved in the exchange of commodities. This would, or should, also mean that those demanding and supplying commodities are seen as doing so in the process of exchange with a view to either directly or indirectly satisfying their consumption desires. A number of Neoclassicals, most notably the New Keynesians, deviate from this line of argumentation. They see the offer prices of those supplying goods to the market as determined by the costs of their production, and, therefore, equilibrium prices as determined by both preferences and costs of production for a given institutional and technological setting.[41]

One problem with this explanation of price magnitudes is the sense to be made of the explanation of input prices. The implication of the Neoclassical approach is that they reflect the preferences of traders for inputs and that these preferences are in turn derived from those for the outputs produced with these inputs. This means, to repeat a point made earlier, that those 'agents' demanding the inputs are effectively seen as consumers whose purpose in purchasing the inputs is one of indirect consumption satisfaction. For Marx, and most non-Neoclassical economists, inputs are purchased by producers with a view to the generation and appropriation of a profit, which may or may not be used to satisfy their consumption desires. In fact, for Marx, profit in capitalism essentially serves to facilitate the continuing expansion of production and not the purchase of consumer goods to satisfy the consumption desires of the capitalist. That is to say, the purpose of production for the capitalist is wealth accumulation and not consumption.

A further problem with the general Neoclassical explanation of the magnitude of equilibrium relative price is that it tacitly assumes preferences are, or somehow can be made, commensurable. This permits the aggregation of preferences of individuals for different commodities, making it meaningful to refer to them, i.e., the preferences of different individuals, as wholly or partially determining the magnitude of price of the commodity in question. A corollary of this, incidentally, is the presumption that demand schedules of individuals for different products, linking the prices of the products and the quantity of them demanded by individuals, can be aggregated to give the market demand for the product, thereby allowing the latter to be seen as 'explained by' individual demand. A number of commentators have pointed out that this cannot be done without recourse to highly restrictive assumptions, *viz.*, assuming homogeneous preferences of individuals or that the economy comprises a single individual.[42] Although Austrians are prominent among such commentators, arguing that the construction of the individual demand schedules makes unwarranted assumptions about real economic behaviour, they too fail to explain how the magnitudes of relative prices can be meaningfully argued to be determined by subjective preferences or utility without assuming the latter to be comparable.[43]

The preceding is not intended as arguing that market demand has no bearing on price. Rather, it brings into question the Neoclassical explanation of this demand (as derived by summing individual demand schedules) and, in the process, highlights the importance of seeing this demand as aggregate, social, demand from the outset.

A third and last problem of note with the Neoclassical explanation of the magnitude of relative price is that once it is argued conditions of supply or costs are also important in the determination of price, even if these are taken to be subjectively determined, it is difficult to avoid the conclusion that price is fundamentally determined by costs. That is to say, once it is argued that offer prices are set by producers with a view to covering their costs, it is difficult to avoid the conclusion that demand has an impact on prices only through its impact on costs, at least over the long run. This is certainly the conclusion reached by Marshall in his retreat from the explanation of relative price in terms of demand and supply. Moreover, once it is accepted that price should cover costs so as to facilitate the reproduction of the commodity, one also cannot escape the conclusion that relative price has to be seen as fundamentally determined by the relative physical resources required to produce the commodity. As noted above, it is perhaps to avoid this sort of conclusion, and corresponding theoretical trajectory, that Austrians deny production has any relevance for price determination.

6.6   Changes in equilibrium relative price magnitudes

In keeping with their explanation of the magnitudes of equilibrium relative prices, Neoclassicals see changes in these as due to changes in the demand for, and supply of, commodities in the process of exchange. For reasons given above, these should in turn be seen as due to changes in preferences of individuals for different commodities. However, as with the explanation of the magnitude of price, many Neoclassicals see costs of production as also having a bearing on price, i.e., changes in prices being also due to changes in costs of production.

Obviously, if it is problematic to conceive of aggregate preferences and the summation of individual demand schedules explaining the market demand for a commodity, then it is equally problematic to conceive of changes in the former explaining changes in the latter. One might also note in passing that a number of empirical studies suggest that the influence of changes in demand on prices (even via costs) is in any case fairly limited.[44]

Moreover, and again following from what was said above, if changes in the conditions of supply or costs are also seen as having a bearing on the explanation of changes in equilibrium relative prices, these of necessity must be seen as pivotal to the explanation of the latter – a conclusion that would obviously be anathema to Neoclassicals. From the perspective of Marx's analysis, there are in any case intractable problems with the Neoclassical, or rather New Keynesian, explanation of changes in costs, including the significance to be accorded to technological change in this explanation. Neoclassicals typically see costs rising with output over both the short and long run. They see an increase in costs over the short run as due to the supposed diminishing marginal product of the variable input into production, and over the long run as due to decreasing returns to scale resulting from managerial and other logistical problems. The problems cited by Sraffa with regard to the assumption of fixed inputs and corresponding cost increases over the short run have been noted above and do not require further elaboration here. What needs highlighting is the marked absence of any significant discussion of the managerial and other logistical problems encountered by firms as they expand output levels over the long run. Given the importance of this alleged tendency for decreasing returns, and the resulting upward sloping long run product supply curve in Neoclassical analyses, such an omission in most Neoclassical writings is telling. As noted earlier, there is in any case also considerable evidence pointing to constant or even falling costs (increasing returns to scale) over both the short and long run in manufacturing and other sectors of various economies.[45]

In respect of this evidence, it needs also remarking that Neoclassicals fail to accord technological change any significant role in the explanation of prices. For Neoclassicals, technological change is given exogenously and is therefore sporadic. As such, it is seen as having no systematic bearing on costs and prices. From the perspective of Marx's analysis, what Neoclassicals fail to appreciate is that technological change is, on the contrary, endogenous and continuous, giving rise to unrelenting pressures on firms for expansions in the scale of their production activities and corresponding decreases in their relative unit costs of production and prices.[46] Indeed, for Marx, one of the important historical tendencies of the capitalist system is that of increases in productivity accompanying expansions in the scale of production. It is for this reason Marx argues that the major explanation of changes in relative long-term prices of production is relative productivity changes.

6.7   The magnitude of monopoly price

One area of price theory where there is little agreement among Neoclassicals is the determination of price magnitudes in a monopoly setting. Walrasians typically have no analyses of monopoly prices, while Austrians have a variety of analyses, with some Austrians even denying it is meaningful to distinguish monopoly from non-monopoly prices in a free market setting.[47] Most analyses of monopoly pricing emanate from the New Keynesian tradition, and tend to follow logically from their explanation of prices in a perfectly competitive environment. New Keynesians argue, as noted above, that the main difference between monopoly and competitive industries is the shape of the demand curve faced by individual firms. In a perfectly competitive environment the shape of the demand curve faced by the individual firm is assumed to be horizontal, while the monopolist faces the industry demand curve, which is assumed to be downward sloping with respect to price.[48] In monopoly industries, as in perfectly competitive ones, profit maximising firms are also assumed to maximise profits by setting output so as to equate marginal cost with marginal revenue. Price is then determined by the level of demand corresponding to the profit-maximising level of output. For New Keynesians, the marginal cost curve is not the supply curve of the monopoly producer since marginal revenue does not equal price and, therefore, there is no unique relation between price and the quantity supplied.[49] In a 'pure monopoly' setting, where there is only one firm in the industry, it is argued that the price will be such that there is an excess or above-average level of profits, while in a 'monopolistically competitive' setting, where there is more than one firm producing a differentiated product and no barriers to entry, there is argued to be no excess profit over the long run.

From the perspective of Marx's analysis, the essential problem with the Neoclassical explanation of the magnitude of price in a non-competitive setting is, as with its explanation of the magnitude of price in a competitive setting, that it pays no heed to the requirements of production and reproduction of the commodity, and, in particular, the costs of (re)producing the commodity. This omission, of course, follows naturally from the Neoclassical view that, even in the case of imperfect competition or monopoly, prices are formed in the process of exchange i.e., the process of bargaining between the firm(s) and consumers with a view to the maximisation of their respective consumption satisfactions. As in the case of perfect competition, Neoclassicals see costs of firms in non-competitive industries as mostly relevant for profit-maximising **output decisions** taken by them. For Marx, and most non-Neoclassical approaches, firms in non-competitive industries set prices and not output levels to maximise profits, although they may well manipulate output levels so as to support price levels at certain junctures. Moreover, they set prices with reference to estimated average unit costs of production and include a mark-up on these costs to yield an excess or above-average rate of profit, since the aim of the firm in most non-competitive industries, as in competitive ones, is the expanded reproduction of commodities. It is in any case inconceivable that firms in non-competitive industries would set prices so as to achieve output levels which equate marginal costs with marginal revenues.

A further problem with the Neoclassical explanation of the magnitude of price in non-competitive industries from the perspective of Marx's analysis is, as noted above, the presumption that the mere existence of differentiated products and/or the adoption of more efficient techniques by some firms implies monopolistic price-setting behaviour in the industry, i.e., the setting of a price which allows for an excessive profit to be appropriated by producers producing the bulk of the products in the industry. For Marx, it is entirely possible, and indeed the norm, for some producers in a competitive industry to produce differentiated products and appropriate an excess profit without this having any bearing on the prices of standard products and the rates of profit appropriated by the producers producing a bulk of the products in the industry concerned. This would be the case where the differentiated product only constituted a small part of the market for the generic product. Indeed, as soon as the differentiated product accounts for the bulk of the industry's products, it would constitute the standard product, and producers of this product would only appropriate an average profit. For Marx it is similarly quite possible, and normal, for some producers in a competitive industry to appropriate an excess profit as a result of the adoption of more efficient techniques of production without this having a bearing on the prices of the standard products produced in the industry.

6.8   The value of money and equilibrium money price level

Neoclassicals see equilibrium money prices as determined additionally, i.e., in addition to the factors which determine equilibrium relative prices, by the exchange value of money – its exchangeable worth in relation to commodities. When explaining the determinants of the equilibrium exchange value or price of money, most Neoclassicals subscribe to what was referred to earlier as the modern quantity theory of money (MQM). According to this theory, the proximate determinants of the price of money are the demand for, and supply of, money, and, in the final instance, the relative scarcity of money in relation to commodities. Money is seen as 'an asset' held by individuals for the purpose of carrying out spot and future purchases. The return on money is argued to be the utility derived by the individual from its use as medium of exchange. Individuals are assumed to have a diminishing rate of substitution of money for commodities, and are seen as holding only a certain quantity of money for the purposes of carrying out spot and futures transactions. That is, they are seen as holding a certain quantity of 'real' money balances for this purpose, i.e., a certain quantity of money in relation to the present and expected future money prices of commodities. What constitutes money varies among Neoclassicals, and not merely along sub-group lines. The range is typically from, on the one hand, the cash base of the system (*viz.*, M0) to, on the other hand, cash plus various categories of commercial bank and noncommercial bank financial sector liabilities (*viz.*, M1, M2, M3...etc.). It is argued that increases in the stock of money over and above the requirements of current transactions causes the marginal real rate on money balances held by individuals to fall and, as a result, individuals to increase their expenditures of these balances. This increase in expenditure is assumed to bring the marginal real rate of return on money once again into equality with the marginal real rate on all other assets. As a result, the relation between money stock and money expenditure, i.e., **income velocity of circulation**, is regarded as being fairly stable. The source of the increases in individual holdings of money balances is typically seen as an expansion of the cash base of the financial system, with a constant relation being assumed between the cash base and money stock – the so-called **money multiplier**.[50] Until relatively recently, it has also been argued by Neoclassicals that the prime mover in this expansion is government; the monetary authorities increasing and/or decreasing the amount of cash in the system without regard to demand – the exogenous money stock argument. However, a number of Neoclassicals, mostly from the New Keynesian approach, have come to accept that money stock changes could also be endogenous, i.e., resulting from changes in the demand for money, with the monetary authorities accommodating these changes in order to avoid excessive fluctuations in wholesale and retail money-market interest rates.[51]

Although there are certain superficial similarities between Neoclassical and Marx's explanations of the determinants of money prices, as noted earlier, these belie the more fundamental differences between the two. From the perspective of Marx's explanation of money prices, the main problem with the Neoclassical explanation is that, like the TQM, it implies money acquires its value, and commodities their money prices, in the process of exchange, as a result of their quantitative commensuration. It implies money comes into circulation without a given magnitude of exchangeable worth and commodities without money prices. From what was said above, it should be evident that Neoclassicals see commodities coming into circulation without money prices and money without exchangeable worth because of the way in which they perceive exchange and the formation of price. It results from Neoclassicals explicitly or implicitly denying, on the one hand, that the exchange process is part and parcel of the reproduction of the commodity such that commodities necessarily come into exchange representing certain magnitudes of exchangeable worth, and, on the other hand, that money is fundamental to the exchange process, acting as measure of the exchangeable worth of commodities, and causing commodities to have money prices which reflect their relative exchangeable worth prior to their entry into the process of exchange.

A second problem with the Neoclassical view of the determination of money price from the perspective of Marx's analysis, is that it is unclear what constitutes money. The source of this particular problem is the ambiguity surrounding the perceived functions of money. In early expositions of the MQM, money was seen, as it logically should be seen from a Neoclassical perspective, as primarily held for transactions purposes; for spot and future purchases of commodities. As a consequence, money was conceptualised quite narrowly, as comprising the cash base of the system (M0), or including alongside this cash base non-interest-bearing checking accounts (M1). In more recent times, however, the definition of money has been expanded to include all manner of banking, and even non-banking, financial sector, liabilities (*viz.*, M2, M3, etc.). While it seems fairly clear that the expanded Neoclassical definition of money was motivated by an apparent breakdown in the empirical relationship between narrow money stock and the money price level,[52] the formal theoretical justification for the expanded definition has been the augmentation of money's functions to include those of settling debts and store of value (hoard). This has caused a number of theoretical problems for Neoclassicals, leading to considerable disarray in the conceptualisation of money. The problem with seeing money as functioning as a settler of debts is that it implies what circulates commodities is not simply money but, as Marx and Post Keynesians argue, also credit. If credit is then shown to play a significant role in the circulation of commodities, as well as being independent of (in the sense of being prior to) the accumulation of the requisite bank liabilities to settle debt, it can no longer be argued that there is a direct causal link from money stock to money prices. Indeed, it even opens the door to seeing, as many Post Keynesians typically do, money stock as largely determined by credit, and the direction of causality, if anything, reversed (see Chapter 7). It also opens the door to seeing demand-induced inflation as largely driven by private credit expansion, albeit accommodated by the monetary authorities. The problem for Neoclassicals with seeing money as a store of value is that it allows for the possibility of exogenous increases in money stock simply forming speculative hoards, or, as Marx sees it, facilitating the circulation of interest-bearing capital. This casts further doubt on the alleged causal link between money stock changes and the level of money prices. Certainly, the muted inflationary impact of the recent unprecedented increase in the quantity of money pushed into circulation in advanced countries would appear to lend testimony to this, especially since, as is now only too apparent, most of the increases have found their way into speculative balances. Indeed, the only inflationary consequences of the increases in money stock appear to be via the impact of the increased speculative activity on primary commodity prices.

A third problem with the MQM, and one pointed out by the orthodox literature itself, is that there is clearly something of circuitous reasoning in the 'real balance' approach. Since individuals are seen as holding money to purchase goods, it is apparent that their 'desire' to hold money balances is dependent on the money price level or value of money. That is, the value of money is argued to depend on preferences to hold money balances, yet the latter are necessarily dependent on the value of money.[53] To get out of this circuitous reasoning, some Neoclassicals, most notably Austrians, argue that preferences to hold money balances depend on individual expectations of the future price level. But what proponents of this line of argumentation fail to realise is that it would only provide an escape route for the Neoclassical approach if it can be assumed that the future value of money does not depend on preferences to hold current balances.

Finally, it is unclear that even if there can be said to be an excess of money with respect to the circulation of commodities at given money prices, this would automatically translate into higher money prices as suggested by the MQM. This is because, as argued in Chapter 3, the actual price of money, and therefore money price level, can deviate from its equilibrium level for lengthy periods of time, particularly when money is to a considerable extent replaced in the performance of its functions by tokens of itself and credit, as in the upswing of the business cycle. In fact, the extent to which the excess of money results in a fall in the value of money and a rise in money prices, will depend on, among other things, the nature of demand for money and the range of acceptable substitutes for it at any point in time.

6.9   The price adjustment process

Relative prices

Most Neoclassicals, with the exception of modern Walrasians, accept that actual prices can diverge from equilibrium prices. Austrians even consider such divergences as the norm, seeing the prices which prevail as typically 'disequilibrium' prices. It should be recalled that equilibrium prices are argued by Neoclassicals to be those which balance supply and demand in a way which maximises satisfaction. Most Neoclassicals see the **source** of these divergences as computational or **decision errors** on the part of individuals (and, for some Neoclassicals, also firms) due to **information gaps**. The decision errors are perceived to be with respect to quantities; the quantities of goods and factors which are demanded and supplied. Information gaps refer to the absence, or partial, knowledge of individuals about one another's preferences and endowments. These gaps are seen as naturally arising, the result of some 'market imperfection', including 'missing markets', or due to some 'shock' to the system. The markets which might be missing are typically seen as futures markets.[54] Shocks to the economic system can be almost anything which takes the fancy of the Neoclassical analyst, but a recurring theme is that they are for the most part government inspired and, for Austrians, monetary in nature. Whatever the perceived source of the divergence of actual prices from their equilibrium levels, most Neoclassicals see these divergences as, by nature, isolated, small and random. With individuals involved in exchange seen as being able to discover and learn from their errors instantly or otherwise, adjustments are then seen as rapid, if not immediate. That is, where deviations of actual from equilibrium prices are seen as existing, they are argued to be transient. The exception to this line of thinking among the Neoclassicals is, once again, the Austrians. Austrians are particularly at pains to emphasise that price divergences can be economy-wide, large and protracted, placing considerable emphasis on the arbitraging activities of 'entrepreneurs' – who are assumed to be more knowledgeable than ordinary individuals – for moving prices towards equilibrium levels.

From the perspective of Marx's analysis, the principal drawback of the Neoclassical explanation of divergences and adjustments of prices is that, as with its explanation of prices in general, it locates this in the process of exchange, abstracting from, in the sense of ignoring, the process of the reproduction of commodities. This causes Neoclassicals to ignore the possibility of divergences between actual and equilibrium prices arising from the fundamental separation of the supply of, and demand for, commodities. In fact, supply and demand cannot be regarded as fundamentally separate when seen only in the context of the process of exchange. Moreover, ignoring the possibility of price divergences as arising from the fundamental separation of supply and demand, also means not seeing that the source of price divergences are those forces driving supply and demand apart.

The way in which most Neoclassicals conceive of the exchange process also means that they are unable to see divergences of actual from equilibrium prices as typically widespread. Since most Neoclassicals conceive of exchange as an atomised process, and the economy as the aggregation of these processes, there is no reason to suppose that divergences between actual and equilibrium prices are necessarily widespread, unless, as in the case of Austrians, it is assumed there is a fundamental lack of knowledge on the part of all individuals of each other's preferences and endowments. From the perspective of Marx's analysis, what Neoclassicals, including Austrians, fail to appreciate is that the divergences of actual from equilibrium or reproduction prices are necessarily widespread because of the essential nature of the reproduction process and the fundamental separation of the supply of, and demand for, all commodities underlying it. Given this separation, and the economy-wide forces which drive them apart, it would be unlikely that actual relative prices of most commodities would correspond to those which facilitate the balanced reproduction of the system as a whole.

Locating the possibility and source of divergences of actual from equilibrium prices in the process of exchange also causes most Neoclassicals to not see that the process of adjustment can be protracted. This is because, if the divergences are seen as due to the absence of the requisite knowledge about the preferences and endowments of those involved in exchanges, it seems plausible, at least for many Neoclassicals, to assume that this knowledge can be acquired fairly quickly in the process of exchange, and the preferences and endowments of the contracting parties do not change in the course of this process of knowledge acquisition. Several commentators have noted that even if it can be assumed that preferences and endowments remain unchanged during the process of exchange, there is no compelling reason to suppose that the parties involved in exchanges will acquire the requisite knowledge for trade to take place at equilibrium prices.[55] From the perspective of Marx's analysis, the problem with the Neoclassical view of price adjustments is more fundamentally that it does not, and cannot, accept that the impulses giving rise to divergences of actual from equilibrium prices are both endogenous to the system and continuous, and that the adjustment processes themselves lead to shifts in equilibrium prices. While Austrians admit to the possibility of protracted adjustment processes, seeing these as due to repeated monetary policy interventions by governments inducing recurring and cumulative decision errors by individuals, they fail to explain why (democratically elected) governments would repeatedly make such damaging interventions. Moreover, while they deny that individuals can acquire the necessary knowledge to take the system towards equilibrium, they argue that entrepreneurs have this knowledge,[56] but without explaining how they come to acquire it or how their actions might lead the system towards equilibrium.

Finally, while many Neoclassicals (*viz.*, New Keynesians and Austrians) accept that price divergences can follow a cyclical pattern, they deny that they are recurrent and intrinsic to the operation of the economic system. This is because they see the cycle itself as the result of exogenous shocks to the system, rather than the product of its inner workings, and price divergences accompanying the cycle as due to decision errors of individuals in respect of these shocks, and, therefore, something of an aberration.

Money prices

With the exception of some, but not all, modern-day Austrians, most Neoclassicals that accept the possibility of a divergence of actual from equilibrium money prices analyse these separately from divergences of actual from equilibrium relative prices in keeping with the analytical distinction they draw between the determination of relative and money price magnitudes. The necessary condition for these divergences is also (as with relative price divergences) seen as information gaps of individuals. In this case the information gaps are with regard to the stock of money in relation to the stock of commodities to be circulated. Neoclassicals see the source of these divergences as monetary disturbances, mostly resulting from government monetary policy. As with relative prices, so with money prices, the divergence of the actual level of money prices from its equilibrium level is typically argued to be random and fleeting, unless the system suffers from continuous exogenous monetary and speculative shocks to it. Adjustment of the actual level of money prices to its equilibrium level, a level consistent with a balance in the supply of, and demand for, money (which maximises welfare), is seen as resulting from either the optimising behaviour of individuals in response to changes in real money balances, or adjustments of money stock by the monetary authorities.

From the perspective of Marx's analysis, one problem with the preceding Neoclassical view of money price divergences and corresponding adjustments is that they are seen as separate from those of relative prices, and having no bearing on the latter, at least not over the long run. This is because, as noted above, Neoclassicals see money as, in the final instance, a standard of preferences, one which facilitates exchange according to relative preferences. To the extent that there is an impact of movements in money prices on relative prices, it is seen as short term or temporary. For Marx, in contrast, money is a measure of the exchange values of commodities and, therefore, the direct regulator of exchanges, not a standard of the regulator of exchanges. Divergences of the value of money and money prices from their equilibrium levels have consequences for equilibrium relative prices of commodities because of the bearing these divergences have on the rate of profit and, via this, the level of production of commodities.

A further problem with the Neoclassical approach to the divergences of money prices and the value of money from their equilibrium levels, is that it sees the possibility for such divergences as explained by the conditions governing exchange, in this case those governing the exchange of commodities and money. Again, this follows naturally enough from the fact that Neoclassicals see both money prices and the value of money as determined simultaneously in the process of exchange as a result of the exchange (or commensuration) of commodities and money. But, from the perspective of Marx's analysis, what Neoclassicals are missing in this regard is that this possibility arises from the separation of the supply of, and demand for, money for the purposes of the circulation of commodities. It is a separation which is enhanced by the appearance and development of substitutes of money and the credit system. Locating the possibility of divergences between the actual and equilibrium level of money prices and value of money in the process of exchange (one divorced from the process of reproduction of commodities) leads Neoclassicals to see the source of these divergences as external to the reproduction of commodities, i.e., external to the functioning of the economic system. It causes them to see these divergences as resulting from shocks to the system, mostly in the form of the irrational, not to say wanton, activities of the monetary authorities.

Finally, there are a number of problems with the Neoclassical real balance mechanism, a mechanism which supposedly gives rise to an automatic and rapid adjustment of actual money prices to their equilibrium level. The implicit assumption underlying this mechanism, i.e., that individuals are aware of both the stock of money and (expected) price level at any point in time, has been dealt with above. What needs additional comment here is that the real balance adjustment mechanism also presupposes individuals will spend excess money balances proportionately on all 'assets', including commodities. But there is no reason to suppose this. Indeed, even if it can be argued that printing of money translates into increases in real money balances of all individuals, and we know from recent experience this is not the case,[57] it cannot be argued that individuals will automatically spend these excess balances, or they will do so on all 'assets' in the same proportion at each and every point in time allowing for differences in rates of return on various assets. As we know, the proportions individuals will spend money balances on, say, commodities as opposed to financial assets, will change over the course of the business cycle. Moreover, that Neoclassicals assume the adjustment of the actual money price level to its equilibrium level is rapid, not only assumes the above-mentioned knowledge on the part of individuals regarding the stock of money and expected price level, it supposes there are no changes in the equilibrium value of money in the adjustment process, except for those emanating from exogenous changes in money stock. But this supposition could only be justified on the basis of the further assumption of fixed output of all commodities in the process of adjustment, something Marx would deny given his view of the linkage between money and relative prices.

7
The Post Keynesian Theory of Price

7.1 Introduction

Post Keynesianism is a relatively modern school of economic thought, originating in the mid-1970s, and 'associated with the vision and ideas of the unorthodox Cambridge economists who rose to prominence in the wake of the Keynesian revolution' (Dunn, 2000, p. 345). Sheila Dow, a leading Post Keynesian, suggests that Joan Robinson, who worked with Keynes at Cambridge, was probably the first to coin the term 'Post Keynesian', and credits Alfred Eichner with providing the first general account of Post Keynesian economics (2001, p. 13).[1] Post Keynesianism is usually regarded as a sub-grouping of a broader grouping, the Heterodox school. The Heterodox school is an amalgam of disparate approaches to economics whose sole unifying thread appears to be their opposition to what is deemed to be orthodox economics, which, for the most part, is what has been referred to in this book as Neoclassical economics. It, the Heterodox school, includes *inter alia* Institutionalists, Marxists, neo-Ricardians, neo-Austrians and Post Keynesians. Although, from its inception, Post Keynesianism purported to be more than a collection of those opposed to mainstream economics, it is accepted that it falls well short of representing a settled, coherent, alternative to the mainstream.

In fact, from its inception three distinct strands of Post Keynesianism have been in evidence; the fundamentalist Keynesians (who have spent much time and energy interpreting the writings of Keynes and demolishing what they see as heretical interpretations of these writings emanating from Neoclassical Synthesisers and their heirs, the New Keynesians), the Kaleckians and the neo-Ricardians/Sraffians. It is perhaps fair to say that it is nowadays accepted by most adherents of the school that the neo-Ricardian/Sraffian grouping cannot be accommodated under the Post

Keynesian umbrella due to perceived differences in terms of focus and method.[2] At the most general level, Post Keynesians see their focus as the explanation of 'macroeconomic' phenomena such as output and employment, while the neo-Ricardians/Sraffians could be argued to be more concerned with 'microeconomic' phenomena such as the determinants of the magnitudes of relative prices of commodities. If there is an overlap between the approaches, it is their shared concern with distribution issues. But it is with regard to method that most Post Keynesians see the two approaches really diverging. Post Keynesians argue that neo-Ricardians/Sraffians adopt what may be termed, following Lawson, a closed system approach, while they adopt, in contrast, an open, organic system approach.[3] Post Keynesians are also critical of neo-Ricardians/Sraffians for the relative abstract nature of their analyses and, perhaps as a consequence of this, their failure to take into account uncertainty and historical time.[4] More recently there has been an attempt by certain Post Keynesians to reinforce their coherency credentials. This has come in the form of a plea by one of the founders of the school, Paul Davidson, who is also an editor of the *Journal of Post Keynesian Economics*, for a 'small-tent' definition of Post Keynesianism which would in effect exclude Kaleckians (see Davidson, 2003–4, 2005). Notwithstanding the merits or demerits of Davidson's arguments, I will take Post Keynesianism in the present chapter as including both the fundamentalist Keynesian and Kaleckian sub-groupings, but excluding the neo-Ricardians/Sraffians. The latter are excluded not because of the alleged differences in their focus and method, but because of their very different theory of price. This difference should become apparent in the course of the presentation of Sraffa's theory of price in the next chapter.

It has to be said, however, that even limiting the definition of Post Keynesianism in this way does not make for a clear and agreed Post Keynesian theory of price. Some 60 years after the publication of Keynes's *General Theory*, one prominent Post Keynesian economist confessed that 'there exists no well grounded cohesive and consistent body of economic analysis that can be referred to as Post Keynesian price theory' (Lee, 1998, p. 2), and, more recently, another has lamented that 'apart from Kalecki, those traditionally cited at the heart of Post Keynesian microeconomics do not possess a coherent and fully developed analysis of the *process* of pricing and its embeddedness within a broader conceptualisation of Post Keynesianism' (Dunn, 2008, p. 146). While it is quite apparent that there remain considerable differences between Post Keynesians in respect of their explanations of prices, I argue that there are enough shared elements in these explanations (*viz.*, normal costs, mark-up and target rates of return) to justify reference to 'a Post Keynesian theory of price'. It is these shared elements that I will accord most attention to in what follows, only paying heed to differences among Post Keynesians where I deem these to be consequent.

7.2 Focus and method

The focus of most Post Keynesian economic analyses is primarily aggregate output and employment, and perhaps only secondarily income distribution. Post Keynesians are principally concerned to show that **aggregate demand** drives aggregate output and employment, and also explains income distribution as well as being explained by it. From the perspective of Marx's analysis, the essential deficiency of this focus is that it is entirely too narrow. That is to say, the problems of low growth and unemployment are not for the most part analysed in the framework of a broader analysis of the economic system. As a consequence, when the Post Keynesian analysis is extended to the explanation of other economic phenomena, it is found wanting and requires supplementation using other theoretical frameworks, most of which do not sit easily with it. It needs remarking in this context that Keynes's own purpose in his *The General Theory of Employment, Interest and Money* was primarily to justify activist fiscal and monetary policy, which he felt would spur aggregate demand and bring to an end the problems of low growth and protracted unemployment besetting the advanced economies at the time of his writing.[5] There can be little doubt that it is this limited focus and purpose of his work that caused Keynes himself to ignore the explanation of prices in his analysis, notwithstanding the inclusion of an entire chapter ostensibly devoted to the theory of prices (Chapter 21) in his *General Theory*, and that has allowed a number of disparate theories of price to be subsequently appended to this analysis even though they appear to be at odds with its underlying logic.

The starting point for Post Keynesian statements on method tends to be their criticisms of what they perceive to be the Neoclassical method. Post Keynesians criticise Neoclassical economists for building abstract and ahistoric models to analyse the economy; abstract in the sense that the underlying assumptions of the models bear little relation to reality, and ahistoric in that the models posit 'event regularities'. Against this backdrop, they opt instead for an alternative realist and historical method, where basic assumptions correspond to reality and analysis is historically informed. However, it can be argued that the realist method of Post Keynesianism leads to a denial of the usefulness of abstraction in anything other than what amounts to a partialisation of the concrete, while its historical approach amounts to little more than the repeated assertion of 'the irreversibility of time'. Consequently, from the perspective of Marx's analysis, the Post Keynesian understanding of economic phenomena tends to be quite superficial. It tends to be built on a number of axioms and lacks real awareness of either the essence of the phenomena being explained or their historical evolution. This is no more evident than in the Post Keynesian explanation of price. This explanation, as will be elaborated on below, tends to be largely from the perspective of individual capitalist producers and their perceived needs in the process of production. It pays inadequate heed to the workings of the system at large. The Post Keynesian approach contrasts, incidentally, with the Neoclassical approach outlined above, which effectively analyses price from the perspective of the individual consumer and her/his decisions in the process of exchange.

7.3   The exchange process

Post Keynesians, following Keynes, argue that the exchange which matters in the explanation of price is the exchange of commodities (C) for money (M) for the purposes of the appropriation of a money profit (*viz.*, M-C-M') by producers of the commodities.[6] This is counterposed to exchange as perceived by Neoclassicals and Classical economists, where the purpose of the act of exchange is argued to be one of obtaining another commodity either by means of barter (C-C') or through the use of money as a medium of exchange (C-M-C'). Insofar as Post Keynesians bring production and money into the analysis of exchange from the outset, their understanding of exchange can be said to be in advance of the Neoclassical approach, which was argued to be bereft of either of these. However, from the perspective of Marx's analysis, the Post Keynesian analysis of exchange too can be argued to have its limitations.

The essential problem with the Post Keynesian understanding of exchange as depicted above is that it confuses the circulation of commodities and money with the circulation of capital, and views the latter from the perspective of the individual productive capitalist in a manner akin to Adam Smith.[7] This causes Post Keynesians to have a distorted view of the nature of commodities and money, as well as their relation to one another. Most fundamentally, it results in a failure in Post Keynesian analyses to see commodities as possessing worth or value independent, and outside, of their relation with money and, therefore, money price as in any way reflecting this worth. This is because, when the exchange process is viewed from the perspective of the individual capitalist, there is a tendency to miss the fact that it is part of a generalised system of exchange mediating a division of labour and facilitating the reproduction of the individual commodity alongside other commodities. It will be recalled, that for Marx it is only when commodities are seen in this light, i.e., as produced in the context of a division of labour, that they can be understood as possessing value in relation to one another, irrespective of their relation to money.

It also causes in Post Keynesian analyses a failure to see that the sale of the commodity (C-M) is one side of a two-sided process, where the other side is the purchase of the commodity (M-C), or, more generally, that it is one aspect of a more continuous process involving the sale and purchase of commodities (C-M-C'). Even from the perspective of the individual producer, there is a failure to see that the sale of the commodity is for the purpose of purchasing the required inputs to recommence (expanded) production and not simply to hold on to the money receipts of the sale and notwithstanding the fact that the goal of the reproduction of the commodity is an increase in money profits.

And, lastly, it causes Post Keynesians to tacitly see money as possessing worth outside of the circulation of commodities, as value in opposition to commodities. This view of money is of course the logical corollary of a view of exchange in which **commodities are seen as intrinsically valueless**. It is this view of money, more than anything else, which underpins Post Keynesian contentions regarding the importance of money in solving the fundamental economic problems of the capitalist system (e.g., unemployment and low growth). And, it is this view of money which allows Post Keynesians to see money as emerging 'anterior' to exchange and as a consequence of the emergence of credit relations, as fundamentally credit money.[8] For Marx, in contrast, money cannot meaningfully be understood as emerging outside of the development of the exchange process, even though it changes its form with the emergence and development of the banking and credit systems. For him, one cannot understand the nature of money, let alone credit money, without a prior understanding of money in the context of a simple process of exchange mediating an extensive division of labour, i.e., abstracting initially from the flow of capital.

7.4 Understanding price

The pre-condition for the existence of price

Post Keynesians are critical of the view that scarcity is a pre-condition for the existence of price, at least in the manufacturing sector, since most manufactured goods which are exchanged and have a price are largely produced using producible inputs. Instead, they see this precondition to be the appearance of money. From the perspective of Marx's analysis, what Post Keynesians appear to miss is that commodities acquire prices, in the sense of acquiring exchangeable worth, even before money comes into being. There appears to be no recognition by them that money and the money price form only emerge when production for exchange becomes the norm and exchange is widespread. For Marx, the products of labour can acquire the price form, i.e., the form of exchangeable worth, even when production is for direct consumption and the exchange of goods produced is infrequent, as in a subsistence economy setting, when exchange is between self-contained communities and typically the exchange of the surpluses of goods. In this setting, the surplus that is exchanged will acquire a price form, which is a form indicating its exchangeability, but it will not be a money price form. Indeed, the form will be whatever product comes to serve as the measure of exchangeable worth – typically a subsistence product that is most frequently traded. Whatever the form, it will be a price form, only not a money price form.

Formation of prices

For Post Keynesians then, the formation of prices is the formation of money prices. Many Post Keynesians, following Kalecki, make a distinction between price formation in manufacturing and agricultural/raw materials sectors. The basis for the distinction is the alleged relative fixity of certain of the important inputs used in production. It is argued that where inputs are flexible, such as in manufacturing, prices are formed by individual producers in the process of production, while where inputs are more fixed, such as in agriculture and raw materials goods production, prices are formed in the process of exchange in the manner suggested by Neoclassical economics, i.e., by individuals seeking to maximise their satisfaction through the exchange of their products.[9] When analysing price, most attention is paid by Post Keynesians to commodities produced in manufacturing. This sector is argued to be characterised by imperfect or monopolistic competition. When producers set prices in manufacturing, they do so in the context of the production of differentiated products, the use of varied techniques of production, and appropriation of different rates of profit. The agricultural and raw material goods sectors are, in contrast, argued to be perfectly competitive, in the sense of the term used by Neoclassicals.

Although Post Keynesians, in contrast with the Neoclassicals, accord money a pivotal role in the formation of price, they are unclear **why** or

how it comes to bestow prices on commodities. To the extent that Post Keynesians have something to say about **why** money comes to bestow prices on commodities, it amounts to little more than a tautology; money is seen as bestowing prices on commodities because producers need to use money to purchase the inputs they require for the reproduction of their commodities. Post Keynesians have even less, if anything, to say about **how** money bestows prices on commodities. This is because, with good reason, they pay little or no attention to money's function as measure of exchangeable worth. They do not see money as a measure of the exchange value of commodities because they see it as value and anterior to the circulation of commodities, and, concomitantly, commodities as intrinsically valueless outside of their relation with money.[10]

From the perspective of Marx's analysis of price, Post Keynesians are correct to argue that the relative fixity, or rather non-reproducibility of inputs, has a bearing on price formation (and more importantly on changes in the magnitudes of prices), but are incorrect in seeing this as giving rise to fundamentally different modes of price formation. The use of non-reproducible inputs in production allows owners of these inputs to appropriate an absolute rent, such that a distinction can most certainly be drawn between price formation in those sectors using relatively more non-produced inputs, *viz.*, agriculture and raw materials, and those using relatively few, if any, non-produced inputs, *viz.*, manufacturing. It certainly does not warrant seeing, as many Post Keynesians do, prices of products in sectors using relatively more non-produced inputs being formed in the process of exchange, while those using relatively more produced inputs being formed in the process of production. From the perspective of Marx's analysis, prices in all sectors should instead be seen as formed in the course of the reproduction of the commodity. That is to say, the prices formed should be seen as economy-wide reproduction prices and not individual, firm-level, reproduction prices as suggested by Post Keynesians. They should be seen as formed in the context of the operation of the forces of both supply and demand, and not the forces of only supply (in manufacturing) or only demand (in agriculture and raw materials).

The Post Keynesian approach to price formation, like the other modern theories of price discussed in the present work, also fails to appreciate that tendencies towards product differentiation, the adoption of different methods of production, barriers to entry, and the appropriation of different intra- and inter-industry rates of profit, are not necessarily inconsistent with a competitive environment and competitive processes.

The source of the problem with the Post Keynesian approach in this regard is its implicit, and often explicit, adoption of the static Neo-classical (Marshallian) conceptualisation of competition – which sees competition as implying the production of a homogeneous product by all producers using identical methods of production and appropriating a uniform rate of profit. For Post Keynesians, as for Neoclassicals, any deviation from these norms is taken as implying non-competitive or imperfectly competitive market structures, and, therefore, non-competitive price formation. What Post Keynesians, like Neoclassicals, fail to appreciate about the competitive process under capitalism is its tendency to impose averages in the context of divergences. I will return to this below when discussing Post Keynesian conceptualisations of competitive and non-competitive prices.

Form of prices

Post Keynesians are clear that the price form is necessarily the money form. This is, of course, a logical corollary of the pivotal role they accord to money in the formation of price. But just as the Post Keynesian approach to the formation of price can be criticised for failing to explain why and how money can be conceived of as pivotal to the formation of price, so it can be criticised for failing to explain why the price form is of necessity the money form. What Post Keynesians seemingly fail to appreciate is that prices assume a money form when exchange is widespread and money emerges as a measure of the general exchangeable worth of commodities. When money emerges as measure of exchange value it serves to facilitate the general exchange of commodities by bestowing on them the form of general exchangeability, the money form. Post Keynesians are not able to explain how commodities come to acquire a money price form because they do not recognise that commodities have value outside of their relation with money. They do not see that commodities are able to acquire the form of general exchangeability, the money form, because they have worth in the first place. It will be recalled, that for Post Keynesians only money has value. Commodities are seen as intrinsically valueless.

Purpose of prices

Post Keynesians reject the Neoclassical view that the purpose of price is the allocation of resources to maximise consumer satisfaction. They deny that prices, at least manufacturing prices, have any coordinating (signaling) role to play.[11] Instead, for Post Keynesians, the purpose of price is to meet the **needs of the individual producer** – reproducing the individual commodity and aiding the expansion of production through the provision of the necessary finance.[12] If anything is seen as playing a coordinating role in the economic system, it is, more often than not, 'quantity signals'. Nicholas Kaldor, one of the pillars of Post Keynesianism, explains:

> The important conclusion is that the signal that causes an economic "agent" to do something different – produce more or produce less, or switch his manufacturing facilities from some varieties to others – is always a quantity signal, not a *price* signal. Prices are set by the producers on normal costs of production (or rather, on the costs calculated by reference to normal utilization of capacity) including a customary percentage added for profit; and within limits, the producer will not change his price as a result of a faster (or slower) increase in orders, unless the increase in demand signaled to him is so large that he cannot cope with it without disappointing his regular customers, or else the fall in demand is so large that it causes him to incur standstill costs due to lack of orders (keeping workers and machinery idle), in which case he might try to avoid some of these untoward consequences by some temporary price concession or a price concession that is not formally announced but that he is willing to concede in bargaining. In any case, in the actual adjustment of supply and demand, prices play only a very subordinate role, if any. If prices do change in the course of adjustment, these are incidental to the process of adjustment, and more likely to be a temporary rather than a permanent feature unless the commodity happens to be one in which increasing returns are important, in which case the increase in demand might indirectly lead to a reduction of prices. (1985, pp. 24–5)

From the perspective of Marx's analysis, Post Keynesians can be said to have a distorted view of the purpose of price in that they see these prices as serving to reproduce the individual commodity irrespective of what happens to other commodities. This distorted view of the purpose of price is attributable to the implicit Post Keynesian view of the economy as a set of fundamentally unconnected production activities. It is assumed producers are able to set prices which enable them to reproduce their commodities and realise target rates of return irrespective of the conditions governing the circulation of these commodities and reproduction of all other commodities. Moreover, from the perspective of Marx's analysis, while Post Keynesians are correct in rejecting the notion that prices serve as signals to allocate resources, they are incorrect in seeing this allocation as brought about by quantity signals. As noted in the discussion of the Neoclassical approach in Chapter 6, in commodity producing systems in general it is the incomes of producers that allocate resources. In capitalism the crucial income that performs this function is profits. Capitalist producers will only respond to changes in the quantity of demand for their products through, say, an expansion of their output, if the expansion in demand is seen as giving rise to an increase in profits. It goes without saying, that the source of the problem with the Post Keynesian approach to understanding the purpose of price is much the same as its problem with understanding the economic system as a whole; that it sees the latter through the lenses of the individual capitalist producer.

Nature of prices

Since Post Keynesians see prices as essentially money prices, they necessarily conceive of them as fundamentally reflecting the exchangeable worth of commodities in terms of money. Moreover, to the extent that they draw a distinction between how prices are formed in sectors where inputs are relatively fixed as compared to those sectors in which they are relatively flexible, Post Keynesians also see the nature of price in the two sectors as differing. In the manufacturing sector, prices are seen as relatively fixed, reflecting in the first instance the money costs of production, where the costs comprise the prices of commodity inputs as well as factor services, and, ultimately, reflecting the money prices of factor services used both directly and indirectly (the factor services required to produce inputs) in the production of a good. Keynes himself expressed sympathy for the view that, among factor services, labour can be considered to be the most important, with prices seen as reflecting direct and indirect wage costs. He says:

> I sympathise, therefore, with the pre-classical doctrine that everything is *produced* by *labour*, aided by...technique, by natural resources which are free or cost a rent according to their scarcity or abundance, and by the results of past labour, embodied in assets, which also command a price according to their scarcity or abundance. It is preferable to regard labour, including, of course, the personal services of the entrepreneur and his assistants, as the sole factor of production, operating in a given environment of technique, natural resources, capital equipment and effective demand. This partly explains why we have been able to take the unit of labour as the sole physical unit which we

require in our economic system, apart from units of money and of time. (Keynes, 1973, pp. 213–14)

Although Post Keynesians are silent about the nature of prices in the agricultural and raw material goods sectors, apart from contending that they are relatively more flexible than those in manufacturing, by implication they must see them as ultimately reflecting the relative preferences or demand of individuals for these products (in relation to each other and money) in the manner of Neoclassicals. It is no doubt a reticence to draw this conclusion so explicitly that causes most Post Keynesians to be silent on the nature of prices in agricultural and raw material goods sectors.

From the perspective of Marx's analysis, the basic problem with the Post Keynesian view of the nature of price is that it fails to recognise money prices reflect, on the one hand, the worth of the commodities in relation to one another, and, on the other hand, the worth of all commodities in relation to money. That is, it fails to recognise that to understand the nature of money prices one needs to understand the nature of the exchangeable worth of commodities in relation to one another, as well as, and separately, the relative worth of money in relation to all commodities. The Post Keynesian approach, instead, collapses the two into one, and sees the nature of prices as given by the nature of the worth of commodities in relation to money.

The Post Keynesian view of the nature of prices also mistakenly sees it as differing between sectors. In the same manner that Post Keynesians see the formation and purpose of price as differing between sectors in accordance with the relative flexibility of inputs used in the production of commodities, they see the nature of price in various sectors as differing for much the same reasons. From the perspective of Marx's analysis, the relative flexibility (non-reproducibility) of inputs used cannot be seen as affecting the fundamental nature of price, much as it cannot be seen as affecting the manner of its formation or purpose. If all prices are seen as formed in the process of reproduction of the commodity, and if the purpose of price is to facilitate this reproduction, it cannot be argued that price fundamentally reflects anything other than the resources (labour time) required for the reproduction of the commodity. This is not to say that price cannot be seen as reflecting additionally other factors, such as absolute rent, in sectors like agriculture and raw material production. As Marx argued, it can and does.

From the perspective of Marx's theory of price, Post Keynesians are correct to see the nature of prices of commodities produced in the manufacturing sector as reflecting the conditions of production of the commodity, and in particular its production by labour, rather than, say, the scarcity of the commodity and/or preferences for it. However, from this perspective, it is also evident that they incorrectly see these prices as in the final instance reflecting what is paid to labour as wages, money wages, and not the physical inputs required to produce the commodity reflected in money – not the labour required to produce commodities as reflected in money. Post Keynesians, in any case, provide no justification as to why and how manufacturing prices come to reflect either money factor rewards or, more narrowly, money wage costs.

Finally, and related to the preceding, since Post Keynesians fail to distinguish between relative and money prices, and since they see prices as reflecting money wages, they erroneously see the value of money and, therefore, aggregate money prices, as reflecting the exchange ratio between money and labour. But why the value of money and level of money prices should reflect the exchange ratio between money and labour is unclear. It appears to be simply an assertion of faith.

7.5   Explicit and implicit price constructs

Like all economic theories, Post Keynesians too found their explanations of the magnitudes of prices on a number of explicit and implicit price constructs. Although on the whole these are palpably less artificial than those found in the Neoclassical approach, they too can be regarded as problematic from the perspective of Marx's analysis.

Disequilibrium prices

When explaining the magnitudes of prices, Post Keynesians deny the existence of, and, therefore, the need to conceptualise, economy-wide equilibrium prices, whether in the sense of the term used by the Neoclassicals, or the more limited sense of the Classical economists – giving rise to the economy-wide balancing of supply and demand. If Post Keynesians have a concept of equilibrium price, it is with respect to the individual product of the individual firm. It is the price which facilitates the reproduction of the individual commodity while permitting the individual firm to attain a certain target rate of return.

The Post Keynesian denial of the need to conceive of economy-wide equilibrium prices in the manner of Marx or other Classical economists can be argued to stem from their misconception of the nature of commodity producing systems in general and capitalism in particular. It is because Post Keynesians look at the economic system from the perspective of individual producers seeking to reproduce their individual commodities and meet their individual objectives, whether these are expanded consumption or production, that they see the prices to be explained in the first instance as those set by individual firms and not economy-wide prices. It is also this perspective that causes them to contend that, even if one could conceive of the prices set by individual firms as somehow being equilibrium prices, these would not be the economy-wide equilibrium prices found in Classical and much of Neo-classical economics. This is because, from the Post Keynesian perspective, there is no reason to suppose that the reproduction of the individual commodity in the context of the appropriation of a target return by the individual producer would give rise to, or be consistent with, the balanced reproduction of all commodities where this implies the appropriation of an average rate of profit by producers of all products. The latter is in any case precluded in Post Keynesian analyses by the assumption of barriers to entry in most industries.

What Post Keynesians appear to be missing here is that commodity production systems are essentially those in which the production activities of individual producers are **interconnected** – the output of one group of producers being required as inputs by another group of producers. In capitalism this interconnectedness takes place additionally, i.e., in addition to the exchange of commodities, through the migration of capital between sectors. Hence, prices need to be understood as essentially economy-wide prices of production. They also need to be conceived of in the first instance as reproduction (equilibrium) prices; prices which facilitate a balanced reproduction of all commodities, such that supply and demand in all sectors are in balance. Conceiving of prices as reproduction prices does not imply that actual prices correspond to these most of the time, or that there is an inexorable tendency of actual prices towards these reproduction prices. Rather, if one presumes continuity in the economic system as the necessary starting point for analysis, then one needs to assume prices correspond to these prices at least periodically, in the same way that Post Keynesians presume continuity of the individual firm, and prices facilitating this continuity, when conceiving of (equilibrium) firm-level prices in the first instance.

Long- and short-run prices

Post Keynesians reject the Marshallian distinction between the long run and the short run, and for the most part deny that the prices prevailing over long periods of time can be regarded as analytically separate from those prevailing over shorter periods of time. This causes most Post Keynesians to collapse long-run prices into short-run ones, failing to see that the former are averages of the latter. It causes Post Keynesians to see market prices as in effect some sort of long-term natural prices, i.e., prices which abstract from supply and demand imbalances.

To the extent that Post Keynesians see prices diverging from their longer-run levels, it is in the sense of a divergence of market prices from their 'full-cost plus mark-up' levels as a result of fluctuations in demand. Demand is usually seen as falling short of supply resulting in market prices falling below their full-cost (including target rate of return) levels, even though it is accepted there can also in principle be an excess of demand. Where it is argued that deviations arise only as a result of a shortfall in demand, long-run prices are seen as representing something of an upper limit for short-run, market prices. Where it is argued that demand can also be in excess of supply, long-run prices are seen as **centres of gravity** of short-run market prices, along the lines of Classical economics. From the perspective of Marx's analysis, the problem with the Post Keynesian analysis in both cases is it fails to recognise that deviations of market prices from long-run prices can, and typically do, arise as a result of variations in supply – the over-expansion of supply – and even the conditions governing supply. It is this that prevents Post Keynesians from seeing long-run prices as averages of market prices.

Competitive and non-competitive prices

Most Post Keynesians appear to implicitly, if not explicitly, accept the Neoclassical conceptualisation of (perfectly) competitive prices. It will be recalled that for Neoclassicals competitive prices are those formed in the process of exchange as a result of bargaining, and are taken as given by firms who then proceed to maximise profits by setting output so as to equate (increasing) marginal costs with (perfectly elastic) marginal revenue. Where Post Keynesians appear to part company with Neoclassicals is when it comes to the conceptualisation of non-competitive, or imperfectly competitive, prices. For Post Keynesians, these prices are set by firms in the process of production and not, as for Neoclassicals, in the process of exchange between the monopolist and buyers of the product. Moreover, for Post Keynesians, firms in non-competitive environments set prices, and not levels of output, so as to attain target rates of profit. On the basis of this distinction between competitive and non-competitive prices, it is typically concluded that prices in the manufacturing sector are non-competitive while those in agricultural and raw material producing sectors are competitive.

From the perspective of Marx's analysis, the basic problem with the Post Keynesian conceptualisation of competitive price is that, as with the Neoclassical approach, it is founded on a static conceptualisation of competition. As a result, the very fact that there is product diversification, differential pricing, the use of different techniques of production, and the appropriation of different rates of profit within and between industries, is taken by Post Keynesians as indicative of a non-competitive or imperfectly competitive environment, and the prices formed as non-competitive prices.[13] However, as was noted in the discussion of the Neoclassical conceptualisation of competitive prices, these phenomena are as much a part of the competitive process as the tendency towards the formation of standard products produced by the bulk of the producers using standard techniques of production and appropriating an average rate of profit.

The Post Keynesian conceptualisation of competitive prices also incorrectly suggests that these prices, and the competitive environment which gives rise to them, are attributable to the relative fixity of inputs in much the same way a non-competitive environment and non-competitive prices are attributable to the relative non-fixity of inputs. The underlying logic here is that when inputs are fixed, being non-reproducible, price is more responsive to demand, while when they are more flexible, being reproducible, it is the quantity supplied and not price that responds to demand. What Post Keynesians seem not to appreciate in this regard, however, is that the non-reproducibility of inputs merely permits owners of these inputs to appropriate an absolute rent. Since, as was argued above, the latter is reflected in the price of the product, it is unclear how the prices of goods produced using non-reproducible inputs can be thought of as being any more competitive than those produced using producible inputs. In any case, it is unclear producible inputs in manufacturing are any more flexible than non-producible inputs in agriculture from the point of view of the individual producer – which is the point of view adopted by Post Keynesians. For example, individual producers of agricultural commodities can readily acquire more land. And, it is also unclear why the absence of a price response to changes in demand is indicative of a non-competitive environment. The absence of such a price response might, for example, simply indicate the presence of a large number of producers involved in cut-throat competition with one another. That is, it might, on the contrary, indicate a highly competitive environment.

Relative and money prices

As has already been argued, Post Keynesians make no analytical distinction between money and relative prices. This is because, as was also argued, they see commodities as possessing no exchangeable worth outside of their relation with money. Money is seen as both value and the measure of exchangeable worth. There appears to be no recognition by Post Keynesians that for commodities to have money prices they must have worth in relation to one another outside of exchange, and that this worth should be measured by something apart from money – which measures worth in exchange. More fundamentally, Post Keynesians do not appear to realise that the causes and consequences of the movement of both relative prices and the money price level are essentially quite different, and for much of economic analysis, what matters is an understanding of the relative worth of commodities, and not their money prices *per se*.

7.6   The magnitude of price

From the preceding it follows that the magnitudes of prices Post Keynesians seek to explain are money prices, and that when they explain these price magnitudes they distinguish between prices formed in sectors in which inputs are relatively flexible and those in which they are fixed, *viz.*, between manufacturing and agriculture/raw material sectors, with the almost exclusive focus being on the former. The standard explanation of the magnitudes of prices in the manufacturing sector is that they are determined by the average money costs of production plus a mark-up.[14] Money costs are taken to be either 'direct' or 'normal' costs. The mark-up is either a gross costing margin covering all general costs and salaries as well as anticipated profits, or a net margin covering the financing needs of the firm or yielding a target return on the capital of the firm when sales are sufficient to maintain production at normal capacity utilisation levels.[15] It is denied by most, but not all, Post Keynesians that demand has any bearing on the magnitude of price over the long run. If it has an impact, it is over the short run, and usually, but not always, to push market prices below their longer-term, full-cost levels and profits below target levels. Since the norm is argued to be product differentiation, the use of different technologies and barriers to entry, it is **denied** that there is a tendency towards either intra- or inter-industry average profit rates appropriated by producers. To emphasise this point some Post Keynesians contend that prices are in fact firm-determined or 'administered', and not cost-determined.[16]

Lastly, to the extent that Post Keynesians can be said to explain the determinants of the magnitudes of prices in agricultural and raw material producing sectors, it is for the most part in terms of demand. With the fixity of inputs implying supply of the product is fixed for all intents and purposes, the key factor determining price is necessarily seen as the strength of demand.[17] There is little said about the rate of profit appropriated by producers in these sectors, although the implication of seeing these sectors as competitive is that it is tacitly assumed to be a normal rate, whatever this might mean. Little is also said about the determinants of the magnitude of rent paid to owners of fixed inputs such as land.

One general problem of note with the Post Keynesian explanation of the magnitude of price is that it is unclear whether what is being explained is the magnitude of relative price or money price, or both. This confusion naturally enough follows from the failure of Post Keynesians to make any analytical distinction between the two.

Considering more specifically the Post Keynesian explanation of the magnitudes of manufactured goods prices, it can be argued that this explanation is essentially tautological in that the magnitudes of prices of outputs are explained by the magnitudes of prices (and quantities) of produced inputs as outputs, albeit along with the magnitudes of prices and quantities of factor inputs. In fact, for this explanation to be more than a tautology, the magnitudes of prices of inputs need to be explained by something other than their price magnitudes as outputs. Although most Post Keynesians ignore this problem, the logic of their approach suggests that price magnitudes should be reduced to factor costs, particularly wage costs, with factor costs being seen as independent and antecedent to prices.[18] Since such an explanation of price is akin to that adopted by Adam Smith once he jettisoned the labour theory of value, it is appropriate to recall Marx's criticisms of this explanation by Smith; that it appears to be oblivious of the fact there will always be a residual constant capital component when costs are reduced to factor costs, and it suggests factor prices can be seen as independent of, and antecedent to, price. If there is always a residual component, then price cannot be said to be reducible to factor costs. Moreover, and perhaps most fundamentally, for Marx, factor prices cannot be seen as independent of, and antecedent to, prices of commodities, since they are influenced by the latter, particularly in respect of labour costs and the prices of wage goods.

A further problem with Post Keynesian explanations of the magnitude of prices in manufacturing from the perspective of Marx's analysis is the way in which wages and profits components are explained. For Marx, it is not the wage rate which matters in the explanation of the wage cost component of price, but rather the amount of labour time required for the production of the commodity, i.e., the productivity of labour. Moreover, for Marx, the rate of profit which pertains to prices of manufactured goods is not that determined by individual producers, varying within and across sectors. Rather, it is the rate pertaining to the price of the standard commodity of a given type, which is formed in the context of the performance of surplus labour in all sectors and its transfer between sectors as a result of competition within and between sectors. Although Marx accepted that, for a variety of reasons, the rates appropriated by individual capitalists and sectors could deviate from the average, he argues that the tendency is for the appropriation of an economy-wide average rate by the producers of a standard commodity.

Lastly, it would appear that there is no explicitly Post Keynesian explanation of price in the context of fixed, non-reproducible, inputs, at least not one that is even remotely consistent with the Post Keynesian explanation of price in the context of non-fixed, producible, inputs. In fact, in the Post Keynesian approach we are left with the somewhat incongruous conclusion that in sectors making considerable use of non-produced inputs price depends on demand. But, as noted above, it is unclear why production using non-produced inputs should imply any more fixed output than in sectors using produced inputs. Why should long-run prices of commodities produced using non-produced inputs be determined exclusively by demand, and not costs of production? As also noted above, it is in any case unclear that inputs are more 'fixed' in sectors where they are relatively more non-reproducible than in other sectors. Much will depend on how the sector is defined and the perspective adopted with respect to price formation.

7.7   Changes in price magnitudes

The Post Keynesian explanation of changes in price magnitudes follows from their explanation of these magnitudes. Thus, Post Keynesians see changes in prices of manufactured commodities as fundamentally due to changes in the magnitudes of money values of rewards to factor services, especially labour, and with respect to the latter, changes in wage rates. And, in line with their explanation of the magnitudes of agricultural and raw material commodity prices, it follows that Post Keynesians must see changes in these as due mostly to changes in demand.

The problems with Post Keynesian explanations of changes in price magnitudes from the perspective of Marx's analysis follow naturally enough from the problems with its explanation of those magnitudes. To begin with, much as it is unclear whether Post Keynesians are explaining the magnitudes of money or relative prices, so it is unclear whether they are explaining changes in relative or money prices, or both. For example, it is unclear whether a change in money wages is seen as impacting on the relative money price of products through its impact on relative money costs or through its implied impact on the value of money,[19] or even some combination of the two in the context of **differential increases** in money wages.

From the perspective of Marx's analysis, perhaps the major deficiency of the Post Keynesian explanation of price changes is its relative neglect of the impact of changes in labour productivity when explaining price changes in the manufacturing sector. In keeping with their explanation of manufacturing price magnitudes, Post Keynesians emphasise changes in factor prices. This is not to say that, for Marx, changes in, for example, the wage (and profit) rate will have no impact on prices. Rather, it is to emphasise that changes in labour productivity will have a considerably greater impact on prices, and in any case changes in the wage (and profit) rate are themselves considerably influenced by changes in the productivity of labour.

Post Keynesian explanations of changes in the magnitudes of manufacturing prices also neglect the impact of demand. Post Keynesians do, of course, admit to the possibility of a shortfall in demand causing prices to fall below their full-cost levels, with rates of profit falling below their target levels. And, some Post Keynesians see fluctuations in demand as explaining deviations of market prices around their long-term levels. However, for the most part, they deny that changes in demand can have long-term consequences for prices. For Marx, in contrast, changes in demand can have an impact on prices over the long-term due to their impact on average techniques of production and, therefore, the productivity of labour. For example, major surges in demand could give rise to capital inflows into a sector and, as a consequence, major changes in techniques of production – quite possibly the adoption of entirely new and more efficient techniques, or simply more efficient existing techniques.

And, to the extent that Post Keynesians subscribe to the Neoclassical approach in the explanation of agricultural and raw material commodity prices, it can be argued that they miss the importance of supply-side factors in the explanation of these prices, especially productivity changes and factors which have a bearing on changes in absolute rent. This is because, in the context of an assumed fixity of supply in these sectors, the emphasis of Post Keynesians in the explanation of changes in agricultural and raw material commodity prices is, or must be, as for Neoclassicals, changes in demand.

7.8   The value of money and the aggregate money price level

Post Keynesians see money as anything that purchases goods and settles debt obligations. Like Neoclassicals, they see money as an asset, but unlike Neoclassicals, and following Keynes, they see it as a certain type of asset; **a financial asset** which is substitutable by other financial assets. Strictly speaking, Keynes himself saw money as a 'non-interest bearing' financial asset, or cash, while Post Keynesians see it as including commercial bank liabilities.[20] Given the substitutability of bank liabilities for other financial assets, some Post Keynesians have even argued for considerably broader definitions of money.[21] Post Keynesians usually refer to this money as credit money because it is seen as coming into existence with the contraction of debt – by the monetary authorities and the banking system.[22] Credit money is seen as either inhabiting the sphere of circulation or held in deposits in the banking system to make future purchases, settle debt obligations, engage in speculative activity or serve as a safeguard for an uncertain future.[23] The important characteristics of money which make it money are argued to be zero elasticity of production – something which cannot be produced through the exertion of labour – and zero elasticity of substitution with respect to liquid assets and goods which are readily reproducible through the exertion of labour.[24]

In line with this view of money, most Post Keynesians see the value of money and the magnitudes of money prices as determined by producers on the basis of exchange ratios between money and factor services, particularly labour.[25] Keynes himself hints at the importance of labour in the determination of the value of money in his *General Theory* when he says '...we must have *some* factor, the value of which in terms of money is, if not fixed, at least sticky, to give us any stability of values in a monetary system' (1973, p. 304). Davidson, interpreting Keynes, sees money as representing generalised purchasing power because of its exchange with labour:

> What permits money to possess purchasing power is, ultimately, its intimate relationship to 'offer contracts' in general and contracts

involving labour offers specifically. Thus it is the money-wage rate, that is the number of units of the money-of-account which labour is willing to buy for a given unit of effort, which is the anchor upon which the price level of all producible goods is fastened. (1978a, pp. 152–3)

In a similar vein Moore states:

For modern post-Keynesians, in contrast, the rate of inflation is determined primarily by the rate of increase of nominal money wages relative to labor productivity. Over wide sectors of the economy, prices are largely cost-determined, based on a mark-up over unit labor costs. (1979b, p. 131)

Post Keynesians further argue that money and commodities come into exchange with value and money prices, respectively. The value of money and money prices of commodities are determined **in the process of production**. The amount of money in the process of exchange and in deposits with the banking system is seen as determined by the demand for money. That is to say, the quantity of money in circulation is **endogenous**.[26] It is argued to be endogenous in the sense that changes in the money in circulation or money stock (cash and bank liabilities) are driven by the demand for loans by the private sector, and the resulting demand for cash to support the expanded money stock is accommodated by the central bank, albeit at an interest rate of its own choosing.[27] Concomitantly, most Post Keynesians deny that there can be an excess supply of money which could spill over into higher money prices.[28]

From the perspective of Marx's analysis, the Post Keynesian explanation of money price magnitudes is arguably founded on a fundamental misconception of money. To begin with, and as argued in the appraisal of the Neoclassical approach, money is not an asset *per se* – something which permits the owner of money to appropriate a return for its use. Rather, money can assume the form of an asset, in the same way that commodities can and do. Seeing money as essentially an asset causes Post Keynesians to confuse money's existence as money with its existence as capital, and in particular interest-bearing capital. It is this confusion that causes Post Keynesians to emphasise money's store of value function and define money stock as including interest-bearing bank and other financial sector liabilities, especially when discussing its worth in relation to commodities. To repeat, for Marx, the holding of money as a store of value or wealth virtually disappears in capitalism since money only preserves its value as capital. That is to say, money held as a store is typically held as interest-bearing capital. This means, as also noted in the discussion of the Neoclassical approach, that when considering money in the circulation of commodities, money which serves to circulate interest-bearing capital should be excluded.

More fundamentally, from the perspective of Marx's analysis, Post Keynesians incorrectly see money as representing generalised purchasing power because it represents command over factor services in general or labour in particular. To argue that money represents generalised purchasing power because it exchanges with labour, as Post Keynesians implicitly and explicitly do, is to argue that money is capital, or, more precisely, money is money because it is capital. This is because money typically represents a command over labour services in capitalism as capital. It is also to argue, tautologically, that labour accepts money in payment for its services because money is exchangeable with these services. For Marx, however, money represents generalised purchasing power because it represents a command over all commodities. Hence, the value of money, and, therefore, money price level of all commodities, is given by the exchange ratio of money and all commodities and not money and labour – the money wage. Indeed, for Marx, the money wage is itself conditioned by the value of money as given by the exchange ratio of money and all commodities. Or, to put it somewhat differently, the bargaining of workers for a money wage is conditioned by the value of money determined independently of this bargaining.

Lastly, although Marx would most certainly agree that commodities come into circulation with money prices and money with value, he would deny that these are formed in the process of **production** *per se*. For Marx, as argued earlier, money prices of commodities and the value of money are formed in the process of the **reproduction** of all commodities. The value of money and level of money prices need not correspond to what may be referred to as their intrinsic levels at any given point in time but can be either above or below these levels, with attendant consequences for price adjustment processes. Crucially, this means for Marx there can be an excess of money in circulation much as there can be a deficiency.

7.9   The price adjustment process

For the most part, as noted above, Post Keynesians deny the possibility of a divergence of actual from equilibrium prices since they deny the existence of equilibrium prices as separate from actual prices. However, as also as noted above, to the extent that they admit to the possibility of a divergence, it is in the sense that actual market prices diverge from those pertaining to full-cost plus mark-up levels, and, in particular, that market prices fall short of these levels. The source of such divergences is seen as fluctuations (a shortfall) in demand, particularly aggregate demand. For at least one branch of Post Keynesians, what may be referred to as the fundamentalist branch, these fluctuations, especially the shortfall in demand, are seen as arising from the peculiar characteristics of money – zero elasticity of production and substitution. Adjustments of prices are then seen as movements of market prices back to their full-cost levels as a result of the return of demand to more normal levels. Where the divergences in prices take the form of a decline in market prices below their full-cost level, adjustments are seen as taking place through a rise in aggregate demand, induced in large part by accommodative monetary and fiscal policies. In the absence of such accommodative policies, adjustment will, so it is argued, take the form of contractions in output and employment.

From the perspective of Marx's analysis, Post Keynesians mistakenly conceive of the divergences of prices in terms of money prices alone, and attribute the source of such divergences to fluctuations in aggregate demand. That is, Post Keynesians fail to see the divergences in prices as divergences in both money and relative prices, and (at least for some Post Keynesians) divergences of market prices above and below equilibrium or reproduction prices, and not simply below the latter. Also, Post Keynesians erroneously attempt to understand the adjustment process in terms of the supply of money and the demand for commodities, and not, as for Marx, the demand for, and supply of, commodities and money. They fail to see that the source of divergences of market from equilibrium prices can be, and typically are, due to a tendency for an unlimited increase in the supply of commodities accompanied by an expansion of surrogates of money permitting a fictitious increase in the demand for commodities, and not a shortfall in the demand for commodities *per se* brought about by a shortfall in the supply of money. They also fail to see that price adjustments typically take place in the context of contractions in the supply of, and demand for, commodities, as well as the supply of money and credit, and can involve both increases and decreases of market and reproduction relative and money prices.

8
Sraffa's Theory of Price

The third and last of the modern theories of price to be considered in the present work is that of the great Italian economist, Piero Sraffa. Sraffa's major (published) contributions to price theory are to be found in three works. The first of these is his 1926 *Economic Journal* article on Marshallian price theory, which served to undermine the foundations of this theory, but not enough to prevent successive generations of economists from continuing to use these. Then there is the aforementioned excellent 1951 *Introduction* to the Collected Works of David Ricardo. The third, and perhaps most important, work by Sraffa on price is his 1960 *magnum opus*, *Production of Commodities by Means of Commodities* (hereafter *Commodities*). It is in this work that Sraffa provides his own theory of price, and to which most attention will be paid in what follows.[1] Although Sraffa's theory of price has often been regarded as an important pillar of the general Post Keynesian theory of price, it will be argued below, in keeping with what was already argued in Chapter 7, that the two theories are very different.

The presentation and critical appraisal of Sraffa's theory of price which follows is accorded special attention in the present study for two interrelated reasons. Firstly, it represents an important development of the Classical theory of price, and in particular that of its 'best exponent', David Ricardo. Certainly, when viewing what is generally accepted as Sraffa's major contribution to economic thought, his *Commodities*, against the backdrop of his *Introduction*, one is left with the distinct impression that his purpose in *Commodities* is essentially to complete Ricardo's theory of price. His concern with the impact of changes in wages on prices and his attempt to construct an invariable standard of prices are perhaps the clearest testimony to this. Since Marx highlighted his own contribution to the theory of price through constant reference to, and critique of, the Classics, especially Ricardo, it would seem appropriate to end this book by critically appraising the work of Sraffa on price, as a work which seeks to complete that of Ricardo's. A second, but less important, reason for according Sraffa's theory of price special attention is because it is seen by many of its adherents (and non-adherents) as explaining prices in the manner of Ricardo and Marx but without the unnecessary baggage of the labour theory of value.[2] Naturally, the aim of critically appraising Sraffa's work in the present chapter will also be to show this view is mistaken.

8.1   Focus, method and approach

The focus of Sraffa's theory of price in *Commodities* is the determinants of the magnitudes of prices, and in particular the link between prices and distributive variables – wages and profits.[3] Specifically, Sraffa's main aim in his *Commodities* appears to be to show, in the manner of Ricardo's opposition to Smith, that changes in wages have no predictable impact on prices, and not to explain the magnitudes, or changes in the magnitudes, of prices *per se*. In contrast with the Post Keynesian approach, the prices Sraffa considers to be most important, and the necessary point of departure for analysis, are what are referred to in the present work as reproduction prices. In this regard, Sraffa is clearly within the tradition of Classical economics, which sought primarily to begin the analyses of prices with the analysis of reproduction prices, seeing market prices as fluctuating around these.[4]

In the presentation of his price theory, Sraffa draws a distinction between price formation in subsistence and surplus production economic systems. He sees a subsistence economy as one that produces no physical surplus, in contrast with a surplus economy. He sees the production of a surplus as the production of an output in excess of what is required to replace inputs. The inputs he is referring to are the commodity inputs required to maintain non-expansionary output levels. Sraffa also considers it important when explaining the magnitudes of prices in surplus-producing economic systems to draw a distinction between single- and joint-product systems, and pay heed to fixed capital and non-produced inputs. He sees the explanation of the magnitudes of prices in subsistence production systems as forming the basis for their explanation in all exchange-based economic systems, but argues that important modifications to this explanation are called for when considering surplus production economic systems, especially when moving from the case of single- to joint-product industries and taking into account the existence of fixed capital and non-produced inputs in certain sectors.

While, from the perspective of Marx's analysis, Sraffa is to be praised for focusing in the first instance on reproduction prices, he is to be criticised for focusing narrowly on the determinants of the magnitudes of these prices and, perhaps more fundamentally, changes in their magnitudes. This focus causes Sraffa to pay little or no attention to how (market) prices come to be formed. It will be recalled that this is the same deficiency seen by Marx in Ricardo's work on price.

Moreover, if Ricardo's method can be criticised from the perspective of Marx's analysis for not adequately investigating the links between the essence and surface appearance of capitalism, then Sraffa's method can be criticised for not really getting to grips with either – the essence or surface appearance. The source of this problem in Sraffa's work is that his conceptualisation of the inner essence of the economic system – what may be regarded as the basic building blocks of his analysis – bears little or no relation to reality, being instead driven by theoretical necessity and logic. This is perhaps most evident in his conceptualisation of commodity-producing systems in general and surplus commodity-producing systems in particular. I will begin with Sraffa's conceptualisation of commodity-producing systems in general.

As the title of his *Commodities* suggests, he sees these systems as essentially characterised by **the production of commodities by means of commodities**. Most importantly, this eliminates the performance of labour from his analysis. Sraffa in fact tacitly justifies this by assuming that the labour input is substitutable by the commodities consumed by it, i.e., by wage goods. A close reading of his *Introduction* would suggest that the reason Sraffa eliminates labour from his analysis in this way is because he believed that the labour theory of value in Ricardo and Marx suffered from certain logical flaws, particularly in respect of the explanation of magnitudes of relative prices in terms of labour time expended in production (see Sraffa, 1981).[5] From the perspective of Marx's analysis, replacement of the labour input by commodities is entirely unacceptable. Not only is the labour input very different from the commodity input (i.e., the expenditure of labour time is not the same thing as the payment for this expenditure), the substitution of one by the other leads to a distorted view of the nature of commodity-producing systems and, therefore, the prices of commodities in these systems. It leads, most fundamentally, to a denial of commodities possessing value which is distinct from their exchangeable worth. For Marx, it will be recalled, commodity producing systems are fundamentally **social systems of production** involving the expenditure of labour time in the production of a certain mass of commodities to meet social demand. Commodities produced in such systems acquire worth or value in relation to one another because they are products of what is in effect a collective labour effort to produce a given mass of commodities. When such systems become exchange-based, the commodities acquire exchangeable worth or prices which necessarily reflect, but are distinct from, this worth.

The problems which the elimination of labour gives rise to in Sraffa's analysis become particularly manifest when he moves to the explanation of magnitudes of prices in a surplus-product economic setting. First and foremost, it causes Sraffa to misunderstand the source and nature of the surplus produced and, therefore, the fundamental nature of these systems. It causes him to see the surplus as simply a surplus of commodities, and to implicitly see the latter as resulting from the physical productivity of commodities as inputs. It also results in Sraffa tacitly not seeing anything distinctive about the source and nature of the surplus in capitalism as opposed to other surplus commodity-producing systems, or understanding how a general rate of profit comes into being in capitalism. From the perspective of Marx's analysis, what Sraffa appears to formally overlook is that a surplus product arises in all surplus-producing societies as a result of the direct producers spending more time in the production of the total output of a system than is required to produce those goods necessary to sustain them. To put it another way, what Sraffa appears to overlook is that a surplus arises when the direct producers produce more output than is given to them by way of remuneration for their labour. When it comes to surplus production in capitalism, Sraffa appears to miss, additionally, that the surplus appropriated by businesses is not that generated in the processes of production under their individual control, but is part of the surplus generated in the system at large – the exchangeable worth of the surplus being appropriated in proportion to the exchangeable worth of the inputs and wage goods advanced to undertake production.

The elimination of labour time from his analysis also requires Sraffa to differentiate between types of commodities in order to make his explanation of prices more than a mere tautology – with prices of commodities explained by the prices of commodities. It requires him to distinguish between basic commodities and non-basic commodities, and assume that there is at least one basic commodity. For Sraffa basics are those commodities which enter either directly or indirectly the production of all other commodities while non-basics do not.[6] On the basis of this distinction, he conceptualises commodity-producing systems, including surplus commodity-producing systems, as those in which **basic commodities produce themselves and other commodities**. The basic commodities are in effect Sraffa's surrogates for the labour input. While the distinction between basics and non-basics certainly allows Sraffa to put more flesh on his conceptualisation of commodity-producing systems, there are nevertheless problems with the distinction. One is that it is unclear what exactly the dividing line is between basics and non-basics. The problem here is the meaning to be attached to the word 'indirectly'. A narrow interpretation of 'indirectly' would tend to cast doubt on the assumption that there is at least one basic which enters the production of all commodities in the way the expenditure of labour time does (also over time), while a broad interpretation would imply that the 'basics' domain includes practically all commodities, making the distinction between basics and non-basics meaningless.[7]

A further consequence of the elimination of labour time from Sraffa's analysis in *Commodities* is that it causes him to see the explanation of prices of commodities produced in industries using shared inputs, what Sraffa refers to as joint-product industries, as fundamentally different from the explanation of prices of commodities where inputs are not shared, what he refers to as single-product industries. This is because in joint-product industries commodities are argued by Sraffa to be produced with shared commodity inputs such that the rate of profit which matters to producers is that with respect to outlays on all commodity inputs required for the production of the joint products, while in single-product industries, since there is no sharing of inputs in the production of different commodities, the rate of profit which matters is that pertaining to the inputs required for the production of the particular commodity in question. Obviously, in a modern economic setting, most products would typically conform to those defined as joint products by Sraffa. It would be inconceivable for a large modern corporation to only have product-specific inputs. Sraffa argues that, given the prevalence of joint-product production processes, it would in fact be more useful to conceive of 'industries' not in terms of the commodities they produce but rather the proportions in which they produce, and the proportions in which they use, the various commodities (see 1960, p. 45). What possible operational meaning this conceptualisation of industries has is entirely unclear.

Marx would not have denied that the norm in capitalism is for commodities to be produced using shared inputs, but he would most certainly have denied that this suggests these products should be treated fundamentally differently from those produced in a single-product system. This is because, for Marx, whether commodities are produced with or without shared inputs, their prices reflect their relative physical (and ultimately labour) input content. Prices reflect their physical input content, even when inputs are shared, because businesses apportion the costs of shared inputs to the different commodities produced with these inputs and compute rates of profit, or mark-ups on costs, in respect of the production of individual products. Where certain commodities prove to be unprofitable on the basis of these calculations, their production would be discontinued and capital moved to the production of more profitable commodities, whether these happen to be existing commodities or entirely new ones. In contrast, Sraffa's joint-product analysis precludes such a movement of capital since the costs of individual commodities are assumed to be unobtainable and the rate of profit is deemed to be with respect to clusters of commodities. Actually, Sraffa's joint-product analysis would suggest that the norm for businesses is to carry dead-weight losses in respect of individual commodities, since the production of certain combinations of commodities is tacitly assumed to be somehow technologically given and the movement of capital is between clusters of commodities to equalise the rate of profit between these clusters. That is to say, in Sraffa's joint-products world there is no mechanism to adjust for excesses or shortfalls in the production of individual commodities.

Since Sraffa uses his conceptualisation of joint products as a basis for that of fixed capital, it should come as little surprise that from the perspective of Marx's analysis there are also problems with this latter conceptualisation. One problem is that it causes Sraffa to see fixed capital, whatever its age and degree of wear and tear, as a produced commodity having a price, even though it is neither produced (unless it is new) nor marketed (except in a limited number of instances). Reading between the lines of his *Commodities*, it is clear that Sraffa himself accepts that fixed capital cannot really be regarded as either produced or having a price in the same way that a normal commodity can. He even concedes that the price of fixed capital should be seen as an 'effective price' in recognition of the fact that it is not typically bought and sold in organised markets in the way other commodities are.[8] However, the necessity for Sraffa to see fixed capital in this way, as a produced commodity with a price, arises from the elimination of labour from his analysis and the resulting need to see all inputs as commodities with determinate prices in order to arrive at an explanation of the magnitudes of prices of outputs in terms of commodities as inputs. I will return to the point below.

An added problem with Sraffa's conceptualisation of fixed capital from the perspective of Marx's analysis is that it leads to a confusion of fixed and circulating capital, i.e., between capital which transfers its value to the commodity over long periods of time and that which transfers the entirety of its value in one production period. This confusion in turn blurs the distinction between constant and variable capital, making it much easier to see all capital advances as purchases of material inputs, and all such purchases giving rise to a surplus, with labour and capital sharing in this surplus.[9] That is, it causes all capital to be seen as variable capital – capital which gives rise to an expansion of value. It also leads to an incorrect formulation of the rate of profit as a rate on outlays of inputs excluding those accruing to labour (which is regarded as, like capital, sharing in the surplus).

Finally, Sraffa's elimination of labour time and value from his analysis, and the consequences this has for how he perceives the source and nature of the surplus produced under capitalism and manner of its appropriation by capital, causes him to also misrepresent the nature of returns to owners of (scarce) non-produced inputs such as land. For Sraffa, even though land can be said to have a price in the form of rent, since it is a non-produced input it cannot represent a cost element in the price of the product. As a consequence, rent can only be admitted as arising from differences in the fertility of land, with more fertile lands yielding a positive rent for given prices of agricultural commodities. In other words, it causes Sraffa to deny the existence of what Marx calls absolute rent, and only admit to the existence of differential rent (or what Marx refers to as DR1) in the manner of Ricardo. As will be argued below, this (mis)understanding of land and rent causes Sraffa to have a quite distorted view of the determination of the magnitude of agricultural commodity prices and changes in these magnitudes.

8.2   The exchange process

Sraffa conceives of exchange in commodity production systems as in the first instance (in a subsistence economy setting) the exchange of commodities for one another (C-C′) by the producers of these commodities for the purpose of their reproduction. That is to say, Sraffa, like Marx and the Post Keynesians, sees exchange as taking place in the context of the reproduction of the commodity. Also like Marx, but unlike Post Keynesians, Sraffa appears to consider it necessary from the outset to conceive of the individual act of exchange as part of a generalised system of exchange which facilitates the reproduction of the individual commodity alongside the reproduction of all other commodities. As I will argue below, it is because of this that he, like Marx, sees the appropriate point of departure for the explanation of the magnitude of price to be economy-wide reproduction prices. This said, there are nevertheless problems with Sraffa's conceptualisation of exchange from the perspective of Marx's analysis. The most important of these is Sraffa's failure to see the exchange process as mediating a division of **labour**. In fact, Sraffa's conceptualisation of exchange results in him seeing it as effectively mediating a certain distribution of basic commodities – the commodity inputs needed to produce the commodity outputs. This is because, as remarked on above, he sees the commodities produced as in effect produced by other (basic) commodities without the intervention of labour. A second problem with Sraffa's conceptualisation of the exchange process is that it ignores money. To be clear, when Sraffa considers the exchange of commodities for one another he is not abstracting from money in the manner of Marx, but rather excluding money altogether from his analysis, in the manner of the Neoclassicals. As I will show below, this leads to all manner of problems in Sraffa's work, as well as distorted theories of money in the works of his followers.

8.3 Understanding price

Formation of prices

As with the Neoclassical and Post Keynesian explanation of prices, Sraffa does not appear to be concerned with how prices come to be formed, apparently considering this irrelevant to his major purpose in *Commodities*; the explanation of the impact of changes in the wage share on price magnitudes. However, one can certainly discern from this explanation a number of implications for how prices are, or must be, seen as being formed in a manner which is consistent with this analysis. To begin with, Sraffa's input–output framework coupled with his assumption of a single price for a given commodity and the appropriation of an average rate of profit by all producers suggests that he sees prices as formed in the context of the reproduction of all commodities and competition between producers within and between industries. From the perspective of Marx's analysis, this puts Sraffa's view of price formation in advance of both the Neoclassical and Post Keynesian views. It will be recalled, Neoclassicals erroneously see prices as formed in the process of exchange, with competition being that between those engaged in trade, while Post Keynesians see prices as formed in production, by individual producers seeking to reproduce their individual commodities without reference to the reproduction of all other commodities, and in an essentially non-competitive environment. The problem with Sraffa's view of price formation in this regard, however, is that it provides no explanation of how prices are formed in the economy-wide process of reproduction of all commodities, and in particular intra- and inter-industry competition.

Specifically, Sraffa provides no explanation of how the competitive process gives rise to a standard product with a single price which is produced using industry-standard technologies. Instead, Sraffa simply argues that a determinate set of prices for a given number of commodities can be said to exist where the number of commodities equals the number of production processes. In a single-product, surplus-economy setting, this causes Sraffa to deny different methods of production for the production of the same commodity and also different varieties of the same commodity. In a joint-product setting, where more than one product is produced by any given production process, this requires Sraffa to assume, without explanation, that a given product has a single price even though it is produced using more than one method of production. Where one of the joint products is fixed capital, this requires Sraffa to assume the existence of a single price for a given product even though the product is produced by fixed capital of different vintages, levels of efficiency and degrees of wear and tear. And, lastly, where some of the inputs are non-produced, such as land, it requires Sraffa to assume, again without explanation, equality of the number of production processes and commodities plus non-produced inputs. The non-produced inputs are assumed to have prices given by the rent paid for those of superior quality (what Marx refers to as DR1). It also requires Sraffa to deny the possibility of rent arising from the adoption of more intensive (productive) techniques of production, or what Marx refers to as DR2.

Sraffa's failure to explain how prices come to be formed in the context of inter-industry competition also requires him to simply assume the existence of an average rate of profit. For example, in the case of a joint-product economic setting, Sraffa simply assumes the existence of an average rate of profit without explaining how and why such an average profit can be expected to come about. To elaborate, Sraffa fails to explain why capital would move between **production processes** characterised by different proportions of commodities used as inputs and produced as outputs so as to equate the rate of profit between them, or in which way this movement can be seen as facilitating the reproduction of the system. Sraffa similarly assumes the existence of an average rate of profit for the joint production of fixed capital and goods produced using the fixed capital without explaining how an average rate of profit for the production of different clusters of similar goods (only in different proportions) using various techniques of production might be expected to come into being. And, finally, Sraffa assumes equal average rates of profit for the production of the same commodity using a non-produced input like land, even though different techniques for the production of the commodity are possible – in the context of the use of land of the same quality. Indeed, to assume this, Sraffa recognises he also needs to assume, somewhat counter-intuitively, that the more productive techniques are necessarily the higher costs techniques (see *Ibid.*, p. 75).[10]

It might be noted in passing that Sraffa's failure to analyse the competitive process also has implications for any attempt to extend his analysis to an understanding of price formation in a monopoly setting. As with Neoclassical and Post Keynesian analyses, it causes non-competitive price formation to be seen as occurring wherever there are differentiated products, a variety of prices for the same product, and the use of different production techniques in the production of a standard product in a given sector. It also leads to a failure to appreciate the fact that the greater the profit appropriated by the monopoly sector the lower the rate of profit prevailing in the remainder of the economy, particularly when the sector in question happens to be an important one.

A second implication to be drawn from Sraffa's *Commodities* for the formation of price relates to non-produced inputs, and the bearing these have on price formation in sectors which use a considerable amount of them. From his tacit denial that rent has any bearing on prices in sectors using relatively greater amounts of non-produced inputs, except in the unlikely case of homogeneity of the non-produced inputs, it would appear that he sees the prices formed in these sectors (*viz.*, agriculture) as being formed in much the same way as those formed in sectors using mostly produced inputs, *viz.*, manufacturing. From the perspective of Marx's analysis, while Sraffa is correct to see prices in sectors using non-produced inputs as not being formed in an entirely different way from those in manufacturing in the manner of certain Post Keynesians, he is incorrect in denying that it has no significance, except in the case of homogeneous non-produced inputs. For Marx, the existence of non-produced inputs such as land allows the owners of these inputs the possibility of intercepting some part of the total surplus produced in the system in the form of absolute rent, and not simply a part of the surplus resulting from differences in the quality of non-produced inputs, or even differences in technical conditions of production, i.e., Marx's differential rents 1 and 2. For Sraffa, the use of non-produced inputs in production allows for only the appropriation of differential rent resulting from differences in the quality of the non-produced inputs. Hence, the use of non-produced inputs, and, therefore, rent, would only have a bearing on price formation in the context of the homogeneity of these inputs.

Lastly, the absence of money from Sraffa's analysis suggests he sees money as having no role in the formation of prices. This is most certainly not because he was unaware of the fact that prices are in the final instance money prices, or that money has a fundamental role to play in the reproduction of commodities and the economic system at large. Rather, it would appear he ignores money because he sees it as irrelevant to his above-mentioned purpose in *Commodities*; the completion of Ricardo's explanation of the impact of changes in the wage share on relative price magnitudes without the cumbersome baggage of the labour theory of value. In fact, given this purpose, the choice or construction of an 'invariable standard' of the relative worth of commodities seems to him to be entirely more useful. For Sraffa, the invariable standard should be such that its own price is invariable with respect to changes in conditions of production affecting the prices of all other commodities, particularly a change in the wage share. Noting that the invariable standard could not, because of this, be any single commodity, Sraffa constructs in *Commodities* his well-known **standard commodity**. The standard commodity is an artificial construct made up of inputs whose proportion to one another as inputs is the same as their proportion to one another as outputs. It is argued that the construct is derived from the real economic system through the application of an appropriate vector of multipliers.[11] I will return later to the nature of this construct, as well as the validity of Sraffa's quest for an invariable standard. However, what needs emphasis here is Sraffa's view that it is the relative price of the standard commodity, and the *numéraire* in a subsistence economy setting, that reduces all other commodity prices to equivalence and facilitates their exchange. That is to say, for Sraffa it is the *numéraire* commodity or invariable standard, and not money, which functions as the measure of exchangeable worth of commodities and facilitates their exchange. Sraffa does not explain, however, why or how the *numéraire* or invariable standard performs this function.

From the perspective of Marx's analysis, what Sraffa appears to overlook is that it is money as the generally accepted representative of exchangeable worth that reduces commodities to exchangeable worth and not any arbitrarily chosen or constructed commodity. Money is able to reduce commodities to equivalence in terms of exchangeable worth for Marx because commodities are already equivalent to one another as values, as embodiments of social labour time. Because all commodities reflect their relative worth in money it, money, is accepted as the general representative of social labour time. I will argue below that it is this failure of Sraffa to analyse the role played by money in the formation of price that has led many of his followers to arrive at erroneous conceptualisations of money and corresponding mistaken explanations of money prices. I will argue it has caused them to see money as one among the produced commodities in an economic system (as the *numéraire* commodity or standard of this *numéraire*), and to adopt explanations of money prices which are along the lines of the TQM and MQM.

Form of prices

Needless to say, as much as there is no explicit analysis of the formation of price in Sraffa's *Commodities*, so there is no explicit analysis of the form of price in this work. However, as with the formation of price, so with the price form, it is possible to deduce what is implicit in this work. Following from what was argued to be his implicit view of the formation of prices, it can be argued that Sraffa necessarily sees this form to be **a commodity form**. That is, Sraffa's approach precludes the possibility of seeing the price form as a money form, the form of a general equivalent, because, as was just noted, the logic of his analysis suggests that what reduces the relative prices of commodities to equivalence, and thereby regulates their exchange, is either a particular commodity (in subsistence production systems) or a cluster of basic commodities (the standard commodity in surplus commodity production systems). To the extent that commodity prices can be argued to have a money form which is distinct from the form of the *numéraire* or standard commodity, it is merely as a reflection of the latter, with money being a standard of the *numéraire* or the standard commodity.

Purpose of prices

In the tradition of the Classical economists, Sraffa sees the purpose of price as facilitating the reproduction of the individual commodity in the context of the reproduction of the system as a whole. Prices facilitate the reproduction of the individual commodity by enabling producers to appropriate the necessary commodity inputs to reproduce their commodities. In the course of his explanation of price magnitudes in a subsistence production setting, Sraffa states, 'There is a unique set of exchange-values which if adopted by the market restores the original distribution of the products and makes it possible for the process to be repeated' (1960, p. 3).

This view of the purpose of price contrasts with the Post Keynesian view which, it will be recalled, sees prices as either facilitating the (expanded) reproduction of the individual commodity or, more usually, meeting the needs of the individual producer in terms of financing expanded production and the like, without reference to the reproduction of the system as a whole. From the perspective of Marx's analysis, Sraffa's view of the purpose of price, like his view of the formation of price, is certainly in advance of that of the Post Keynesians in that he sees price as facilitating the reproduction of the individual commodity alongside, and with reference to, the reproduction of all other commodities. However, the weaknesses with Sraffa's view are: a) he does not see that prices facilitate the reproduction of the individual commodity alongside all other commodities because it allows producers to appropriate the required social labour time and not commodities *per se*; and b) he does not see that price facilitates the reproduction of the commodity alongside all other commodities in accordance with the social **demand** for the individual commodities and all other commodities.

That price is not seen as facilitating the appropriation of requisite social labour time by Sraffa is understandable, at least in the context of subsistence production, given that what is commanded through the sale of the commodity by the direct producer is the commodity inputs needed for the reproduction of the commodity in question, and also given Sraffa's desire to eliminate labour from the analysis. However, the elimination of labour from the analysis means that he necessarily sees prices as in the final instance facilitating the required allocation of commodities for the purpose of producing commodities. From the perspective of Marx's analysis, this view of the purpose of price is not so much wrong as limited. For Marx, since exchange mediates a division of labour, with 'labour' being the operative word, prices which govern the exchange process must necessarily facilitate the appropriation of the necessary quantities of social labour time to enable the reproduction of the system.

That Sraffa ignores demand in his analysis of price is, similarly, entirely intentional, and is tacitly justified by him on the basis of the limited purpose of his study and the assumption of fixed output. From the perspective of Marx's analysis, however, this omission in Sraffa's analysis gives rise to a distorted view of price, which in turn has deleterious consequences for his broader understanding of the determinants of the magnitudes of prices and changes in these magnitudes. For Marx, since prices facilitate the reproduction of an economic system characterised by a division of labour and mediated by exchange, they must of necessity serve to link, to one degree or another, the reproduction of commodities to the demand for them. I will return to this point below in the discussion of Sraffa's explanation of the magnitude of price.

Nature of prices

For Sraffa, whether commodities are produced in subsistence or surplus economic systems, their prices fundamentally reflect the technical conditions of their production and, ultimately, the **commodity inputs** required to produce them. In the case of surplus economic systems, Sraffa sees prices as additionally reflecting the distribution of the surplus product between wages and profits. He sees no reason for a distinction to be drawn between the nature of prices in sectors using only produced inputs and those also using non-produced inputs, *viz.*, between agricultural and manufacturing sectors. And, to the extent that Sraffa's approach can be used as a basis for the explanation of money prices, it suggests these prices reflect additionally the value of money as given either by the value of the commodity inputs required to produce the money commodity when money is deemed to be the *numéraire* commodity, or the quantitative relation of money to the *numéraire* when money is seen as a token or standard of the *numéraire*.

Although there is a certain superficial similarity between Sraffa's and Post Keynesian views of the nature of prices in that both approaches see prices as reflecting what may loosely be termed supply-side factors, they are nevertheless fundamentally different. Post Keynesians, it will be recalled, see prices as ultimately reflecting factor rewards, particularly wages, while Sraffa sees them as fundamentally reflecting commodity inputs. From the perspective of Marx's analysis outlined above, it should be apparent that Sraffa's understanding of the nature of price is superior to that of the Post Keynesian approach because of the emphasis he places on the physical requirements of production, one which he continues to adhere to even when acknowledging that in surplus systems prices must additionally reflect the distribution of the surplus product. However, it should also be apparent that from the perspective of Marx's analysis, there are also a number of problems with Sraffa's understanding of the nature of price.

In keeping with what has been argued above, the most fundamental of these is that it assumes it is commodities and not labour that produce commodities and, therefore, that the labour input can be substituted by the wage goods required to sustain labour in the course of the production of commodities. As pointed out above, this in turn presumes that in commodity production systems exchange mediates the required distribution of commodities and prices facilitate their allocation, and not that exchange mediates a division of labour with prices facilitating the allocation of labour time in the final instance. Where Marx sees prices as reflecting the direct and indirect labour time required for the production of commodities, Sraffa sees them as reflecting (the prices of) the direct and indirect commodity inputs required for the production of commodity outputs.

Sraffa's view that prices reflect commodity inputs is also founded on the dubious distinction between basics and non-basics. As argued above, Sraffa makes this distinction in order to avoid the impression that his explanation of price is a mere tautology by providing more substance to his contention that commodity output prices reflect the commodity inputs required for the production of the outputs. Distinguishing between basics and non-basics allows him to conceive of prices of commodities as reflecting the basic commodity inputs required for their production. However, as I have also argued above, this distinction between basics and non-basics is conceptually quite vague. Moreover, how commodity prices might be seen as reflecting basic commodity inputs when commodities are regarded as joint products comprising basics and non-basics is anyone's guess, and a problem Sraffa himself acknowledged (see below).

Related to this, Sraffa's view of the nature of price also, problematically, requires commodity inputs or basics to be seen as reducible to equivalence. For Sraffa this equivalence can be achieved through the choice of an appropriate *numéraire*. This is because, for Sraffa, the prices of outputs cannot reflect the relative quantities of heterogeneous physical inputs, but rather their exchangeable worth. The magnitudes of exchangeable worth of commodity inputs are given by the quantities of inputs multiplied by their relative prices. The *numéraire* is required to reduce the relative prices of all inputs and outputs to equivalence. To see the relative prices of outputs as reflecting the relative worth of the physical commodity inputs required for their production means, in effect, seeing them as reflecting the prices of inputs. It means tautologically seeing **prices as reflecting prices**. It also means accepting that an arbitrarily chosen, or artificially constructed, *numéraire* can be seen as reducing the relative prices of commodities to equivalence.

Sraffa's view that prices in surplus economies also reflect the distribution of the surplus product between wages and profits is founded on what is, from the perspective of Marx's analysis, a misconception that the surplus product comprises profits and wages components. For Marx, relative prices do not reflect the distribution of the surplus product so much as the general rate of profit. There is a very important distinction to be made between the two, which I will also return to below.

Finally, it should by now be fairly evident that Sraffa's implicit views on the nature of money prices are founded on a misunderstanding of money. As noted in the discussion of his implicit views on the formation of prices, the logic of Sraffa's analysis suggests that money as *numéraire* is a particular commodity, say an input, or a standard of the *numéraire*. There seems to be no appreciation, and indeed cannot be any appreciation, by those using Sraffa's analysis that money is neither just any particular commodity nor a token of the *numéraire* commodity, but is rather the general commodity or universal equivalent. As universal equivalent the worth of money is given by its worth in relation to all other commodities. That is, its value is given by the average labour time required to produce all those commodities it circulates over a given period of time. It is not given by the relative exchangeable worth of inputs required to produce it as a particular commodity, as would be the case when it is seen as a *numéraire*, or the amount of it in existence in relation to the amount of the *numéraire*, as would be the case when it is seen as the standard of the *numéraire*.

8.4 Implicit price constructs

Like the Post Keynesian analysis, Sraffa's approach to the analysis of prices does not formally contain a number of explicit price constructs in the same way as, for example, the Neoclassical approach does. He does not, in contrast with the Neoclassical approach, formally conceive of equilibrium prices, competitive prices, etc. However, as with the Post Keynesian approach, a number of these conceptualisations are implicit in Sraffa's work, and warrant some attention here since they provide certain insights into how he understands prices and explains their magnitudes.

Equilibrium and long-run prices

For Sraffa, as for Marx, the starting point for the explanation of price is what has been referred to as reproduction prices – the prices which facilitate the reproduction of commodities by permitting producers to command the requisite inputs for their production. It is this notion of prices that Sraffa uses in the first instance when explaining the magnitudes of prices in subsistence-economy and single-product, surplus-economy settings. It can be argued they are **equilibrium prices** in the sense that they imply the relative economy-wide balance of demand for, and supply of, the individual product alongside all other products, as well as the appropriation of an average rate of profit by producers of all products.[12] Since, as was argued above, Marx too sees reproduction prices as equilibrium prices in this sense, Sraffa cannot be criticised from the perspective of Marx's analysis for conceiving of equilibrium prices as the point of departure for his explanation of the magnitude of prices. Rather, the problem with Sraffa's implicit conceptualisation of prices as equilibrium prices has to do with how he conceives of these prices in relation to actual prices. Specifically, the implication of Sraffa's analysis is that reproduction or equilibrium prices are **centres of gravity** for the movement of actual prices rather than, as for Marx, averages of actual prices. This implication arises because Sraffa appears to tacitly deny that the movement of actual prices, resulting from demand and supply imbalances, has any bearing on the movement of reproduction or equilibrium prices. It will be recalled that for Marx demand and supply imbalances can have an impact on reproduction prices through their impact on the scale and techniques of production adopted by producers in an industry. Although Sraffa may have actually recognised the possibility of such an impact,[13] his assumption of fixed output and a given technology lead in effect to a denial of this possibility. Sraffa appears to justify his assumptions of fixed output and given technology by, once again, his limited purpose in *Commodities*; the explanation of the impact on price magnitudes of changes in the wages share. However, at the very least, this raises the question of the validity of his analysis for a more general understanding of prices and their dynamics, especially given that the wage share itself can be argued to be impacted by changes in the level of output and technology.[14]

To the extent that Sraffa's prices can be thought of as equilibrium or reproduction prices, it is also difficult to know what sense to make of these when moving to a joint-product world. It is difficult to understand in which way the prices of individual products comprising joint products can be said to be either reproduction or equilibrium prices when, a) it is unclear that they correspond to a balance of supply and demand for individual products, and b) the profit rates for the production of a given product necessarily diverge between producers of that product, and can even move in different directions. In fact, since it is unclear how movements of profit rates in respect of the production of different clusters of goods can be expected to induce changes in the supply of an individual product in accordance with changes in demand for it, the prices of individual products in a joint-product setting must of necessity be **disequilibrium** prices. What all of this suggests is that, when Sraffa explains the magnitudes of prices in subsistence and single-product, surplus-economic settings, the prices of individual products can be thought of as equilibrium prices, while when he moves to an explanation of price magnitudes in a joint-product, surplus-economy setting, they are by definition disequilibrium prices.

It might also be noted that Sraffa's conceptualisation of reproduction prices, and the implied view in his analysis of their relation to market prices, suggests that the former can also be seen as long-run prices and the latter as short-run prices. From the perspective of Marx's analysis, the problem with such a distinction in Sraffa's work is that the former would be seen as moving independently of the latter. In modern parlance the problem is that it would suggest a tendency to see long-run prices as not being path dependent. Although it is unlikely that Sraffa actually believed this to be the case, much as it is unlikely that he did not see supply and demand imbalances as having a bearing on reproduction prices, it is difficult to see how such a conclusion can be avoided given his approach to the analysis of prices. The implicit view of the distinction between long- and short-run prices in Sraffa's work contrasts with the implicit view of this distinction in Marx's analysis of price. In Marx's analysis long-run prices are very much dependent on the movement of prices over the short run, since they are seen as the **averages** of the latter.

Competitive and non-competitive prices

The reproduction prices Sraffa analyses, at least in the single product surplus economic setting, can also be argued to be competitive prices, or, to be more precise, competitive equilibrium prices. They can be argued to be competitive prices because a competitive environment gives rise to a single price for a single product which is produced using a homogenous technology and where producers appropriate an economy-wide average rate of profit.[15] From the perspective of Marx's analysis, the problem with this implicit conceptualisation of price in Sraffa's work is that, as with the similar Neoclassical conceptualisation of competitive price, it is devoid of any understanding of the competitive processes giving rise to the formation of these prices. This point was already noted above when discussing the absence in Sraffa's work of an understanding of how prices come to be formed. It was argued there that a major source of this *lacuna* is his failure to explicitly analyse the process of competition underlying price formation. This in turn, it was also argued, gives rise to a number of problems in Sraffa's work when he seeks to extend his explanation of the magnitude of price from a single-product, surplus-economy setting to that of joint products and non-produced inputs. To repeat, among other things it causes Sraffa to assume, without explanation, the existence of a single price for a homogeneous product, even though technologies and rates of profit differ between producers of the same product.

What needs additional mention here is the implications this absence of an explicit analysis of the process of competition has for the distinction to be drawn between competitive and non-competitive prices in Sraffa's work when he goes beyond the single-product, surplus-economy setting.

As with both the Neoclassical and Post Keynesian approaches, the absence of an explicit analysis of the competitive process underlying price formation in Sraffa's work allows for the conceptualisation of non-competitive prices as those which are formed in the context of, among other things, firms using different technologies to produce the same product thereby appropriating different rates of profit, with some firms appropriating an excess profit. In Sraffa's work this raises the question of whether the prices he conceives of in economic settings characterised by joint products and/or the use of non-produced inputs are competitive or non-competitive, given that in these settings the same product can be produced with several techniques of production and certain producers may be appropriating an excess profit in respect of the production of a given product. As with the question of whether the prices he is explaining in joint-product and non-produced input settings are equilibrium or disequilibrium prices, this is hardly a semantic issue. If such prices are seen as both non-equilibrium and non-competitive, this must surely have implications for how the magnitudes of prices are to be explained, something which is tacitly denied in Sraffa's analysis.

Relative and money prices

Like Marx, but unlike the Post Keynesians, it is implicit in Sraffa's analysis that a distinction needs to be drawn between relative and money prices, and that the explanation of the magnitude of price should begin with an explanation of the magnitude of the former. However, unlike Marx, it would seem Sraffa does not (at least formally) recognise relative prices are in essence money prices. He does not appear to recognise that the relative exchangeable worth of commodities is always expressed in terms of money, and that it is money, as the general equivalent (and not a particular commodity) that governs exchange. In fact, seeing relative prices as divorced from money prices, reinforces the tendency in those adopting Sraffa's framework of analysis to see what governs the actual exchange of commodities as something other than money, as a commodity *numéraire*, and money itself as a mere standard of the *numéraire* – a veil.[16] As a standard of the *numéraire*, money converts relative prices into money prices which simply reflect relative prices denominated in terms of the *numéraire*.

8.5   The magnitude of relative price

Subsistence production

Sraffa begins his explanation of the magnitude of price in a subsistence commodity production setting because, it would seem, he sees this as providing the essence of the explanation of price magnitudes in all commodity production systems, including surplus ones, whether single or joint product, and whether inputs are produced or non-produced. He argues that in a subsistence economy setting the magnitudes of relative prices of commodity outputs (which are also inputs) are determined by the relative exchangeable worth of the commodity inputs required for the production of the outputs. The relative worth of commodity inputs is given by the quantities **and** relative prices of the inputs required for the production of the commodity, and the relative prices of the inputs are in turn determined by the 'methods of production' used in their production. These methods of production are, incidentally, also the methods of production used in the production of the outputs since all outputs are assumed to also be inputs in the subsistence system. By methods of production, Sraffa means the physical inputs required for the production of the inputs as outputs. For a given level of output, the relative prices of the inputs will be such that they permit the reproduction of the inputs according to the technical requirements of production. That is, for a given level of output, it is the methods, or technical conditions, of the production of inputs that determine the amounts, and therefore proportions, of basics that need to be exchanged with each other to facilitate their reproduction. Crucially, Sraffa denies that the determination of the magnitudes of relative prices can be linked to relative **quantities of inputs** measured independently of, and prior to, the determination of their **prices**, although he argues that the amounts of material inputs and labour should be ascertainable in quantitative terms without need of knowing these prices. Actually, Sraffa denies that his explanation of relative prices can be called a 'cost of production' explanation because a) cost of production explanations have come to be identified with approaches which suggest relative prices can be linked to quantities of inputs that are measurable independently of, and prior to, the determination of the prices of products, and b) the relative worth of inputs also depends on their relative worth as outputs (*Ibid.*, p. 9).[17] With the magnitudes of prices of outputs given by the quantities and prices of inputs, Sraffa argues there is still need for one further step in order to arrive at a determinate solution for prices. This step is to choose as *numéraire* one of the commodity prices. Once this is done, the prices of all commodities can be expressed in terms of the *numéraire*, thereby making them comparable.

From the perspective of Marx's analysis, the positive aspects of Sraffa's explanation of price magnitudes, albeit in a subsistence economy setting, are, firstly, it recognises the need to locate this explanation in the context of the reproduction of the individual commodity alongside all other commodities, and, secondly, the importance it accords to the technical conditions of production ('methods of production') in this explanation. It is these two aspects of Sraffa's explanation of the magnitudes of relative prices that arguably make it superior to the Post Keynesian approach. These positive aspects notwithstanding, there are nevertheless a number of problems with Sraffa's explanation of prices in a subsistence commodity production economic setting from the perspective of Marx's analysis.

The major problem is, not surprisingly, the way in which Sraffa conceives of the methods of production, and in particular the labour input. As noted above, in an attempt to overcome what critics have argued to be the logical flaws of the labour theory of value, Sraffa replaces the expenditure of labour time with the goods purchased by labour using wages paid to them for their labour time. I have already discussed the question of the validity of this substitution. Here I will consider the consequences it has for his explanation of price magnitudes. To begin with, it causes Sraffa to explain the magnitudes of output prices in terms of the magnitudes of input prices, albeit alongside quantities of inputs. To avoid reducing the explanation to a tautology, i.e., the explanation of prices by prices, Sraffa then proceeds to explain input prices by the technical conditions of their production in terms of themselves.[18] The problem with this explanation, however, is the meaning to be ascribed to the production of inputs in terms of themselves. Even leaving aside the deficiencies noted above with such a conceptualisation, one can seriously doubt whether the magnitudes of commodity prices can be accepted as meaningfully explained by the methods of producing the required inputs in terms of themselves. Is it meaningful, for example, to argue that the magnitudes of prices of all goods can be explained by the methods of producing oil (and a limited number of other inputs) in terms of itself (themselves)? The vacuous nature of this explanation becomes even more apparent when it is extended to consider **changes** in price magnitudes (see below).

A second consequence of omitting labour time in the explanation of the magnitudes of prices in a subsistence economy setting is that it requires Sraffa to make one of the relative prices of the commodities produced in the system a *numéraire* in order to arrive at a determinate set of prices.[19] The problem with this, as noted above when discussing the formation of prices, is that Sraffa fails to explain **why** and **how** the *numéraire* reduces commodities to equivalence and what this means for the role of money. Although it is implicit in Sraffa's analysis that the *numéraire* should be an input into the production of all commodities, since as an input it can be seen to be something of a common denominator in terms of the relative worth of outputs, this does not explain **why** the relative price of an arbitrarily chosen input would reduce the relative prices of all other commodities to equivalence. Of course, it could be argued that the *numéraire* reduces commodities to equivalence as exchange values because it is required in the production of all commodities. That is, because it is required in the production of all commodities, it causes commodities to have worth in relation to one another. However, this would suggest that for Sraffa commodities come to acquire relative worth when they are produced by a certain commodity – the *numéraire* – in the context of their production by other commodities, and not when they are produced by the expenditure of labour in the context of a division of labour.

Perhaps even more problematic for Sraffa, is **how** the *numéraire* can be seen as reducing commodities to equivalence. This is because it would require seeing producers (and other market participants) using the *numéraire* as the measure of exchangeable worth. But this would beg the question why producers would use something other than money as measure of exchangeable worth, and, if they did, what this would imply for money. For something to function as the measure of exchangeable worth, it should be accepted as the most exchangeable of all commodities possessing certain specific characteristics, *viz.*, homogeneity, divisibility, transportability, etc., which contribute to its acceptability. It is unclear that an (arbitrarily chosen) input would meet these requirements. Moreover, for something other than money to function as measure of exchangeable worth, raises the question of money's relation to it. As noted above, it would necessarily cause money to be seen as a mere standard of the chosen *numéraire*.

Surplus production

When Sraffa moves to the explanation of price magnitudes in a surplus product setting, he feels it necessary to distinguish between the cases of single-product industries, joint-products industries, fixed capital, and production using non-produced inputs alongside produced inputs. In assessing this explanation, I will follow the trajectory of his presentation in terms of these distinctions.

Single-product industries

Sraffa argues that when we move to a surplus product setting it is no longer possible to explain the magnitudes of prices simply in terms of the exchangeable worth of the inputs required for the production of the commodity outputs. In this setting it becomes necessary to bring into the analysis additionally the magnitude of the surplus and its constituents, wages and profits. That is, beginning with a single-product setting, Sraffa explains the magnitudes of output prices by, on the one hand, the prices of the commodity inputs required for their production (their quantities and prices) and, on the other hand, the rates of profits and wages (times the quantities of commodity inputs and labour, respectively, required for the production of the commodities).[20] It warrants emphasising that, although Sraffa recognises the need to bring the rates of profit and wages into the explanation of the magnitude of price in the surplus-product setting, it is clear from his concern to show that changes in the wage share have no predictable impact on this magnitude that he continues to adhere to the view that it is the commodity-input requirements which remain the most important determinant of price magnitudes. The parallels between Sraffa's insistence on commodity inputs continuing to be the major determinant of reproduction prices in a surplus economy setting and Marx's insistence on value as measured by labour time continuing to be the major determinant of reproduction prices in the context of the formation of a general rate of profit are striking and, obviously, not coincidental.

I have just elaborated on the problems with Sraffa's commodity inputs explanation of prices in the context of the subsistence economy setting. What requires additional mention in the surplus economy setting is his explanation of the profits and wages components. From the perspective of Marx's analysis, the major deficiency with this explanation is that it suggests the rate of profit and/or the wage rate can be taken as given exogenously. Marx would no doubt have particularly objected to Sraffa's view that the rate of profit can be taken as given by the money rate of interest. This is because for Marx the former conditions the latter; interest being in fact a deduction from profits.[21]

A further modification to Sraffa's subsistence economy explanation of the magnitude of price in a single-product, surplus-economy setting which requires some attention is his replacement of the *numéraire* by the standard commodity. The purpose of the standard commodity is, like the *numéraire* commodity in the subsistence economy setting, to reduce commodity prices to equivalence and arrive at a determinate set of prices. As noted earlier, Sraffa's standard commodity is in fact an artificially constructed composite of basic commodities where the ratio of basics to one another as outputs is the same as their ratios to one another as inputs. With the standard commodity, Sraffa aimed to express all commodity prices in terms of a standard whose relative worth does not change with changes in the wage share (where this share is seen as part of the surplus product) and, therefore, the rate of profit. Sraffa hoped the standard commodity would help him demonstrate that changes in the wage share have no predictable impact on relative prices without the 'noise effect' of a change in the exchangeable worth of the measure of exchangeable worth interfering. Although Sraffa denies it, in constructing the standard commodity he appears to be attempting to complete Ricardo's search for 'an invariable standard'.[22] I will take up the validity of this endeavour shortly, but here some consideration needs to be given to Sraffa's standard commodity and related **dated labour** constructs. Most importantly, it needs pointing out that the standard commodity is made invariant to changes in the conditions of production affecting the relative prices of all commodities by assuming fixed technology.[23] If technological change is allowed, then the ratios between inputs, and therefore the relative worth of the standard commodity, would vary along with the relative prices of all other commodities. It also needs pointing out that Sraffa's conceptualisation of dated quantities of labour is directly related to his standard commodity. This is because dated quantities of labour for Sraffa are the quantities of **labour time commanded** by a unit of the standard commodity. Reducing commodities to equivalence as magnitudes of dated labour then translates relative prices of commodities in terms of the cumbersome standard commodity into relative prices in terms of wage costs, albeit wage costs in terms of the standard commodity. This means Sraffa's dated labour measure of exchangeable worth is not so much a measure of exchangeable worth as a standard of the measure of exchangeable worth, i.e., it is a standard of the standard commodity. Hence, the problems noted in connection with his reduction of commodity prices to equivalence using the standard commodity apply equally to their reduction to equivalence in terms of dated labour.

Joint-product industries

It will be recalled that Sraffa defines joint-product industries as those where the same inputs are used to produce two or more commodities. He assumes the individual commodities comprising joint products can be produced using more than one technique of production. He further assumes that the relative prices of individual commodities and profit rates in respect of the production of the joint products will be the same. He then argues that, for there to be a determinate set of prices of individual commodities in such an economic setting, there only needs to be the same number of production processes as commodities (*Ibid.*, p. 44).

The first and most obvious problem with this explanation of the magnitudes of prices in a joint-products setting, and one already alluded to above, is that it simply assumes the existence of a determinate set of prices. No explanation is offered as to why there should be an equal number of production processes as commodities. In reality there are likely to be many different production techniques employed in the production of similar commodities, or even the same commodity, notwithstanding the fact that there is likely to be a standard technique used by the average producer, much as there is likely to be many different varieties of the same commodity produced notwithstanding the fact that there will tend to be a certain standard type of each and every commodity produced using a certain standard technology.

Secondly, as Sraffa himself candidly admits, in the case of joint products it is no longer possible to talk of methods of production of basics determining the magnitudes of prices of all products, including the basics themselves (*Ibid.*, p. 49). This is because in a joint-products economic setting the production of basics may involve the production of non-basics in the same production process. From the perspective of Marx's analysis, the source of the problem with Sraffa's analysis in this regard is his failure to appreciate that whether inputs are shared or not, their costs can be, and are, apportioned to the exchangeable worth of commodities which they help produce. Sraffa does not see this because he does not consider how prices come to be actually formed.[24]

A third problem with Sraffa's explanation of price magnitudes in a joint-products setting is that it suggests these magnitudes are in fact **indeterminate**, and can even be **negative**. Price magnitudes are indeterminate because the profit components of the prices of the individual products comprising the joint products necessarily vary inversely with one another. Indeed, the profits components of the prices of individual commodities comprising the joint product can take on a whole range of values, including negative values. Recognising this latter theoretical possibility, Sraffa explicitly precludes it by appeal to 'reality' (see *Ibid.*, p. 59).

A last problem of note with Sraffa's attempt to extend his explanation of the magnitude of relative price to a joint-product setting is the conceptual difficulties it gives rise to with regard to the standard commodity and associated dated labour constructs. With joint products, Sraffa notes the construction of the standard commodity involves negative multipliers (*Ibid.*, p. 47). The multipliers used in the construction of the standard commodity, it will be recalled, are those which link the standard system to the actual system. Negative multipliers arise in the construction of the standard commodity in a joint-product setting because the proportion in which individual production processes produce two or more basics in the actual system do not correspond to the proportion in which they are required as inputs into the standard system. This is because the production of basic commodities in the actual joint-product system is hypothesised by Sraffa to involve simultaneously the production of non-basic commodities which are not required in the standard system. Hence, to enable the inclusion of such basics in the standard system without the accompanying non-basics, the production processes which produce them alongside the non-basics will need to have negative multipliers applied to them. The problem is, as Sraffa himself notes, that it is difficult to give precise meaning to the notion of negative multipliers (*Ibid.*, p. 48).[25]

With joint products, Sraffa also finds that it is no longer possible to reduce the prices of commodities to dated quantities of labour (*Ibid.*, p. 56). This is because it is not possible to 'track back' on a single track in respect of costs, since some costs would be unique to the production of one or another of the individual products comprising the joint product. Moreover, even if this were possible, it would require assigning **negative values** to some dated labour components. Apart from the problem of interpreting such negative values, it would mean there is in principle no limit to the reduction process. Some Sraffians have taken these results as further proof, if such proof were needed, of the inconsistency of Marx's labour theory explanation of magnitudes of prices and changes in these.[26] However, not only does it warrant repeating that Sraffa's dated labour analysis is very different from Marx's labour theory of value, it should be apparent that the logical problems encountered by Sraffa with his dated labour analysis really stem from the problems with it noted above. These problems are: a) the assumption that when two commodities or more are produced using the same inputs, their costs in terms of these inputs are not decomposable while their implied individual rates of profit move in opposite directions to one another for a given general rate of profit, and b) the assumption that prices reflect historic costs. Once these assumptions are granted it follows logically that 'tracking back' in terms of dated labour values gives rise to negative quantities of dated labour and no limit to the reduction process.

Fixed capital

When taking into account fixed capital, and, therefore, the exchange value of the long-lasting inputs to be transferred to the exchange value of the product, Sraffa makes a number of important points which have a bearing on his explanation of the price magnitudes of commodities. He argues that the value of fixed capital transferred to the final selling price of the commodity in a certain period of time, say a year, is given by the **depreciation quota**. This quota is determined by the initial price of the fixed capital, its expected life, efficiency and intensity of use. The magnitude of profit transferred to the price of the final commodity is given by the rate of profit and the 'book-value' of the fixed capital at the beginning of the production process. Sraffa refers to the depreciation quota plus the profit as the **depreciation charge** for the fixed capital (*Ibid.*, p. 66). That is:

$$C = Q + rK$$

where C is the depreciation charge, Q is the depreciation quota (the value of fixed capital transferred to the final selling price in a year), r is the rate of profit, and K is book value of fixed capital at the beginning of the production process. Taking fixed capital to be machines, Sraffa assumes the depreciation charge for each machine is the same irrespective of its age. As machines get older, the profit on the outstanding capital which they comprise falls, so that the depreciation quota will have to rise to compensate. Sraffa contends that the depreciation charges for the individual machines will not be constant over their lives, but will tend to fall as the machines get older due to declines in their physical productivity and increases in wear and tear (*Ibid.*). Lastly, when considering the implications of his analysis of fixed capital for the construction of the standard commodity, Sraffa argues that it causes the problem of negative multipliers which arises in the general joint-products setting to disappear (*Ibid.*, pp. 72–3).

From the perspective of Marx's analysis, one problem with Sraffa's explanation of the magnitude of the depreciation charge, is his contention that a fall in the average rate of profit implies higher depreciation quotas in the early years of the use of fixed capital by producers of a given product – i.e., it gives rise to accelerated depreciation charges. It should be apparent, however, this conclusion depends on the assumption that the prices of commodities produced with the fixed capital remain unchanged as the rate of profit falls. But, for Marx, as also for Sraffa, prices change with changes in the rate of profit. Moreover, for Marx, the source of changes in the rate of profit are, more often than not, the same sources as those of the changes in prices, *viz.*, relative productivity changes (in wages goods industries).

Perhaps more importantly in this regard is that Sraffa's focus on the impact of the rate of profit on the depreciation charge gives rise to a certain myopia in his analysis with respect to the sources of the differences in the charges between sectors. It results in his failure to see that the major reason for some sectors having relatively higher depreciation charges in the early years of the lives of fixed capital is that these sectors are characterised by more rapid technological change. As Marx argued when introducing the notion of a 'moral element' in depreciation charges, rapid technological change increases the risk that falling prices of the commodities produced in the sector will not permit businesses to recover fixed capital costs over the expected lives of the fixed capital elements.[27] Hence, the accelerated depreciation charges in such industries.[28]

A further problem with Sraffa's explanation of the magnitude of depreciation charges is that it implicitly assumes these charges pertain to a standard producer producing a standard product for a standard price and appropriating an industry (and economy-wide) average rate of profit. That is, it implicitly assumes the existence of intra-industry competition giving rise to these averages. However, while this assumption can be justified in Sraffa's single-product setting, it cannot be so justified in his joint-product setting. Building on what was said above in the context of a discussion of Sraffa's implicit conceptualisation of competitive price, in a joint-product setting technologies and rates of profit of producers of the same products are necessarily different, making it in principle impossible to conceive of standard depreciation charges for a standard product. Indeed, such standard charges can only be conceived of in a joint-product setting by assuming, as Sraffa does, that a) the joint products comprise only fixed capital and marketable commodities produced with the fixed capital, and b) the processes of production of the marketable commodities are broadly similar, such that the same type of fixed capital of the same vintage, etc., can be found in the production of all commodities. That is, standard depreciation charges for standard products can only be conceived of in a joint-product setting by assuming the joint-products setting is in effect a single-product one.

It may, similarly, be seen that it is this same assumption, i.e., that the joint-product system is in effect a single-product one, that permits Sraffa to argue that the negative multipliers found in a joint-product setting disappear in the fixed capital setting. To quote Sraffa,

> The similarity between the several processes which employ a durable instrument in its successive stages of wear will generally make it possible for the Standard system to be constructed by means of exclusively positive multipliers. As a result, a system which contained no other element of joint production besides what is implied in the presence of fixed capital would in general have an all-positive Standard commodity, thus reproducing in this respect the simplicity of the system of single-product industries. (1960, p. 73)

Non-produced inputs

Sraffa sees non-produced inputs as occupying 'among means of production a position equivalent to "non-basics" among products' (1960, p. 74). He sees such inputs as attracting a rent when they are in short supply, and only having significance for the determination of price magnitudes in the exceptional case where the non-produced input is scarce and of the same quality. In all other circumstances it will have no significance. Sraffa also argues that with non-produced inputs negative multipliers once again reappear in the construction of the standard commodity, but suggests they can be dealt with through an appropriate redefinition of the economic system.

When he considers the specific case of land, and the determination of the magnitudes of prices of agricultural commodities, Sraffa distinguishes between, on the one hand, an economic setting where land is scarce and of different qualities and, on the other hand, where it is scarce and of the same quality. In both cases, since land is deemed to be scarce, it will attract a rent. In the former setting Sraffa sees the magnitude of price as determined by the costs of production on the worst land, which he argues to be the no-rent land. If rent arises in this setting it is in respect of production of the same types of agricultural commodities on better quality land. The source of this rent is then the implied greater productivity of the better quality land. Where land is scarce and of the same quality, Sraffa tacitly accepts that rent will have a bearing on the price of the product. In such a setting he also assumes, as was noted above, that it is possible for there to be more than one technique of production. This means, however, that for there to be homogeneous prices and equal rates of profit, the more efficient technique needs to be assumed to also be the higher costs technique.

For Marx too non-produced inputs need to be scarce to attract a rent. However, for him, they will have a bearing on the magnitudes of prices of commodities produced using them whether they are of the same or different quality. This is because, for Marx, the existence of such inputs, when they are scarce, typically allows their owners to appropriate a part of the surplus produced in the specific sector, or even other sectors of the economy, in the form of absolute rent. The appearance of absolute rent causes the relative prices of commodities produced with non-produced inputs, where they are not substitutable by produced inputs, to be higher than they otherwise would be.[29]

Although Marx too saw prices of agricultural commodities as determined by conditions of production on the worst lands where land is of different quality, the logic, if not the letter, of his analysis, suggests that for him they would be determined by the average techniques of production used by producers of the same product on this land, i.e., producers using average cost techniques on the worst lands. He would most certainly have denied that different qualities of land imply that producers could not use more than one technique of production as argued by Sraffa. Also, where there is more than one producer, he would deny that the more efficient producer needs to be seen as also the higher cost producer for there to be a single price for the standard commodity produced on this land and the appropriation of an average profit by producers of this standard commodity. This is because, for Marx, a standard product of a given type is produced with a certain average technique of production, where producers using this technique appropriate an average rate of profit. More efficient producers would typically be lower-cost producers appropriating an excess profit or differential rent, not high-cost producers. High-cost producers would be those using less efficient techniques and appropriating a lower-than-average profit.

Finally, it should be apparent that in order to eliminate negative multipliers in the construction of the standard commodity when some of the inputs are non-produced, Sraffa simply, and arbitrarily, redefines an economic system as one in which the number of production processes equals the number of commodities and non-produced inputs. Sraffa recognises that the troublesome negative multipliers reappear when he seeks to construct the standard system and standard commodity in the context of non-produced inputs (1960, p. 77). This is because the existence of non-produced inputs in his system allows for the possibility of a multiplicity of production processes each producing the same commodity (even though each process is assumed to produce no more than a single product on the basis of the assumptions made under fixed capital production). With the redefinition of the economic system in the manner noted above, Sraffa has no need to apply negative multipliers since there is no longer need to eliminate some of the production processes (apart from those involving the production of non-basic outputs) to get equivalence between production processes and commodities in the standard system.

8.6 Changes in relative price magnitudes

The core arguments

Sraffa's explanation of changes in the magnitudes of relative prices follows directly from his view of the determinants of these magnitudes. His major concern in this explanation is to show that **changes** in the magnitudes of relative prices are primarily to be explained by **changes** in both the immediate conditions of production of the commodity concerned and the basics required for its production, and, concomitantly, that changes in the wage share have no determinate impact on the magnitudes of prices. As an adjunct to the latter, he also attempts to show that changes in the magnitudes of relative prices cannot exceed changes in the wage share. It is these conclusions that Sraffa arrives at by the end of his explanation of price magnitudes and changes in these in subsistence and single-product, surplus-economy settings.

From the perspective of Marx's analysis, in the same way that Sraffa's explanation of the magnitude of price is to be praised for the importance it accords to the material conditions of reproduction of the commodity, so his explanation of changes in the magnitudes of relative prices is to be praised for the emphasis it places on the importance of changes in the material conditions of production. Indeed, Sraffa even continues to emphasise the latter when the logic of his own analysis appears to contradict it – as in the case of price changes in a joint-product setting. However, also in the same way his fundamental explanation of the magnitude of price is to be criticised for the elimination of the expenditure of labour time, so his explanation of changes in magnitudes of prices is to be similarly criticised.

To begin with, the elimination of the expenditure of labour time in Sraffa's analysis results in a failure to (formally) recognise that productivity changes in the immediate process of production which give rise to changes in relative prices are those with respect to the labour input, i.e., are changes in labour productivity. With the elimination of labour from his analysis, Sraffa is unable to see that relative prices of commodities fall when the same amount of labour produces more output in the same amount of time. Sraffa is unable to conceive of this even implicitly, because in his analysis the labour input is converted into a given amount of wage goods, and there is no reason to suppose, following the logic of this analysis, that wage goods are any more productive of outputs than any other commodity inputs.

The elimination of labour creates analogous problems for Sraffa when he explains changes in relative prices of outputs in terms of changes in relative prices of inputs or basics. This is because, to argue that changes in the prices of basics are the result of changes in techniques of production of these basics, would require Sraffa to argue that changes in the relative prices of basics are due to changes in the methods of production of basics **in terms of themselves**. Even if it could be assumed that there is at least one basic commodity which enters the production of all commodities, say oil, it cannot surely be argued that a fall in the relative price of oil is for the most part due to a rise in the productivity of the oil in terms of itself.

Sraffa's arguments concerning the unpredictable impact of changes in the wage share on relative prices crucially requires one to accept that it is meaningful to layer inputs *ad infinitum*, see costs as historic costs, and reduce costs to equivalence in terms of a *numéraire*. I have noted earlier the problems with seeing inputs and costs in this manner, and I will return to the problem of the *numéraire* below. What needs mention here is that, for Marx, in contrast, changes in the wage share can be seen having a predictable impact on relative prices via their impact on the average rate of profit. An increase in the wage share will in general result in a fall in the average rate of profit for a given rate of surplus value, causing the relative prices of industries with above average organic compositions of capital (or, crudely speaking, higher-than-average capital to labour ratios) to rise, and those with below-average organic compositions of capital to fall. Changes in the wage share can only be said to have no predictable impact on relative prices when the changes in it result from changes in the relative prices of wage goods, and these in turn are due to productivity changes in the wages goods industries which are accompanied by changes in their organic compositions of capital.

Sraffa's argument that the rate of fall in relative prices cannot exceed the rate of fall of the wage share, depends on his assuming away productivity changes in the immediate processes of production and/or the processes of producing inputs. Thus, the relative price of a commodity can fall faster than the fall in wage share if productivity in the immediate process of production is rising. Of course the magnitude of the wage contained in each commodity price will fall in proportion to the increase in labour productivity, but this fall cannot be argued to be due to a fall in the wage share at the aggregate level.

Following from what was said earlier regarding Sraffa's failure to analyse the formation of the general rate of profit, it can be argued that this failure causes Sraffa to mistakenly argue that changes in the conditions of production of non-basics, unlike basics, have no bearing on the relative prices of all commodities. However, to the extent that these changes can be argued to impact on the aggregate surplus produced in the system, and this in turn impact on the general rate of profit, changes in the conditions of production of non-basics can in principle be argued to impact on the relative prices of all commodities, in opposition to Sraffa.

Finally, it can be argued that Sraffa is misguided in seeing his standard commodity construct as aiding him show that changes in the wage share have no determinate impact on relative prices. For Sraffa, the standard commodity is needed to show this because its own relative worth is unresponsive to changes in the wage share. From the perspective of Marx's analysis, it can be argued Sraffa does not seem to appreciate that to show what he wants to show all that is necessary is to demonstrate that all commodities change equiproportionately to the standard in question, and not that this standard is invariable.

This is the case when the standard is money, but not when it is an arbitrarily chosen commodity. To repeat what was said earlier in relation to Ricardo's quest for an invariable standard, money's relative worth is given by its average exchange ratio with all commodities and, as such, whatever impact changes in the wage share have on all commodities, including money, changes in the prices of commodities in relation to one another will remain the same when expressed in terms of money. This also means, incidentally, that when money is a commodity, there is no reason why the relative worth of the measure of price should be invariant to conditions affecting the relative prices of all other commodities.

Extensions

Although most of the discussion of the determinants of changes in relative prices in Sraffa's *Commodities* is to be found in his analysis of prices in a single-product, surplus-economy setting, some discussion of these matters is to be found in the extension of his analysis beyond this setting.

Joint products

When Sraffa moves to a consideration of joint product systems he finds that the conclusions he arrives at by the end of his study of prices in a single-product, surplus-economy setting become more difficult to sustain. Specifically, he finds that in a joint-product, surplus-economy setting improvements in the methods of production of basics may not lead to corresponding falls in the relative prices of commodities. This is because, as noted above, in joint-product systems basics may be produced alongside non-basics such that changes in the rate of profit pertaining to the individual product may offset the implied movement in costs. This conclusion notwithstanding, however, Sraffa argues that while it can no longer be said that an improvement in the methods of production of basics would necessarily lead to a corresponding change in the prices of commodities (and the rate of profit), one could nevertheless 'find an equivalent in a tax (or subsidy) on the production of a particular commodity' (1960, p. 55). The problem with this defence of his major line of argumentation is it suggests he is admitting that in a joint-product setting changes in the relative prices of basics cannot be 'explained' by changes in their methods of production, leaving one with the tautological conclusion that in this setting the changes in the prices of outputs are to be 'explained' by changes in the prices of inputs.

Sraffa also notes that the existence of joint products makes it possible for prices of individual products to fall faster than the wage share and, perhaps more problematically, for a fall in the wage share to not necessarily be accompanied by a corresponding rise in the general rate of profit. Given this, it becomes difficult to show that a change in the wage share gives rise to a corresponding change in the rate of profit and, therefore, a determinate change in relative price. Indeed, as Sraffa also notes, much depends on the specification of the standard in which the wage share is denominated. (*Ibid.*, p. 62)

Non-produced inputs

When taking into consideration non-produced inputs, it would appear that Sraffa sees changes in the magnitudes of prices of commodities produced with these inputs as additionally (in addition to changes in the methods of production) due to changes in the quality of the non-produced inputs used. Taking land as the non-produced input, and agricultural commodities as the output, it would suggest that, where there are several qualities of land used for the production of the same commodity, changes in the relative price magnitudes of agricultural commodities would result from changes in the worst quality of land used in the production of these commodities. This means that, for Sraffa, relative agricultural commodity prices would tend to rise as a result of the extensive development of production – bringing less and less fertile soil into production.

Although Marx's analysis too suggests that where commodities are produced with non-produced inputs changes in the quality of the non-produced input will impact on the price of the commodity in much the same way as that suggested by Sraffa's analysis, Marx's analysis also points to other sources of changes in relative prices of these commodities. Most importantly, it points to the importance of changes in those factors impacting on the level of absolute rent. For example, in the case of land and the production of agricultural commodities, it points to the importance of changes in the strength of demand and imports of agricultural commodities as sources of changes in the relative prices of these commodities. Since Sraffa tacitly denies absolute rent has a bearing on the prices of agricultural commodities, he necessarily fails to see the significance of the above-mentioned changes for these prices.

8.7 The magnitudes of money prices

Mention should also be made of the explanation of money price magnitudes and changes in these magnitudes which emerges from Sraffa's work. To repeat what was said above, Sraffa did not provide any explanation of either money or money prices in his *Commodities*. However, as has been argued above, his work does nevertheless have implications for such an explanation. One implication derived by a number of adherents to Sraffa's thinking is that money is the *numéraire*, and the value of money, like the value of commodities in general, is fundamentally given by the exchangeable worth of basics required to produce it.[30] Not surprisingly, little is said about the value of money and money prices when money is not a produced commodity.

One problem with Sraffian analyses which see money as a *numéraire* is that it ends up explaining the value of money in terms of the methods of producing money in terms of itself. This follows from the fact that money is also necessarily seen by these approaches as a basic commodity.

The more fundamental problem with these analyses from the perspective of Marx's analysis, however, is they do not seem to appreciate that it is not any particular commodity that reduces commodities to equivalence as prices, but the general commodity, or general equivalent. As the general equivalent, even when it is a commodity, the value of money is not (only) determined by the resources (labour time) required for its production, but rather (also) by the average resources (average labour time) required for the production of all commodities it exchanges with. This means that, for Marx, unlike for Sraffian analyses which see money as the *numéraire*, there is no problem with explaining the value of money and money prices when money is state-issued paper money and not a commodity.

A further possible line of thinking emerging from Sraffa's analysis is to see money as the standard of the *numéraire*. In this case, the value of money and the level of money prices would be given by the quantitative relation of money and the *numéraire*. However, what this presupposes is that it is the *numéraire*, and not money, that reduces commodities to equivalence in exchange. I have already discussed the problem with such a supposition.

9
Concluding Remarks

The preceding study has sought to show that Marx's economic analysis of capitalism contains an intelligible and coherent theory of price which is distinct from that of Ricardo and has not been made redundant by the work of Sraffa. The interpretation of Marx's theory of price provided in this study is very different from most modern sympathetic interpretations of this theory and could, in certain respects, be said to revert to more traditional interpretations. It offers what may be described as a physical cost interpretation of Marx's theory of price, including **a physical cost explanation** of commodity inputs, wages and profit. This contrasts with the other interpretations discussed above, that attribute to Marx a neo-Ricardian (Sraffian) explanation, with price being in effect explained by price – the prices of both commodity inputs and commodities comprising wages and profits, albeit denominated in terms of labour time.

9.1 Marx's contribution to the theory of price, or why choose Marx?

Pivotal to the interpretation provided in the present study is how Marx understands price. It is this that permits an appreciation of his explanation of price magnitudes in the form in which he left it in *Capital*. Of importance in this regard is how Marx sees the emergence, purpose, formation and nature of prices. It was argued that Marx sees values as the relative worth of commodities measured by labour time, and that commodities acquire values when they are produced in the context of a division of labour. It was further argued that for Marx commodities acquire **price forms** when the division of labour comes to be mediated by exchange. Prices indicate the exchangeability of the commodities with each other. Commodities acquire a **money price form** when exchange is in turn mediated by money. This form indicates the exchangeability of commodities with money, and through money, the exchangeability of all commodities with each other. That is, the money form of the prices of commodities indicates their general exchangeability. Marx denies that prices are formed in either exchange or production, or even at the end of the production process. Rather, he sees prices as formed in the course of the **reproduction** of commodities. Money plays a vital role in the process of price formation. Ignoring this role is the source of many erroneous theories of money and prices. In capitalism prices are additionally formed in the context of competition between capitalists. Failure to understand how prices are formed in the process of competition in capitalism is a further reason for flawed explanations of prices. Marx sees the purpose of prices to be the reproduction of commodities alongside all other commodities commensurate with social demand. Accordingly, he would have regarded the view that prices facilitate the reproduction of the commodity to meet the needs of the individual producer as superficial, and would have been entirely dismissive of the notion that they facilitate the allocation of resources to maximise consumer satisfaction. For Marx, it is in any case incomes of producers and not price (or quantity) that facilitates the allocation of resources in commodity producing systems.

The preceding view of the emergence, formation and purpose of price leads Marx to see (money) prices as necessarily reflecting both the worth of commodities in relation to one another and the worth of the quantity of money commodities exchange with on average. Specifically, he sees the worth of commodities in relation to one another as reflecting the relative direct and indirect social labour time required for their production, and the worth of money these commodities exchange with as reflecting their relative worth in terms of the relative worth of the money they exchange with, where the latter is given by the average labour time required for the production of the commodities that a given quantity of money circulates over a given period of time. For Marx, prices must reflect values – the physical resources required to produce commodities as measured by labour time – if the reproduction of commodities is to continue, and the price of money must reflect the average labour time required for the production of the commodities circulated by a given quantity of money if money is to serve as the measure of the exchange values of commodities and regulator of commodity exchange in the process of the reproduction of all commodities.

Marx's view of the nature of price strongly suggests that he would have been critical of those views which see relative commodity prices as either reflecting the satisfaction derived from the consumption of commodities or the commodity/factor inputs required for their production. To see relative prices as reflecting utility in the manner of Neoclassicals, it was argued, presumes that the relative prices are formed in the process of exchange between individuals who are naturally endowed with commodities and who exchange them primarily for the purposes of satisfying individual consumption desires. As noted in the discussion of Sraffa's theory of price, to see prices of commodity outputs as reflecting the exchangeable worth of commodity inputs required to produce these outputs misrepresents the very essence of all social production systems; production involving human labour – the expenditure of social labour time. And, to see prices as reflecting the exchangeable worth of factor inputs in the manner of Post Keynesians implies seeing the latter as somehow theoretically and historically antecedent to price.

Marx's view of the nature of price also suggests that he would have been critical of those views of the value of money which see it as reflecting either the demand for money as a medium of exchange in relation to its availability, or the command of money over the goods required to sustain labour. Marx would have been critical of the former because he sees money as being held for purposes other than that of only the medium of exchange (circulation), and, in the context of state-issued paper money, that its quantity could not in any case be seen as given in relation to demand for it. He denies that money's value reflects its command over factor inputs, especially labour, because there is no reason to suppose this.

It is the preceding understanding of prices (and money) that conditions Marx's approach to the explanation of their magnitudes in all commodity production systems in general, and capitalism in particular. Specifically, it is this understanding of prices that causes Marx to make an analytical distinction between relative and money prices, and begin his explanation of the magnitudes of prices with an explanation of the former. This is because, if it is accepted that the purpose of prices is the reproduction of commodities, then what matters in the final instance as far as the magnitudes of prices is concerned, is the inputs commanded by commodities for their reproduction, i.e., the worth of commodities **in relation to** one another. Of course, since Marx sees money as mediating exchange and prices as necessarily assuming money forms, there is also a need for an explanation of the magnitudes of money prices and their linkage with relative prices. Further, if the purpose of prices is the reproduction of commodities, then the prices whose magnitudes must be explained in the first instance should also be seen as **equilibrium** or **reproduction prices** – prices which facilitate the balanced reproduction of commodities. Marx sees these prices as the appropriate point of departure for the explanation of actual price magnitudes, because the explanation of the latter must logically be the explanation of prices as deviations from their equilibrium levels. In this regard, Marx would have criticised those approaches which begin their explanation of price magnitudes with actual or disequilibrium prices, *viz.*, Post Keynesian and Austrian approaches. Lastly, since Marx sees reproduction price as also formed in the process of competition in a capitalist setting, he conceives of the equilibrium prices whose magnitudes are to be explained in the first instance as also competitive prices – prices of production. It was noted on a number of occasions that, in contrast with many modern theories of price, the notion of competition underlying Marx's theory is not a static one. Rather, for him, competition needs to be seen as a process, and competitive prices need to be seen as formed in this process. This means that he would most certainly have rejected the view that there is need for the explanation of prices as non-competitive as opposed to competitive ones simply because there are different prices for the same product, and/or different products, and/or different techniques used in the production of the same good, and/or the appropriation of different rates of profit within a sector or between sectors.

Seeing prices as formed in the process of the reproduction of commodities, for the purpose of facilitating the latter, and reflecting social labour time, causes Marx to see the magnitudes of prices as fundamentally determined by the magnitudes of social labour time required for the reproduction of commodities. That is, it causes him to see the magnitudes of the prices of commodities as determined by their respective values. Marx does not deny that prices could deviate from values when explaining price magnitudes in the context of capitalism. Rather, his argument is that values remain the most important determinant of prices in spite of this deviation. He is also not opposed to the idea that supply and demand must be seen as in balance when explaining price magnitudes as reproduction or equilibrium price magnitudes. He simply considers it nonsensical to explain these price magnitudes by the balance of supply and demand. He would, in any case, most certainly have opposed the view that price magnitudes could be explained by the (marginal) preferences attached by individuals to the consumption of different commodities because for him, among other things, preferences or utility cannot be meaningfully reduced to equivalence. It was noted in the discussion of the Neoclassical approach that seeing preferences of individuals as revealed preferences does not help in this regard, since it only ends up jettisoning the explanation of price magnitudes by preferences and replacing it with one in which prices are explained by prices – prices being tautologically argued to be the manifestation of preferences which are 'revealed' in the process of exchange (see fn 43, Chapter 6). Marx would also have opposed the view that prices are explained by the prices of commodity inputs because this would mean accepting, on the one hand, that it is possible and meaningful to differentiate between commodity inputs and outputs and, on the other hand, that commodity inputs can be reduced to equivalence by something other than labour or money – at least money as a non-produced commodity. And, lastly, Marx would have denied that commodity prices could be seen as explained by the prices of factor inputs because this would require accepting the view that the prices of commodity inputs could be reduced to the prices of factor inputs. It is evident from his discussion of the theory of price in Adam Smith that he considered such a reduction to be impossible, and in effect a rejection of the existence of fixed capital.

Since Marx sees money playing a vital role in the formation of price as the measure of exchangeable worth, and since, as a consequence, he sees price as assuming a money form, it follows that he sees prices as determined additionally (in addition to its determination by relative labour time) by the value of money. For Marx, money is not necessarily commodity money, but can and does assume a paper form, including a state-issued paper money form. He sees money as held not only for the purposes of facilitating spot and future commodity transactions, but also to settle debts and as a store of value (although he sees this as a limited function in capitalism). He sees the value of money as given by the average labour time of the commodities which a given quantity of money circulates over a given period of time, and, where money is a commodity, ultimately by the resources required to produce the commodity that functions as money. Commodities, in turn, are seen as acquiring money price magnitudes which reflect the labour time they are notionally expected to command for the purposes of their reproduction. It is with these prices that they enter the process of exchange. Although Marx sees the value of money as given by the quantitative relation of money and commodities, even when money is a commodity, he is not a quantity theorist in the sense that he sees the value of money and money prices as given in the process of circulation and determined by the quantitative relation of money and commodities at each and every point in time. It was argued above that, for a variety of reasons, Marx considered it unlikely that the exchangeable worth of money as given by the quantitative relation of commodities and money (including what is accepted as performing the functions of money) would reflect the (equilibrium) value of money at any given point in time. Indeed, although Marx sees commodities as coming into circulation with given money prices and money with a given value, it is entirely possible for there to be an excess or shortfall in the quantity of money in relation to its intrinsic, equilibrium worth at any point of time.

Finally, it is because Marx sees commodity production systems as characterised by a separation of sale from purchase, that he sees **actual money prices** as mostly disequilibrium prices, albeit disequilibrium prices which on occasion must gravitate towards equilibrium ones but which can nevertheless deviate from the latter quite significantly and for considerable periods of time. Moreover, because he sees capitalism as a system in which the conditions of production and products are constantly changing as a result of continuous revolutions in technology, he sees equilibrium prices as in continuous flux. He argues that there are forces at work in capitalism tending towards the cumulative and widespread deviation of actual from reproduction prices, much as there are also economy-wide forces, including crises, which tend to bring them back together in the context of constantly shifting equilibrium prices. Accordingly, he would reject those theories of price which deny such deviations of actual from equilibrium price, or see them as random, isolated, and the product of errors in decision-making owing to information gaps. For Marx, to see price deviations in this manner is to misunderstand both how prices are formed and their fundamental nature. It is typically to see prices as formed in a process of exchange which is devoid of any link to the (expanded) reproduction of commodities and without any reference to the incessant technological change underlying and conditioning this reproduction.

9.2   Locating Marx's theory of price

In the spectrum of price theories, Marx's theory can be located among those often referred to as supply-side, objective theories as opposed to demand-side, subjective theories. This does not mean that Marx paid no heed to demand factors. He did. However, for him, if demand has a fundamental bearing on prices over the long run, it would be through its impact on the conditions of production. Even over the short-run, demand would only have an impact on price if there were significant changes in its level (the level of demand). Otherwise, the impact of changes in demand would tend to be on output levels. Among the supply-side approaches, Marx's theory of price is to be clustered with the physical cost of production approaches as opposed to, say, the commodity and factor input price approaches. That is, within the supply-side camp, it places Marx on the other side of the fence from Sraffa and the Post Keynesians, but alongside Ricardo and non-Sraffian neo-Ricardians. While Marx and Ricardo are to be found in the same grouping, and while it is evident that Marx's theory of price owes a great deal to the work of Ricardo, it should be apparent from what was argued above that Marx's theory of price is very different from that of Ricardo in a number of crucial respects. Undoubtedly the most important of these is the distinction drawn by Marx between value and price, and, related to this, their respective theories of money.

9.3   The significance of rehabilitating Marx's theory of price

The significance of the preceding account of Marx's theory of price is not only that it shows Marx had an intelligible, logical and consistent theory of price, but also that it contributes to a growing debate regarding the validity of the accepted foundations of what is seen to be orthodox or mainstream economic theory. There can be little doubt that these foundations have been shaken badly by the recent, on-going, turmoil in the world economic system, with some of the most important devotees of economic orthodoxy expressing concerns about the fundamental principles of economics which have guided them for most of their working lives. One need only recount in this connection the astonishingly forthright, and widely quoted, testimony of the previous chairman of the US Federal Reserve, Alan Greenspan, to the US Congress, in which he candidly stated that:

> I found a flaw in the model that I perceived is the critical functioning structure that defines how the world works. That's precisely the reason I was shocked...I still do not fully understand why it happened, and obviously to the extent that I figure it happened and why, I will change my views. (Testimony to the Congressional Committee for Oversight and Government Reform, 28 October 2008)

Thus far most of the discussion within the mainstream has been in terms of the perceived weaknesses of certain of these foundations with a view to strengthening them. What the presentation of Marx's theory of price and accompanying critique of modern theories of price hopefully has shown is that there are intractable problems with these foundations, requiring a tearing down of the entire edifice and a new beginning. In this regard, one can only echo the words of the winner of the 2001 Nobel Memorial prize in economics, Joseph Stiglitz:

> Changing paradigms is not easy. Too many have invested too much in the wrong models. Like the Ptolemaic attempts to preserve earth-centric views of the universe, there will be heroic efforts to add complexities and refinements to the standard paradigm. The resulting models will be an improvement and policies based on them may do better, but they too are likely to fail. Nothing less than a paradigm shift will do. (*Financial Times*, 19 August 2010)

Most certainly Stiglitz was not thinking of a paradigm shift to Marx's economics when he penned these words. However, it is hoped what the preceding study has shown is that nothing short of such a shift will really do.

Notes

Chapter 1   Introduction

1 See, for example, Colander et al. (2009), and Lawson (2009).
2 See, for example, Steedman (1977, 1991), Roncaglia (1978, 2009), Keen (2001), and Sinha (2003, 2010).
3 More recently, the validity of Marx's value analysis has been questioned on the grounds that we have shifted to a phase of 'cognitive capitalism' in which the production and dissemination of knowledge are alleged to be pivotal in defining the economic system. The labour theory of value of Marx is considered to be irrelevant in this context because labour increasingly produces immaterial things, including knowledge, whose value cannot be measured in terms of labour time. See Fine et al. (2010) for an elaboration and critique of the cognitive capitalism rejection of Marx's theory of value, and De Angelis and Harvie (2009) for an example of how cognitive labour can be integrated into Marx's labour theory of value framework.
4 A far from exhaustive list includes Sweezy (1968), Mandel (1968), Howard and King (1975), Fine (1975), Rosdolsky (1977), Fine and Harris (1979), Harvey (1982), Foley (1986), Itoh (1988), Fine and Saad-Filho (2004) and Kliman (2007).
5 See Meek (1977, Chapter 5) for an elaboration of this point.
6 See, for example, Baumol (1974).

Chapter 2   Marx's Theory of Price in the Simple Circulation of Commodities

1 This also means, incidentally, that the study of the simple commodity circulation in Marx should not be seen as akin to the study of Smith's 'early and rude state', i.e., the study of a distinct, antecedent, economic system. See Rubin (1972) and Banaji (1979) on this point.
2 See Chapter 6, Section 3, below for an elaboration of the Neoclassical view of the exchange process.
3 See Marx (1976, pp. 162–3).
4 It is perhaps pertinent to note here the criticism of Marx's view of the emergence of money by Ingham (see for example Ingham, 2001, 2004 and 2006). According to Ingham, Marx sees money and money prices as emerging in the process of **bilateral** exchange or barter. He argues that the latter need not, and routinely does not, produce a single price for a given commodity (Ingham, 2006, p. 260). Rather, for such prices to emerge, there would necessarily have to be multilateral exchanges, and for **multilateral** exchanges to take place money would have to exist. In other words, money would have to be 'logically anterior' to the market (*Ibid.*). However, it should be evident from the preceding that Ingham misrepresents Marx's view of the emergence of money

and money prices. He incorrectly attributes to Marx what is really a Neoclassical view of the emergence of money; that money emerges to overcome the difficulties of barter (see Chapter 6, Section 2). Since, for Marx, money emerges when one commodity begins to mediate an increasing number of interdependent exchanges, it is difficult to see how he could be interpreted as seeing money emerging in the context of bilateral exchanges. As will be argued again below, it is because Marx sees money as emerging in a multilateral exchange process that he refers to it having a 'medium of circulation' as opposed to a 'medium of exchange' function. Moreover, while Marx saw money as also facilitating the development of the multilateral exchange process, he would most certainly have denied that its emergence is anterior to this process.

5 It needs emphasising that this does not mean that Marx sees prices as facilitating the allocation of productive resources in the manner of Neoclassicals since, most importantly, there is no sense in his analysis of prices providing 'signals' to either individuals or entrepreneurs. I will elaborate further on this point when discussing the Neoclassical approach in Chapter 6, Section 3.

6 It is interesting to note here that Marx sees commodities continuing to be values in a post-capitalist, possibly socialist, system. He says, '...after the abolition of the capitalist mode of production, but still retaining social production, the determination of value continues to prevail in the sense that the regulation of labour time and the distribution of social labour among the various production groups, ultimately the book-keeping encompassing all this, become more essential than ever' (Marx, 1981, p. 851).

7 The term reproduction price is preferred to that of equilibrium price because of the connotation of equilibrium price as representing an unchanging centre of gravity.

8 In the analysis of the simple circulation of commodities it is presumed that the producers of commodities are the direct producers.

9 See Moseley (2000, 2008) for this textual evidence.

10 It is for this reason that it is mistaken to argue, as for example Sinha (2010, p. 173) does, that Marx implicitly assumes the labour that produces money is necessarily unskilled, simple labour.

11 See, for example, Foley (1982) and other interpreters of Marx from the New Interpretation school.

12 Marx notes that tokens appear as replacements for money in the process of circulation because of certain tendencies for the natural and artificial degradation of the media of circulation and not any conscious activity on the part of the state. Natural degradation refers to the erosion of the metal as a result of the use of the media, and artificial degradation to such actions as 'clippings' and dilution of the metal content of money as circulating media with other metals (see 1970, pp. 107–16).

13 For an account of the historical origins of the quantity theory of money see Bordo (1989).

14 See also Brunhoff (1976, p. 40) and Lapavitsas (2000, pp. 642–3).

15 This does not mean that Marx regards abstract labour as homogenous labour in the manner of Ricardo. To establish the equivalence of labour, Ricardo simply assumed that the type of labour performed, the actual concrete labour performed, is homogenous. For Marx the labour expended is in fact of many different concrete types. However, what all labour has in common is the fact

that it represents human effort in general. That is, for Marx, different concrete types of labour are also abstract general labour.
16   Marx makes a distinction between simple and complex general labour seeing the latter as multiples of the former.

Chapter 3   Marx's Theory of Price – Capitalist Commodity Production

1   See Marx (1972, pp. 455–61; 1981, pp. 459–79, pp. 515–24) for an elaboration of the distinction between productive and interest-bearing capital.
2   For details of the logic and structure of Marx's presentation in *Capital* the interested reader is referred to Nicolaus (1973), Foley (1986), Saad-Filho (2002) and Fine and Saad-Filho (2004).
3   It warrants noting here that Marx refers to prices of production in *Theories of Surplus Value* as 'cost-prices', i.e., as including the profit on capital advanced, while in *Capital* he distinguishes between prices of production and cost-prices, seeing the latter as only referring to the capital advanced component of price.
4   See Fine and Saad-Filho (2004, Chapter 10) for an elaboration of this.
5   See Ochoa and Glick (1992), Duménil and Lévy (2002) and Tsoulfidis and Tsaliki (2005) for examples of empirical attempts to validate the tendency towards an equalised inter-industry rate of profit.
6   As Shaikh has argued, none of this should be taken as implying that producers are aware of the economy-wide average rate of profit and set prices of production accordingly (1982). Rather, the price of production should be seen as the outcome of a competitive process in which producers seek to reproduce their commodities while simultaneously attempting to maximise returns on outlays (see *Ibid.*, p. 77).
7   Marx refers to the ratio of C to V as, *inter alia*, the technical, organic and value compositions of capital. The technical composition of capital refers to the physical ratio of means of production to labour inputs e.g., numbers of machines to labour, the organic composition to the value ratio of the two inputs, and the value composition to the value ratio of the two inputs taking into account the impact of changes in techniques of production on the values of the inputs. In presenting the transformation of values into prices of production and the formation of the general rate of profit, Marx abstracts from technical change, hence he uses the term 'organic composition of capital' to refer to the value ratio of C to V.
8   Foley, 1986, Chapter 6, provides details of these and other problems which result in Marx's analysis from transforming inputs into prices of production.
9   See Fine (1986c) and Saad-Filho (1997).
10   The landmark empirical study showing the existence of significant increasing returns to scale (decreasing costs) in manufacturing is, of course, that of Young (1928). More recent empirical studies along similar lines include those by Griliches and Ringstad (1971), Cripps and Tarling (1973), Scherer (1980), Owen (1983), McCombie (1985), Hall (1988), Fingleton and McCombie (1998), Fingleton (2003) and McCombie and Roberts (2007). Junius (1997) provides evidence for significant levels of increasing returns in services in general, and Hughes and Mester (1998) for the banking sector in particular.

11 Marx also refers to state-issued paper money backed by commodities (see, for example, 1973, pp. 131–6 and 1981, pp. 523–4), but this form of money will not be considered in the present study since it is felt that its inclusion would not add much to the analytical insights derived from the consideration of commodity and inconvertible state-issued paper money.

12 In this respect it is difficult to understand why Marx has been repeatedly branded a 'metallist' by friends (e.g., Nelson, 2005) and foes (e.g., Schumpeter, 1954 and Lavoie, 1986) alike.

13 The logic of Marx's analysis would seem to suggest that the quantity of money in a state-issued paper money environment should be seen as what has come to be referred to as narrow money or M1 (i.e., notes and coins and non-interest bearing liabilities of the banking system). Interest-bearing liabilities are excluded because, even when they are held for the purposes of making purchases and settling debts, they typically need to be converted into either demand deposits or cash before they could be used for these purposes.

14 See, for example, Lapavitsas (2000).

15 'Intrinsic price' is preferred to 'equilibrium price' here, as reproduction price is preferred to equilibrium price in the case of commodity money due, again, to the centre of gravity and static connotation of the latter.

16 See Fine and Saad-Filho (2004) for an elaboration of Marx's theory of agricultural rent.

17 See Marx (1981, p. 797).

18 Ball (1986) makes this point in an enlightening debate with Fine (1986b) on Marx's theory of agricultural rent.

19 Some commentators have argued that Marx failed to recognise that a part of the value transferred to the monopolist could be the consequence of implied lower real wages due to monopolies operating in wage goods sectors (see, for example, Howard and King, 1975, p. 138). However, not only is it unclear that wages goods sectors are particularly monopolistic, it overlooks Marx's discussion of absolute rent and the value of labour power.

20 See Marx (1969b, p. 30; 1981, p. 478).

21 Although Marx sees deviations of market prices from prices of production as typically following a cyclical pattern, it does not mean he denies the possibility for such deviations being random, sectorally isolated (in the case of commodities) and unconnected with the business cycle. For Marx, such random and isolated fluctuations are always possible in capitalism, as in all commodity producing systems, where sale and purchase are separated.

22 See Itoh (1988) and Sherman (1991) for fairly comprehensive accounts of Marx's view of the cyclical movement of capitalist economies.

23 See Marx's letter to Engels 22 April 1868, in Marx and Engels (1983, pp. 131–3).

24 To the extent that the increase in prices leads to a fall in the value of labour power and an increase in the rate of exploitation, it must also be seen as one of the countervailing influences in the tendency for the rate of profit to fall in the upswing of the cycle.

Chapter 4   Marx on Smith and Ricardo

1 Marx also praises Ricardo for arguing, in opposition to Smith, that changes in the aggregate wage share would not cause the aggregate price level to rise

but instead aggregate profits to fall and, as a result of differing organic compositions (capital–labour ratios), some commodity prices to fall and others to rise (see 1969b, pp. 199–200).

2 Marx sees Ricardo's failure in this regard as due to his failure to distinguish between value and price of production and, by implication, his failure to conceive of the transfer of value between sectors in the process of the formation of the general rate of profit and prices. See also Milonakis and Fine (2009, p. 57).

3 It is of note that Sraffa does precisely this in the construction of his own invariable standard, the standard commodity.

4 See Shaikh (1979, 1980).

Chapter 5 Marxist Interpretations of Marx's Theory of Price

1 See Sweezy (1968, p. 115), Dobb (1973, p. 159) and Meek (1977, p. 108).

2 See, for example, Roncaglia (1977) and Steedman (1977, 1991).

3 A notable exception here is Meek, who explicitly accepted that the proposed solutions were along the lines of Sraffa's theory of price, and even proposed accepting Sraffa's models as providing the general technical basis for Marxist analyses of price (see Meek, 1977, p. 132).

4 Marx says in this regard, 'A monopoly price for certain commodities simply transfers a portion of the profit made by the other commodity producers to the commodities with the monopoly price' (1981, p. 1001).

5 It is generally acknowledged to have its origins in the independent works of Foley (1982) and Duménil (1983–4).

6 See Foley (1982, pp. 37–8).

7 See Foley (1986, pp. 98–102).

8 See Duménil (1983–4, pp. 441–2).

9 For more details of the proposed NI solution see Mohun (1994).

10 See Foley (1982, p. 37) and Mohun (1994, p. 404).

11 See, for example, Foley (1982, p. 99).

12 See, for example, Fine et al. (2004).

13 A similar point is made by Fine et al. (2004).

14 See Freeman and Carchedi (1996a), Freeman (1996a, 1996b), Freeman et al. (2004) and Kliman (2007).

15 See, for example, Kliman and McGlone (1988).

16 See, for example, Freeman (1996b).

17 See the various contributions in Freeman and Carchedi (1996a).

18 See, for example, Mongiovi (2002) and Laibman (2004).

19 It warrants adding, but will not be expanded on here, that Marx's reproduction prices are not the same as Walrasian general equilibrium prices, much as his 'actual prices' are not akin to Walrasian disequilibrium prices. To equate the two, as a number of TSSI proponents have done, is to seriously misunderstand both Marx and Walras (and his disciples).

20 See, for example, Marx (1976, pp. 317–18; 1981, pp. 207–9).

21 See, for example, Kliman (2007, p. 98).

22 See Carchedi and de Haan (1996, p. 141).

23 See Kliman and McGlone (1999).

Chapter 6   The Neoclassical Theory of Price

1   Dobb notes that Jevon's *Theory of Political Economy* and Menger's *Grundsätze* both appeared in 1871 and Walras's *Éléments* in 1874, with all three paying tribute to H.H. Gossen's pioneering 1854 work entitled 'Development of the Laws of Human Action and the consequent Principles of Human Commerce' (1973, p. 167, p. 192).

2   It needs recognising that the nature of the break between the Neoclassical school of thought and that of Classical economics is so fundamental that it makes the term 'Neoclassical' something of a misnomer. I refer the reader to the excellent article by Aspromourgos (1986) which makes precisely this point. Notwithstanding this, however, I will retain the term in the present work because of its continued and widespread use in the literature.

3   See Arnsperger and Varoufakis (2008) for an instructive discussion of certain of these principles.

4   See Mankiw and Romer (1991) for what is still widely regarded as the definitive New Keynesian theory of price.

5   See Kreps (1990) for a critical yet sympathetic presentation of the Walrasian General Equilibrium theory of price.

6   See Horwitz (2000) for a modern Austrian view of the theory of price.

7   Walrasian and Austrian approaches sometimes have the prefix 'neo' to indicate that they are modern incarnations of traditional lines of thinking identified with these labels. While recognising that it is frequently useful to make such distinctions in presenting the current thinking of these sub-schools of Neoclassical thought, I will refrain from its use in the present study. I will instead make clear as and when necessary how current thinking diverges from traditional thinking in respect of these two sub-schools.

8   See, for example, Dobb (1973), Himmelweit (1977) and Lichtenstein (1983).

9   The so-called 'Edgeworth box' approach adopted by many Neoclassicals is perhaps the best illustration of this point of departure.

10   Gee (1991) provides an excellent account of the exchange process in Neo-classical economics.

11   See Hahn (1984, p. 91), Tobin (1985), Rogers (1989, p. 6, p. 46), Smithin (2003, pp. 20–1) and Hoover (2007, p. 418).

12   See Horwitz (2000, p. 66).

13   Kirman notes that 'production as it is typically treated in the general equilibrium model can be argued to yield little more than a glorified exchange economy' (1989, p. 135). This is because, if production is brought into the analysis in anything like a meaningful way, it is unclear that the postulated exchange process will lead to unique equilibria. See also Kehoe (1985) on this point.

14   See Horwitz (2000, p. 67).

15   See, for example, Sinha (2010, p. 209).

16   Kreps says of the Walrasian general equilibrium approach in this regard that it fails to provide any sense of how markets work. 'There is no model here of who sets prices, or what gets exchanged for what, when, and where.... Because of this, a Walrasian equilibrium is a *reduced form* solution concept; it describes what we imagine will be the outcome of some underlying and unmodeled process. It seems natural to think that we could increase (or

decrease) our faith in the concept of a Walrasian equilibrium if we had some sense of how markets really do operate' (Kreps, 1990, p. 195).

17   This result is known in the relevant literature as the Sonnenschein-Mantel-Debreu theory, after its main exponents. See Kirman (1989, 1992) and Rizvi (1994) for a technical explanation of this theory.

18   See Hahn (1984), Kirman (1989, 1992) and Rizvi (1994, 2007).

19   See Endres (1997, p. 223) and Horwitz (2000, p. 21).

20   See Debreu (1959, p. 28) and Kreps (1990, p. 195).

21   See Horwitz (2000, p. 123).

22   Roll notes that Menger explicitly draws this inference (see 1973, p. 390).

23   See Horwitz (2000, p. 35).

24   It is not clear what Neoclassicals mean by 'resources' when referring to the 'allocation of resources'. While most Neoclassicals appear to subscribe to the view that it refers to 'factors' of production or 'inputs' into production, there are also differences between them as to what these factors or inputs include, most notably in respect of capital and entrepreneurship.

25   See Horwitz (2000, p. 30).

26   See Hahn (1984, p. 92).

27   A good illustration of the Neoclassical confusion on this point is provided by Friedman when he states, on the one hand, that 'Prices serve as guideposts to where resources are wanted most....' (1976, p. 9) and, on the other hand, 'Prices of products in relation to the costs of producing them determine the distribution of resources among industries....' (*Ibid.*).

28   See Shand (1984, p. 56).

29   One of the seminal Neoclassical works in this regard is considered to be Pigou (1949).

30   Friedman (1956) and Patinkin (1956) are often seen as providing the founding modern Neoclassical analyses of the value of money along these lines.

31   See Endres (1997, p. 215).

32   It is recognised, however, that there can be many sets of *Pareto optimal* equilibrium prices – one for every distribution of income (see Hahn, 1984, p. 74).

33   See Howard (1983), Hahn (1984), Rogers (1989), Kreps (1990) and Blaug (2007) for elaborations of the assumptions made by Walrasians in order to 'prove' the existence of equilibrium prices.

34   '[Hayek] argues that to the extent that economics is an empirical science it is because of the "assertion that such a tendency [towards equilibrium] exists"'(Horwitz, 2000, p. 25).

35   See Shand (1984, p. 38) and Horwitz (2000, p. 24).

36   See Frisch (1971).

37   The concept of a perfectly competitive price comes mostly from New Keynesian analyses.

38   See Shand (1984, pp. 125–30).

39   See Endres (1997, p. 223).

40   See Hortwitz (2000, p. 67).

41   Neoclassicals typically make a distinction between accounting costs and subjectively assessed 'economic' or 'opportunity' costs. Accounting costs are simply those noted by accountants of a firm as being incurred in the production of a good. Economic or opportunity costs are '...what must be fore-

gone to acquire that item' (Mankiw and Taylor, 2010, p. 256). What must be foregone can be both pecuniary and non-pecuniary. It would seem that the particular importance of this concept of economic cost is that it allows Neo-classicals to conceive of profit/interest as part of cost, thereby putting it on the same footing as wages and other necessary costs of production.

42 Kirman comments that '...if we do not deal with the aggregation problem then we should be honest from the outset and assert simply that *by assumption* we postulate that each sector of the economy behaves as one individual and not claim any spurious microjustification' (1989, p. 138). See also Keen (2001, Chapter 2) and Lee and Keen (2004) for elaborations of this point.

43 Some Neoclassicals have invoked the notion of revealed preference to give pref-erences a tangible homogeneous existence. However, it is difficult to avoid the impression that it is little more than a tautology – that relative exchange ratios reflect relative preferences because individuals express their relative preferences in relative exchange ratios. Indeed, to avoid this impression one would need to argue, for example, that exchange or some other economic process reduces pref-erences of different individuals to equivalence. Although one can understand how and why exchange in the context of a division of labour can be argued to reduce concrete heterogeneous labour to abstract general labour, it is difficult to understand how and why it might do this with subjective preferences. Indeed, and to repeat a point made earlier, the notion of **equivalent subjective preferences** would seem to be a contradiction in terms.

44 Brinkman (1999, p. 42) cites a number of these studies.

45 See fn 10 Chapter 3.

46 Why Marx considered technological change to be endogenous and continuous in capitalism is beyond the scope of the present study, but an insightful exposition of this is to be found in Fine and Saad-Filho (2004).

47 See Shand (1984).

48 Keen contends it is mathematical nonsense to argue, as Neoclassicals do, that individual firms in a perfectly competitive market setting face perfectly flat demand curves, while the market demand curve, seen as the sum of the demand curves facing the individual producer, is assumed to be downward sloping. As Keen puts it, 'If you add up a huge number of flat lines, you will get one very long flat line. If you break one downward sloping line into many lines, you will have many downward sloping lines' (2001, p. 98).

49 See for example Lipsey and Chrystal (2007, p. 164).

50 For standard expositions of the MQM see Friedman (1956, 1976 and 1989), Laidler (1982, 1990) and Vane and Thompson (1979).

51 Goodhart (1984, 1989) can be regarded as a notable first in this regard, and F. Mishkin's *The Economics of Money, Banking and Financial Markets*, 2006, as an example of a recent Neoclassical monetary economics textbook which attrib-utes explicit importance to monetary accommodation in aggregate money price level determination.

52 See, for example, the survey article by Judd and Scadding (1982) for a dis-cussion of early empirical studies pointing to volatility in income velocity of circulation of narrow money stock (or, what is the same thing, unstable demand for narrow money). It needs noting, however, that a number of Neoclassicals have rejected these findings of instability in income velocity, arguing that they are the result of, among other things, the time period chosen, the specification

of the model being tested and the statistical methods used (see Hillinger and Süssmuth, 2008, and McCallum and Nelson, 2010, for reviews of the relevant literature).

53 See Shand (1984, pp. 160–1).

54 While Walrasians too acknowledge the possible absence of some futures markets, rather than accepting that this could cause actual prices to deviate from equilibrium prices, they attempt to deal with this phenomenon through the somewhat dubious constructs of temporary equilibrium and contingent commodities. See the excellent elaboration of this point in Howard (1983).

55 See, for example, Hahn (1984, p. 82).

56 See Loasby (1991, p. 65) and Horwitz (2000, pp. 31–2) for Austrian expositions of the role of entrepreneurs in the adjustment process.

57 It is quite evident that the recent massive increases in money printing in the US and other advanced countries have not percolated into the hands of individuals or increased bank liabilities proportionately.

Chapter 7   The Post Keynesian Theory of Price

1 The term itself has been the subject of dispute, with a leading Post Keynesian, Paul Davidson, arguing that there should be no hyphen between Post and Keynesian to differentiate true adherents from less catholic brethren who might be labelled post-Keynesian or even neo-Keynesian (see Davidson, 2003–4). Without entering into the semantics of this debate, the present chapter will use the term Post Keynesian to describe the corpus of theory which is the subject of the present chapter.

2 Notable exceptions are Lavoie (2005, 2006), who explicitly includes Sraffians in his own definition of Post Keynesianism, and Mongiovi (2003) who sees no necessary incompatibility on methodological grounds between the two approaches.

3 See Dunn (2000, p. 350; 2008, p. 45).

4 See Dunn (2008, pp. 29–30).

5 Keynes even says he called his theory 'a general theory' only in the sense that he was '…chiefly concerned with the behaviour of the economic system as a whole, – with aggregate incomes, aggregate profits, aggregate output, aggregate employment, aggregate investment, aggregate saving rather than with the incomes, profits, output, employment, investment and saving of particular industries, firms or individuals…' and not that he sought to develop a general theory of the functioning of the economic system (Keynes 1973, p. xxxii).

6 See Rotheim (1981, p. 577).

7 Rotheim points out that Keynes explicitly considers his view of the exchange process as reflecting the attitude of businesses, as opposed to that of private consumers, which he sees as the Neoclassical approach (*Ibid.*).

8 The Post Keynesian view of money as anterior to the circulation of commodities is most closely identified with the so-called neo-Chartalists subgrouping. According to neo-Chartalists, money comes into existence by state decree and has value prior to, and outside of, the process of commodity exchange. For more on the neo-Chartalist view of money see Wray (2001, 2002, 2003, and 2010) and Ingham (2001, 2004 and 2006).

9 See Kenyon (1979, p. 34). It is perhaps fair to say that this distinction is less common among Post Keynesians nowadays than in the past, although for those not making the distinction it is unclear how prices are seen as formed in sectors using considerable amounts of non-produced inputs as compared with those using relatively few of these inputs.

10 A good example of this line of thinking is provided by the neo-Chartalist, Post Keynesian G. Ingham. In response to criticisms of his views on money by Lapavitsas (2005) and Dodd (2005), Ingham argues 'Money has value not because it comprises a commodity with fixed intrinsic value...but because it is "the value of things without the things themselves" (Simmel, 1978[1907], p. 121)' (2006, p. 261).

11 It is unclear from Post Keynesian analyses what role agricultural and raw material prices play given that these are implicitly, if not explicitly, seen as set in the context of bargaining between individuals in the process of exchange and not by producers seeking to attain target rates of return on capital.

12 See Shapiro and Mott (1995), Lee (1998) and Lavoie (2001).

13 See, for example, Shapiro (2003, 2005).

14 See, for example, Lee (1998, 2003) and Lavoie (2001, 2006).

15 See, for example, Kenyon (1979), Shapiro and Mott (1995), Lee (1998, 2003), and Lavoie (2001, 2006).

16 See, for example, Shapiro and Mott (1995), Lee (2003), and Shapiro and Sawyer (2003).

17 See Kenyon (1979).

18 It should be recalled here the sympathy Keynes expressed for the view that prices mostly reflect direct and indirect wage costs (see 1973, pp. 101–2).

19 It will be recalled that for Post Keynesians a change in the money wage implies a corresponding change in the value of money.

20 See Chick (2000).

21 The so-called Monetary Circuit approach, whose adherents see themselves as belonging to the Post Keynesian school, conceive of money as credit and even consider exchange mediated by coin as barter (see Graziani, 1996, 2003). Victoria Chick, a prominent Post Keynesian, argues in opposition to this approach that 'the feature which distinguishes money from credit is the general acceptability of deposits, as against the personal quality of credit. The central mystery of modern banking is that expenditure against a bank credit agreement gives rise to deposits, which transforms a bilateral contract into a liquid, multi-laterally accepted, asset. In Post Keynesian thinking, the status of money is given to banks' liabilities, not their assets. This does not diminish the importance of credit, but...argues that it is the proximate *cause* of money' (2000, p. 131).

22 The Monetary Circuit approach see credit money as coming into existence through bank lending to entrepreneurs for both working and fixed capital formation (see Graziani, 2003; Rochon, 1999, 2009; Gnos, 2009). It needs noting, however, that the emphasis placed by this approach on bank lending for capital formation tends to diminish the importance accorded to internal sources of finance – a traditional stick used by Post Keynesians to beat the Neoclassical loanable funds theory.

23 See Davidson (1978b), Moore (1988) and Chick (2000).

24 See Davidson (1978b, p. 66).

25 The Monetary Circuit approach tends to see the value of money as given by money's exchange ratio with all factor inputs and not simply labour (see, for example, Rochon, 2009).

26 The endogenous, or horizontalist, view of money is seen as having its origins in the work of Kaldor (1970, 1982) and Weintraub (1978), and subsequently developed by Moore (1979a, 1983, and 1988), Lavoie (1984), Rochon (1999, 2009) and others.

27 It needs to be said that the extreme endogenous money approach is no longer accepted by most Post Keynesians, including some of its earlier proponents, since, among other things, it appears to contradict Keynes' theory of liquidity preference. In Keynes' theory banks are accorded a key role in determining whether or not *ex ante* investment plans of productive enterprises are realised, while in the endogenous money theory (and the Monetary Circuit approach) banks are seen as passively accommodating any and all demands for loans. Critics of the endogenous money approach argue that the passive accommodation of the demand for bank credit is overstated since, even if banks can be argued to accommodate business demand for loans, they may be less accommodating of an increase in demand for liquidity by the general public. In such a situation, so it is argued, the public will probably try and sell-off some holdings of other financial assets to meet their desire for additional liquidity (Wray, 1992). Critics further argue that central banks typically operate under various policy constraints which affect their ability and willingness to pursue a full accommodative reserve policy, in the sense of supplying unlimited cash to banks at given interest rates. More usually, the tendency is for central banks to adjust rates according to policy dictates, making the supply of cash less than horizontal (see Palley, 1991; Dow, 1997; Rousseas, 1998).

28 See Kaldor and Trevithick (1981) and Moore (1988).

Chapter 8   Sraffa's Theory of Price

1 Signorino (2005) provides an interesting discussion of some of Sraffa's unpublished early writings on certain aspects of Marshallian and Classical theories of price.

2 See Howard and King (1975), Roncaglia (1977), Steedman (1977) and Meek (1977).

3 See Roncaglia (1978, 2009).

4 I will return below to the discussion of whether or not Sraffa's prices can be regarded as equilibrium prices – see fn 12.

5 Kurz and Salvadori (2005) provide an illuminating account of the evolution of Sraffa's commodity explanation of price and in particular his reading of James Mill's *Elements of Political Economy* which supports this interpretation of the development of Sraffa's thinking on price.

6 See Sraffa (1960, p. 8).

7 A similar point is made by Samuelson (2000, p. 131).

8 See Sraffa (1960, p. 64).

9 See Chapter 3 for Marx's definitions of fixed, circulating, constant and variable capital.

10 Sraffa is, of course, able to assume this because he assumes throughout *Commodities* that output is fixed.

11 See Roncaglia (1978, 2009) for an elaboration of this construct in Sraffa's *Commodities*.

12 Sraffians appear to be divided on the question of whether Sraffa's prices can be seen as equilibrium prices. Garegnani (1984, 1997 and 1998) and Bellino (1997) can be seen as representatives of the traditional view that Sraffa's prices can indeed be seen as equilibrium prices, while Roncaglia (2009) and Sinha (2010) argue in opposition to this view that there is no textual evidence to support it. I would argue that while there is certainly no direct textual evidence to support the traditional view of Sraffa's prices as equilibrium prices, there is a fair amount of indirect textual evidence to support it including Sraffa's assertion that the prices he is concerned with can be referred to as the 'necessary price', 'natural price' or 'price of production' of Classical political economy (Sraffa, 1960, p. 9) and his contention that the systems he is concerned with are those where '...there is no deficit in the production of some commodities over their consumption...' (*Ibid.*, p. 5, fn 1).

13 See Salvadori (2000).

14 Roncaglia defends Sraffa's abstraction from changes in output levels and technology when considering the impact of changes in the wage share, arguing it is a theoretical device that 'increases our understanding of reality' (2009, p. 50), but without explaining how it does this, especially given that changes in the level of output and technology, as well as product prices themselves, can be argued to impact on the wage share.

15 For Roncaglia the mere assumption by Sraffa of a uniform rate of profit implies that he sees prices as formed in a competitive environment in the sense of the term used by Marx and the Classics, i.e., the free entry and exit of firms into and out of an industry (see 1978, p. 22).

16 See, for example, Hodgson (1981, 1982).

17 Given that Sraffa has been so explicit in denying relative prices can be explained by relative physical quantities of inputs alone, it is surprising to find a number of his followers misrepresenting him in this regard. Ian Steedman, perhaps one of the most prominent of his followers, argues for example that '...the conditions of production and the real wage paid to workers, both specified in terms of physical quantities of commodities suffice to determine the rate of profit (and, less importantly, all prices of production)...' (1977, p. 14). See also Keen (2001, p. 285).

18 It is of note this route is different to that chosen by Post Keynesians, who reduce prices to direct and indirect factor prices – wage costs.

19 See Sraffa (1960, p. 5).

20 Sraffa is explicit about not wanting to use the term 'capital' to describe these inputs, because he wants to avoid the usual connotation which accompanies the use of this term; that the quantity of capital can be measured independently of its price (see *Ibid.*, p. 9).

21 See, for example, Marx (1981, p. 493).

22 Sraffa's attempt to complete Ricardo's quest for an invariable standard is also acknowledged by a number of sympathetic interpreters of his work, including Bellino (2004) and Roncaglia (1978, 2009).

23 See Roncaglia (2009, p. 88).

24   Sinha argues that the problem of basics in Sraffa's multi-product analysis can be dealt with by seeing the multi-product system of production as one '...in which each technique is allowed to produce at most one good that it uses as input and that all other inputs used by the technique are not produced and all other outputs are not used as inputs by the same process' (2010, p. 302). However, it should be evident that this amounts, in effect, to assuming the multi-product system to be a single-product one, something Sraffa also does to overcome the problem of negative multipliers in his explanation of price magnitudes in fixed capital production systems.

25   With his customary intellectual honesty Sraffa says of the appearance of negative multipliers in his analysis, 'The outcome of this, since no meaning can be attached to the "negative industries" which such multipliers entail, is that it becomes impossible to visualise the Standard system as a conceivable rearrangement of the actual processes. We must therefore in the case of joint-products be content with a system of abstract equations, transformed by appropriate multipliers, without trying to think of it as having a bodily existence' (Sraffa, 1960, p. 48).

26   See, for example, Steedman (1977, p. 157) and more recently Sinha (2010, p. 297).

27   See Marx (1976, p. 528; 1981, pp. 522–3).

28   Given Marx's explicit statements on the matter, it is surprising that a number of commentators have attributed to Marx a 'straight-line' method of depreciation. A recent example is in the otherwise instructive paper by Moseley, in which he persuasively refutes Sraffa's contention that Marx analysed fixed capital as a 'joint product' (2009).

29   See Marx (1969b, p. 316).

30   See for example Steedman (1977) and Hodgson (1981, 1982). At one point in his *Commodities* Sraffa himself appears to be suggesting that the standard commodity can be thought of as money and therefore reducing commodities to equivalence. For example, when discussing the emergence of negative multipliers in the construction of the standard commodity in a multi-product system, he says that the 'Standard commodity which includes both positive and negative quantities can be adopted as money of account without too great a stretch of the imagination provided that the unit is conceived as representing, like a share in a company, a fraction of each asset and each liability, the latter in the shape of an obligation to deliver without payment certain quantities of particular commodities' (1960, p. 48).

References

Arthur, C.J. (2005) 'Value and money' in Moseley, F. (ed.), pp. 111–23.

—— (2006) 'Money and exchange', *Capital & Class*, 90, 7–35.

Arnsperger, C. and Varoufakis, Y. (2008) 'Neoclassical economics: Three identifying features' in Fullbrook, E. (ed.) *Pluralist Economics* (London: Zed Books), pp. 13–25.

Aspromourgos, T. (1986) 'On the origins of the term "neoclassical"', *Cambridge Journal of Economics*, 10(3), 265–70.

Ball, M. (1986) 'Debate: On Marx's theory of agricultural rent: A reply to Ben Fine' in Fine, B. (ed.) (1986a), pp. 152–74.

Banaji, J. (1979) 'From the commodity to capital: Hegel's dialectic in Marx's *Capital*' in Elson, D. (ed.) *Value: The Representation of Labour in Capitalism* (London: CSE Books), pp. 14–45.

Baran, P.A. (1957) *The Political Economy of Growth* (New York: Monthly Review Press).

Baran, P.A. and Sweezy, P.M. (1966) *Monopoly Capital: An Essay on the American Economic and Social Order* (New York: Monthly Review Press).

Baumol, W.J. (1974) 'The transformation of values: What Marx "really" meant (an interpretation)', *Journal of Economic Literature*, 12(1), 51–62.

Bellino, E. (1997) 'Full-cost pricing in the classical competitive process: A model of convergence to long-run equilibrium', *Journal of Economics*, 65(1), 41–54.

—— (2004) 'On Sraffa's standard commodity', *Cambridge Journal of Economics*, 28(1), 121–32.

Blaug, M. (2007) 'The formalist revolution of the 1950s' in Samuels, W.J., Biddle, J.E. and Davis, J.B. (eds.), pp. 395–410.

Böhm-Bawerk, E. von (1975) 'Karl Marx and the close of his system' in Sweezy, P.M. (ed.), pp. 3–118, originally published in 1896.

Bordo, M.D. (1989) 'Equation of exchange' in Eatwell, J., Milgate, M. and Newman, P. (eds.), pp. 151–6.

Bortkiewicz, L. von (1975) 'On the correction of Marx's fundamental theoretical construction in the third volume of *Capital*' in Sweezy, P.M. (ed.), pp. 199–221, originally published in 1907.

Brinkman, H-J. (1999) *Explaining Prices in the Global Economy: A Post-Keynesian Model* (Cheltenham: Edward Elgar).

Brunhoff, S. de (1976) *Marx on Money*, translated by Goldbloom, M.J. (New York: Urizen Books).

Carchedi, G. and de Haan, W. (1996) 'The transformation procedure: A non-equilibrium approach' in Freeman, A. and Carchedi, G. (eds.) (1996a), pp. 136–63.

Chick, V. (2000) 'Money and effective demand' in Smithin, J. (ed.) *What is Money?* (London: Routledge), pp. 124–38.

Colander, D., Föllmer, H., Haas, A., Goldberg, M., Juselius, K., Kirman, A., Lux, T. and Sloth, B. (2009) 'The financial crisis and the systemic failure of academic economics', *Kiel Institute for the World Economy*, Kiel working paper, February, No.1489.

Cripps, T.F. and Tarling, R.J. (1973) *Growth in Advanced Capitalist Economies 1950–1970* (Cambridge: Cambridge University Press).

Davidson, P. (1978a) *Money and the Real World*, 2nd edn (London: Macmillan Press).

—— (1978b) 'Why money matters: Lessons from a half-century of monetary theory', *Journal of Post Keynesian Economics*, 1(1), 46–70.

—— (2003–4) 'Setting the record straight on *A history of Post Keynesian economics*', *Journal of Post Keynesian Economics*, 26(2), 245–72.

—— (2005) 'Responses to Lavoie, King, and Dow on what Post Keynesianism is and who is a Post Keynesian', *Journal of Post Keynesian Economics*, 27(3), 393–408.

De Angelis, M. and Harvie, D. (2009) '"Cognitive Capitalism" and the rat-race: How capital measures immaterial labour in British universities', *Historical Materialism*, 17(3), 3–30.

Debreu, G. (1959) *Theory of Value: An Axiomatic Analysis of Economic Equilibrium* (New Haven: Yale University Press).

Dobb, M. (1973) *Theories of Value and Distribution since Adam Smith: Ideology and Economic Theory* (London: Cambridge University Press).

Dodd, N. (2005) 'Reinventing monies in Europe', *Economy and Society*, 34(4), 558–83.

Dow, S.C. (1997) 'Endogenous money' in Harcourt, G.C. and Riach, P.A. (eds.) *A 'Second Edition' of the General Theory: Volume 2* (London: Routledge), pp. 43–55.

—— (2001) 'Post Keynesian methodology' in Holt, R.P.F. and Pressman, S. (eds.), pp. 11–20.

Duménil, G. (1983–4) 'Beyond the transformation riddle: A labor theory of value', *Science and Society*, 47(4), 427–50.

Duménil, G. and Lévy, D. (2002) 'The field of capital mobility and the gravitation of profit rates (USA 1948–2000)', *Review of Radical Political Economics*, 34(4), 417–36.

Dunn, S.P. (2000) 'Wither Post Keynesianism?', *Journal of Post Keynesian Economics*, 22(3), 343–64.

—— (2008) *The 'Uncertain' Foundations of Post Keynesian Economics* (Abingdon: Routledge).

Eatwell, J., Milgate, M. and Newman, P. (eds.) (1989) *The New Palgrave: Money* (London: Macmillan Press).

Eichner, A.S. (ed.) (1979) *A Guide to Post-Keynesian Economics* (London: Macmillan Press).

Endres, A.M. (1997) *Neoclassical Microeconomic Theory: The Founding Austrian Version* (London: Routledge).

Fine, B. (1975) *Marx's 'Capital'* (London: Macmillan Press).

—— (1982) *Theories of the Capitalist Economy* (London: Edward Arnold).

—— (ed.) (1986a) *The Value Dimension: Marx versus Ricardo and Sraffa* (London: Routledge & Kegan Paul).

—— (1986b) 'On Marx's theory of agricultural rent' in Fine, B. (ed.) (1986a), pp. 114–87.

—— (1986c) 'Note: A dissenting note on the transformation problem' in Fine, B. (ed.) (1986a), pp. 209–14.

Fine, B. and Harris, L. (1979) *Rereading 'Capital'* (London: Macmillan Press).

Fine, B. and Saad-Filho, A. (2004) *Marx's 'Capital'*, 4th edn (London: Pluto Press).

Fine, B., Jeon, H. and Gimm, G.H. (2010) 'Value is as value does: Twixt knowledge and the world economy', *Capital & Class*, 100, 69–83.

Fine, B., Lapavitsas, C. and Saad-Filho, A. (2004) 'Transforming the transformation problem: Why the "New Interpretation" is a wrong turning', *Review of Radical Political Economics*, 36(1), 3–19.

Fingleton, B. (2003) 'Increasing returns: Evidence from local wage rates in Great Britain', *Oxford Economic Papers*, 55(4), 716–39.

Fingleton, B. and McCombie, J.S.L. (1998) 'Increasing returns and economic growth: Some evidence for manufacturing from the European Union regions', *Oxford Economic Papers*, 50(1), 89–105.

Foley, D.K. (1982) 'The value of money the value of labor power and the Marxian transformation problem', *Review of Radical Political Economics*, 14(2), 37–47.

—— (1986) *Understanding 'Capital': Marx's Economic Theory* (Cambridge, Mass.: Harvard University Press).

Freeman, A. (1996a) 'The psychopathology of Walrasian Marxism' in Freeman, A. and Carchedi, G. (eds.) (1996a), pp. 1–28.

—— (1996b) 'Price, value and profit – a continuous, general, treatment' in Freeman, A. and Carchedi, G. (eds.) (1996a), pp. 225–79.

Freeman, A. and Carchedi, G. (eds.) (1996a) *Marx and Non-Equilibrium Economics* (Cheltenham: Edward Elgar).

—— (1996b) 'Foreword' in Freeman, A. and Carchedi, G. (eds.) (1996a), pp. vii–xx.

Freeman, A., Kliman, A. and Wells, J. (eds.) (2004) *The New Value Controversy and the Foundations of Economics* (Cheltenham: Edward Elgar).

Friedman, M. (ed.) (1956) *Studies in the Quantity Theory of Money* (Chicago: University of Chicago Press).

—— (1976) *Price Theory* (Chicago: Aldine).

—— (1989) 'Quantity theory of money' in Eatwell, J., Milgate, M. and Newman, P. (eds.), pp. 1–40.

Frisch, R. (1971) 'Alfred Marshall's theory of value' in Townsend, H. (ed.) *Price Theory* (Harmondsworth: Penguin Books), pp. 59–92, originally published in 1950.

Garegnani, P. (1984) 'Value and distribution in the Classical economists and Marx', *Oxford Economic Papers*, 36(2), 291–325.

—— (1997) 'On some supposed obstacles to the tendency of market prices towards natural prices' in Caravale, G.A. (ed.) *Equilibrium and Economic Theory* (London: Routledge), pp. 139–72, originally published in 1990.

—— (1998) 'Sraffa: The theoretical world of the "old classical economists"', *European Journal of the History of Economic Thought*, 5(3), 415–29.

Gee, J.M.A. (1991) 'The Neoclassical school' in Mair, D. and Miller, A.G. (eds.), pp. 71–108.

Gnos, C. (2009) 'Circuit theory supplementing Keynes's genuine analysis of the monetary economy of production' in Ponsot, J-F. and Rossi, S. (eds.), pp. 1–20.

Goodhart, C.A.E. (1984) *Monetary Theory and Practice: The UK Experience* (London: Macmillan).

—— (1989) 'Monetary base' in Eatwell, J., Milgate, M. and Newman, P. (eds.), pp. 206–11.

Graziani, A. (1996) 'Money as purchasing power and money as a stock of wealth in Keynesian economic thought' in Deleplace, G. and Nell, E.J. (eds.) *Money in Motion: The Post Keynesian and Circulation Approaches* (Basingstoke: Palgrave Macmillan), pp. 139–54.

—— (2003) *The Monetary Theory of Production* (Cambridge: Cambridge University Press).

Griliches, Z. and Ringstad, V. (1971) *Economies of Scale and the Form of the Production Function: An Econometric Study of Norwegian Manufacturing Establishment Data* (Amsterdam: North-Holland).

Hahn, F. (1984) *Equilibrium and Macroeconomics* (Oxford: Basil Blackwell).

Hall, R.E. (1988) 'The relation between price and marginal cost in U.S. industry', *Journal of Political Economy*, 96(5), 921–47.

Harvey, D. (1982) *The Limits to Capital* (Oxford: Basil Blackwell).

Hilferding, R. (1981) *Finance Capital: A Study of the Latest Phase of Capitalist Development*, translated by Watnick, M. and Gordon, S. (London: Routledge & Kegan Paul), originally published in 1910.

Hillinger, C. and Süssmuth, B. (2008) 'The quantity theory of money is valid. The New Keynesians are wrong!', *University of Munich*, Munich discussion paper, No.2008-22.

Himmelweit, S. (1977) 'The individual as basic unit of analysis' in Green, F. and Nore, P. (eds.) *Economics: An Anti-Text* (London: Macmillan Press), pp. 21–35.

Hodgson, G. (1981) 'Money and the Sraffa system', *Australian Economic Papers*, 20(36), 83–95.

—— (1982) *Capitalism, Value and Exploitation: A Radical Theory* (Oxford: Martin Robertson).

Holt, R.P.F. and Pressman, S. (eds.) (2001) *A New Guide to Post Keynesian Economics* (London: Routledge).

Hoover, K.D. (2007) 'A history of postwar monetary economics and macroeconomics' in Samuels, W.J., Biddle, J.E. and Davis, J.B. (eds.), pp. 411–27.

Horwitz, S. (2000) *Microfoundations and Macroeconomics: An Austrian Perspective* (London: Routledge).

Howard, M.C. (1983) *Profits in Economic Theory* (London: Macmillan Press).

Howard, M.C. and King, J.E. (1975) *The Political Economy of Marx* (Harlow: Longman).

Hughes, J.P. and Mester, L.J. (1998) 'Bank capitalization and cost: Evidence of scale economies in risk management and signaling', *Review of Economics and Statistics*, 80(2), 314–25.

Ingham, G.K. (2001) 'Fundamentals of a theory of money: Untangling Fine, Lapavitsas and Zelizer', *Economy and Society*, 30(3), 304–23.

—— (2004) *The Nature of Money* (Cambridge: Polity).

—— (2006) 'Further reflections on the ontology of money: Responses to Lapavitsas and Dodd', *Economy and Society*, 35(2), 259–78.

Itoh, M. (1988) *The Basic Theory of Capitalism: The Forms and Substance of the Capitalist Economy* (Basingstoke: Macmillan Press).

Judd, J.P. and Scadding, J.L. (1982) 'The search for a stable money demand function: A survey of the post-1973 literature', *Journal of Economic Literature*, 20(3), 993–1023.

Junius, K. (1997) 'Economies of scale: A survey of the empirical literature', *Kiel Institute of World Economics*, Kiel working paper, May, No.813.

Kaldor, N. (1970) 'The new monetarism', *Lloyds Bank Review*, July.

—— (1982) *The Scourge of Monetarism* (Oxford: Oxford University Press).

—— (1985) *Economics Without Equilibrium* (Cardiff: University College Cardiff Press).

Kaldor, N. and Trevithick, J. (1981) 'A Keynesian perspective on money', *Lloyds Bank Review*, January, 1–19.

Keen, S. (2001) *Debunking Economics: The Naked Emperor of the Social Sciences* (London: Zed Books).

Kehoe, T.J. (1985) 'Multiplicity of equilibria and comparative statics', *Quarterly Journal of Economics*, 100(1), 119–47.

Kenyon, P. (1979) 'Pricing' in Eichner, A.S. (ed.), pp. 34–45.

Keynes, J.M. (1973) *The General Theory of Employment, Interest and Money* in *The Collected Writings of John Maynard Keynes, Volume VII* (London: Macmillan Press), originally published in 1936.

King, J.E. (ed.) (2003) *The Elgar Companion to Post Keynesian Economics* (Cheltenham: Edward Elgar).

Kirman, A.P. (1989) 'The intrinsic limits of modern economic theory: The emperor has no clothes', *Economic Journal*, 99(395), Supplement: Conference papers, 126–39.

—— (1992) 'Whom or what does the representative individual represent?', *Journal of Economic Perspectives*, 6(2), 117–36.

Kliman, A.J. (2007) *Reclaiming Marx's 'Capital': A Refutation of the Myth of Inconsistency* (Plymouth: Lexington Books).

Kliman, A.J. and McGlone, T. (1988) 'The transformation non-problem and the non-transformation problem', *Capital & Class*, 35, 56–83.

—— (1999) 'A temporal single-system interpretation of Marx's value theory', *Review of Political Economy*, 11(1), 33–59.

Kreps, D.M. (1990) *A Course in Microeconomic Theory* (Hemel Hempstead: Harvester Wheatsheaf).

Kurz, H.D. (ed.) (2000) *Critical Essays on Piero Sraffa's Legacy in Economics* (Cambridge: Cambridge University Press).

Kurz, H.D. and Salvadori, N. (2005) 'Representing the production and circulation of commodities in material terms: On Sraffa's objectivism', *Review of Political Economy*, 17(3), 413–41.

Laibman, D. (2004) 'Rhetoric and substance in value theory: An appraisal of the new orthodox Marxism' in Freeman, A., Kliman, A. and Wells, J. (eds.), pp. 1–18.

Laidler, D. (1982) *Monetarist Perspectives* (Oxford: Philip Allan).

—— (1990) *Taking Money Seriously* (Hemel Hempstead: Philip Allan).

Lapavitsas, C. (2000) 'Money and the analysis of capitalism: The significance of commodity money', *Review of Radical Political Economics*, 32(4), 631–56.

—— (2005) 'The social relations of money as universal equivalent: A response to Ingham', *Economy and Society*, 34(3), 389–403.

Lavoie, D. (1986) 'Marx, the quantity theory, and the theory of value', *History of Political Economy*, 18(1), 155–70.

Lavoie, M. (1984) 'The endogenous flow of credit and the Post Keynesian theory of money', *Journal of Economic Issues*, 18(3), 771–97.

—— (2001) 'Pricing' in Holt, R.P.F. and Pressman, S. (eds.), pp. 21–31.

—— (2005) 'Changing definitions: A comment on Davidson's critique of King's history of Post Keynesianism', *Journal of Post Keynesian Economics*, 27(3), 371–6.

—— (2006) *Introduction to Post-Keynesian Economics* (Basingstoke: Palgrave Macmillan).

Lawson, T. (2009) 'The current economic crisis: Its nature and the course of academic economics', *Cambridge Journal of Economics*, 33(4), 759–77.

Lee, F.S. (1998) *Post Keynesian Price Theory* (Cambridge: Cambridge University Press).
—— (2003) 'Pricing and prices' in King, J.E. (ed.), pp. 285–9.
Lee, F.S. and Keen, S. (2004) 'The incoherent emperor: A heterodox critique of Neoclassical microeconomic theory', *Review of Social Economy*, 62(2), 169–99.
Lichtenstein, P.M. (1983) *An Introduction to Post-Keynesian and Marxian Theories of Value and Price* (London: Macmillan Press).
Lipsey, R.G. and Chrystal, K.A. (2007) *Economics*, 11th edn (Oxford: Oxford University Press).
Loasby, B.J. (1991) 'The Austrian school' in Mair, D. and Miller, A.G. (eds.), pp. 40–70.
Mair, D. and Miller, A.G. (eds.) (1991) *A Modern Guide to Economic Thought: An Introduction to Comparative Schools of Thought in Economics* (Aldershot: Edward Elgar).
Mandel, E. (1968) *Marxist Economic Theory*, translated by Pearce, B. (London: Merlin Press).
Mankiw, N.G. and Romer, D. (eds.) (1991) *New Keynesian Economics, Volume 1, Imperfect Competition and Sticky Prices* (Cambridge, Mass.: MIT Press).
Mankiw, N.G. and Taylor, M.P. (2010) *Economics* (Andover: Cengage Learning EMEA).
Marshall, A. (1920) *Principles of Economics: An Introductory Volume*, 8th edn (London: Macmillan).
Marx, K. (1969a) *Theories of Surplus Value: Part I*, translated by Burns, E. (London: Lawrence & Wishart).
—— (1969b) *Theories of Surplus Value: Part II*, translated from German by Simpson, R. (London: Lawrence & Wishart).
—— (1970) *A Contribution to the Critique of Political Economy*, translated from German by Ryazanskaya, S.W. (Moscow: Progress).
—— (1972) *Theories of Surplus Value: Part III*, translated from German by Cohen, J. and Ryazanskaya, S.W. (London: Lawrence & Wishart).
—— (1973) *Grundrisse*, translated by Nicolaus, M. (Harmondsworth: Penguin Books).
—— (1976) *Capital: Volume I*, translated by Fowkes, B. (Harmondsworth: Penguin Books).
—— (1978) *Capital: Volume II*, translated by Fernbach, D. (Harmondsworth: Penguin Books).
—— (1981) *Capital: Volume III*, translated by Fernbach, D. (Harmondsworth: Penguin Books).
Marx, K. and Engels, F. (1983) *Letters on 'Capital'*, translated by Drummond, A. (London: New Park).
McCallum, B.T. and Nelson, E. (2010) 'Money and inflation: Some critical issues', *Federal Reserve Board*, Washington D.C., Finance and economics discussion series, Working paper, 2010–57.
McCombie, J.S.L. (1985) 'Increasing returns and the manufacturing industries: Some empirical issues', *Manchester School*, 53(1), 55–75.
McCombie, J.S.L. and Roberts, M. (2007) 'Returns to scale and regional growth: The static-dynamic Verdoorn law paradox revisited', *Journal of Regional Science*, 47(2), 179–208.

Meek, R.L. (1973) *Studies in the Labor Theory of Value*, 2nd edn (London: Lawrence & Wishart).

—— (1977) *Smith, Marx, & After: Ten Essays in the Development of Economic Thought* (London: Chapman & Hall).

Milonakis, D. and Fine, B. (2009) *From Political Economy to Economics: Method, the Social and the Historical in the Evolution of Economic Theory* (Abingdon: Routledge).

Mishkin, F.S. (2006) *The Economics of Money, Banking, and Financial Markets*, 8th edn (Boston: Pearson/Addison-Wesley).

Mohun, S. (1994) 'A re(in)statement of the labour theory of value', *Cambridge Journal of Economics*, 18(4), 391–412.

Mongiovi, G. (2002) 'Vulgar economy in Marxian garb: A critique of temporal single system Marxism', *Review of Radical Political Economics*, 34(4), 393–416.

—— (2003) 'Sraffian economics' in King, J.E. (ed.), pp. 318–22.

Moore, B.J. (1979a) 'The endogenous money stock', *Journal of Post Keynesian Economics*, 2(1), 49–70.

—— (1979b) 'Monetary factors' in Eichner, A.S. (ed.), pp. 120–38.

—— (1983) 'Unpacking the Post Keynesian black box: Bank lending and the money supply', *Journal of Post Keynesian Economics*, 5(4), 537–56.

—— (1988) *Horizontalists and Verticalists: The Macroeconomics of Credit Money* (Cambridge: Cambridge University Press).

Moseley, F. (2000) 'The "New Solution" to the transformation problem: A sympathetic critique', *Review of Radical Political Economics*, 32(2), 282–316.

—— (ed.) (2005) *Marx's Theory of Money: Modern Appraisals* (Basingstoke: Palgrave Macmillan).

—— (2008) 'The "Macro-monetary" interpretation of Marx's theory: A reply to Ravagnani's critique', *Review of Radical Political Economics*, 40(1), 107–18.

—— (2009) 'Sraffa's interpretation of Marx's treatment of fixed capital', *Review of Political Economy*, 21(1), 85–100.

Nelson, A. (2005) 'Marx's objections to credit theories of money' in Moseley, F. (ed.), pp. 65–77.

Nicolaus, M. (1973) 'Foreword' in Marx, K., pp. 7–63.

Ochoa, E.M. and Glick, M. (1992) 'Competing microeconomic theories of industrial profits: An empirical approach' in Milberg, W. (ed.) *The Megacorp & Macrodynamics: Essays in Memory of Alfred Eichner* (Armonk: M.E. Sharpe), pp. 225–50.

Owen, N. (1983) *Economies of Scale, Competitiveness, and Trade Patterns within the European Community* (Oxford: Clarendon Press).

Palley, T.I. (1991) 'The endogenous money supply: Consensus and disagreement', *Journal of Post Keynesian Economics*, 13(3), 397–403.

Patinkin, D. (1956) *Money, Interest, and Prices: An Integration of Monetary and Value Theory* (Evanston, Ill.: Row, Peterson).

Pigou, A.C. (1949) *The Veil of Money* (London: Macmillan).

Pilling, G. (1986) 'The law of value in Ricardo and Marx' in Fine, B. (ed.) (1986a), pp. 18–44.

Ponsot, J-F. and Rossi, S. (eds.) (2009) *The Political Economy of Monetary Circuits: Tradition and Change in Post-Keynesian Economics* (Basingstoke: Palgrave Macmillan).

Rizvi, S.A.T. (1994) 'The microfoundations project in general equilibrium theory', *Cambridge Journal of Economics*, 18(4), 357–77.

—— (2007) 'Postwar Neoclassical microeconomics' in Samuels, W.J., Biddle, J.E. and Davis, J.B. (eds.), pp. 377–94.

Robinson, J. (1964) *Economic Philosophy* (Harmondsworth: Penguin Books).

Rochon, L-P. (1999) *Credit, Money and Production: An Alternative Post-Keynesian Approach* (Cheltenham: Edward Elgar).

—— (2009) 'The existence of profits within the monetary circuit: Some unanswered questions revisited' in Ponsot, J-F. and Rossi, S. (eds.), pp. 56–76.

Rogers, C. (1989) *Money, Interest and Capital: A Study in the Foundations of Monetary Theory* (Cambridge: Cambridge University Press).

Roll, E. (1973) *A History of Economic Thought*, 4th edn (London: Faber and Faber).

Roncaglia, A. (1977) 'Sraffa and price theory: An interpretation' in Schwartz, J. (ed.) *The Subtle Anatomy of Capitalism* (Santa Monica: Goodyear), pp. 371–80.

—— (1978) *Sraffa and the Theory of Prices*, translated from Italian by Kregel, J.A. (Chichester: John Wiley & Sons).

—— (2009) *Piero Sraffa* (Basingstoke: Palgrave Macmillan).

Rosdolsky, R. (1977) *The Making of Marx's 'Capital'*, translated by Burgess, P. (London: Pluto Press).

Rotheim, R.J. (1981) 'Keynes' monetary theory of value (1933)', *Journal of Post Keynesian Economics*, 3(4), 568–85.

Rousseas, S. (1998) *Post Keynesian Monetary Economics*, 3rd edn (Basingstoke: Macmillan Press).

Rubin, I.I. (1972) *Essays on Marx's Theory of Value*, translated by Samardźija, M. and Perlman, F. (Detroit: Black & Red).

Saad-Filho, A. (1997) 'An alternative reading of the transformation of values into prices of production', *Capital & Class*, 63, 115–36.

—— (2002) *The Value of Marx: Political Economy for Contemporary Capitalism* (London: Routledge).

Salvadori, N. (2000) 'Sraffa on demand: A textual analysis' in Kurz, H.D. (ed.), pp. 181–97.

Samuels, W.J., Biddle, J.E. and Davis, J.B. (eds.) (2007) *A Companion to the History of Economic Thought* (Malden: Blackwell).

Samuelson, P.A. (1957) 'Wages and interest: A modern dissection of Marxian economic models', *American Economic Review*, 47(6), 884–912.

—— (2000) 'Sraffa's hits and misses' in Kurz, H.D. (ed.), pp. 111–80.

Scherer, F.M. (1980) *Industrial Market Structure and Economic Performance*, 2nd edn (Boston: Houghton Mifflin).

Schumpeter, J.A. (1954) *History of Economic Analysis* (London: George Allen & Unwin).

Seton, F. (1957) 'The "Transformation Problem"', *Review of Economic Studies*, 24(3), 149–60.

Shaikh, A. (1979) 'Foreign trade and the law of value: Part I', *Science and Society*, 43(3), 281–302.

—— (1980) 'Foreign trade and the law of value: Part II', *Science and Society*, 44(1), 27–57.

—— (1982) 'Neo-Ricardian economics: A wealth of algebra, a poverty of theory', *Review of Radical Political Economics*, 14(2), 67–83.

Shand, A.H. (1984) *The Capitalist Alternative: An Introduction to Neo-Austrian Economics* (Brighton: Wheatsheaf Books).

Shapiro, N. (2003) 'Competition' in King, J.E. (ed.), pp. 65–7.

—— (2005) 'Competition and aggregate demand', *Journal of Post Keynesian Economics*, 27(3), 541–9.

Shapiro, N. and Mott, T. (1995) 'Firm-determined prices: The Post-Keynesian conception' in Wells, P. (ed.) *Post-Keynesian Economic Theory* (Boston: Kluwer Academic), pp. 35–48.

Shapiro, N. and Sawyer, M. (2003) 'Post Keynesian price theory', *Journal of Post Keynesian Economics*, 25(3), 355–65.

Sherman, H.J. (1991) *The Business Cycle: Growth and Crisis Under Capitalism* (Princeton, NJ.: Princeton University Press).

Signorino, R. (2005) 'Piero Sraffa's lectures on the advanced theory of value 1928–31 and the rediscovery of the Classical approach', *Review of Political Economy*, 17(3), 359–80.

Sinha, A. (2003) 'Some critical reflections on Marx's theory of value' in Westra, R. and Zuege, A. (eds.) *Value and the World Economy Today: Production, Finance and Globalization* (Basingstoke: Palgrave Macmillan), pp. 171–87.

—— (2010) *Theories of Value from Adam Smith to Piero Sraffa* (Abingdon: Routledge).

Smithin, J. (2003) *Controversies in Monetary Economics*, revised edn (Cheltenham: Edward Elgar).

Sraffa, P. (1926) 'The laws of returns under competitive conditions', *Economic Journal*, 36(144), 535–50.

—— (1960) *Production of Commodities by Means of Commodities* (Cambridge: Cambridge University Press).

—— (1981) 'Introduction' in Sraffa, P. (ed.) *The Works and Correspondence of David Ricardo, Volume I on the Principles of Political Economy and Taxation* (Cambridge: Cambridge University Press), pp. xiii–lxii, originally published in 1951.

Steedman, I. (1977) *Marx after Sraffa* (London: New Left Books).

—— (1991) 'The irrelevance of Marxian values' in Caravale, G.A. (ed.) *Marx and Modern Economic Analysis, Volume I: Values, Prices and Exploitation* (Aldershot: Edward Elgar), pp. 205–21.

Sweezy, P.M. (1968) *The Theory of Capitalist Development: Principles of Marxian Political Economy* (New York: Monthly Review Press).

—— (ed.) (1975) *Karl Marx and the Close of His System By Eugen von Böhm-Bawerk & Böhm-Bawerk's Criticism of Marx By Rudolf Hilferding* (London: Merlin Press).

Tobin, J. (1985) 'Theoretical issues in macroeconomics' in Feiwel, G.R. (ed.) *Issues in Contemporary Macroeconomics and Distribution* (London: Macmillan Press), pp. 103–33.

Tsoulfidis, L. and Tsaliki, P. (2005) 'Marxian theory of competition and the concept of regulating capital: Evidence from Greek manufacturing', *Review of Radical Political Economics*, 37(1), 5–22.

Vane, H.R. and Thompson, J.L. (1979) *Monetarism: Theory, Evidence & Policy* (Oxford: Martin Robertson).

Veblen, T. (1900) 'The preconceptions of economic science', *Quarterly Journal of Economics*, 14(2), 240–69.

Weintraub, S. (1978) *Keynes, Keynesians and Monetarists* (Philadelphia, PA.: University of Pennsylvania Press).

Wheen, F. (2006) *Marx's Das Kapital: A Biography* (London: Atlantic Books).

Winternitz, J. (1948) 'Values and prices: A solution of the so-called transformation problem', *Economic Journal*, 58(230), 276–80.

Wray, L.R. (1992) 'Commercial banks, the central bank, and endogenous money', *Journal of Post Keynesian Economics*, 14(3), 297–310.

—— (2001) 'Money and inflation' in Holt, R.P.F. and Pressman, S. (eds.), pp. 79–91.

—— (2002) 'State money', *International Journal of Political Economy*, 32(3), 23–40.

—— (2003) 'Money' in King, J.E. (ed.), pp. 261–5.

—— (2010) 'Money', *Levy Economics Institute*, Bard College, Working paper, December, No.647.

Young, A.A. (1928) 'Increasing returns and economic progress', *Economic Journal*, 38(152), 527–42.

Author Index

Subject Index

abstraction, 7, 12, 16, 32, 33, 37, 78, 91–2, 102, 114, 121, 123, 132, 149, 188, 197

accommodative monetary policy, 59–60

accumulation
of capital, *see under* capital
of wealth, 7, 19, 21, 52, 83, 90, 106, 139

allocation of resources, 88, 89, 96–7, 100, 126, 128, 179, 187, 192

auctioneer, 93, 94, 101

Austrians, 5, 89–108, 113–16, 119, 181, 191, 194
see also neo-Austrians

bank
credit, 195, 196
liabilities, 42–3, 57, 58, 111, 112, 138, 139, 189, 194, 195;
see also financial sector liabilities

banking system, 17, 22, 42, 53, 123, 138, 139
see also financial system, credit

barriers to entry, 2, 50, 75, 103, 109, 125, 131, 134
see also migration of capital

barter, 8, 90–1, 122, 186, 187, 195
see also exchange

basic- and non-basic commodities, *see under* Sraffa

bills of exchange, 53

business cycle, ix, 46, 54, 56, 58–60, 85, 102, 113, 116, 118, 189
downswing, 46, 60
upswing, 46, 56, 58–9, 113, 189
see also crisis

capital
accumulation of, 21, 52
circulating, 68, 148, 196

concentration and centralisation of, 2, 4, 31
constant, 32, 33, 135, 148, 196
fixed, 32, 143 144, 147, 148, 150, 151, 168–70, 182, 195, 198
interest-bearing, 91, 112, 139–40, 188
variable, 33, 148, 196

capitalism
competitive, 2, 4, 5, 30–1, 50, 71, 74–6, 93–4, 102–3, 124–6, 150–1, 197
monopoly, 2, 4, 51, 71, 74–6, 102

cash
base, 42,110, 111, 112; *see also* money
demand for, 58, 111, 139
supply of, 58, 139, 196

central bank, 139, 196

Classical political economy, 40, 61–9, 143, 197

competition
as a process, 4, 30–1, 75, 93–4, 102–3, 125–6, 133, 150–1, 160, 181
imperfect, 109, 114, 124, 126, 132–3
inter-industry, 30–1, 150–1
intra-industry, 30, 75, 169–70
monopolistic, 75, 103, 109, 124, 189
oligopolistic, 103
perfect, 35, 108, 124, 192, 193

composition of capital
organic, 36, 39, 42, 44, 48–9, 76, 174, 188, 190
technical, 188
value, 188

computational errors, 25, 114, 115, 116, 183

constant of proportionality, 78, 81–3, 84, 87
see also MELT